WEBSITE NEWS UPDATED WEEKLY
WWW.INDEXONCENSORSHIP.ORG • CONTACT@INDEXONCENSORSHIP.ORG
TEL: 020 7278 2313 • FAX: 020 7278 1878

Editor-in-chief Ursula Owen • **Editor** Judith Vidal-Hall • **Associate Editor** Rohan Jayasekera • **Eastern Europe Editor** Irena Maryniak • **Editorial Production Manager** Natasha Schmidt • **Publisher** Henderson Mullin • **Development Manager** Hugo Grieve • **Membership and Promotions** Tony Callaghan • **Project Manager** Ruairi Patterson • **Director of Administration** JM Thomson • **Volunteer Assistants** Michelle Ayre, James Badcock, Ben Carrdus, Gulliver Cragg, Julie-Ann Davies, Ioli Delivani, Veronique Dupont, Hanna Gezelius, Monica Gonzalez Correa, Javier González-Rubio, Andrew Kendle, Gill Newsham, Jason Pollard, Shifa Rahman, Lorenzo Sabbadini, Jugoslav Stojanov, Mike Yeoman • **Proofreading** Katherine Fry, Roger Thomas
Cover design Sheridan Wall • **Design and production** Jane Havell Associates • **Printed by** Thanet Press, UK

CONTENTS

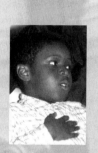
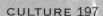

AMERICA THE CONTRADICTORY
URSULA OWEN

America has always colonised people's minds in contradictory ways – a place of freedom, plurality and openness scarred by stark inequalities; a country relied on to solve international problems whose ruthless use of power is feared and resented. But after 11 September and the war in Iraq, attitudes are hardening.

Many commentators, in and out of government, seem now to regard free expression as inconvenient or unpatriotic. The attack on civil liberties, the marginalising of dissent, the treatment of immigrants (p112) have all aroused anger, yet three out of four Americans believe that the US is making the world a safer place.

So what is America becoming? Is it merely reinventing itself, as it does endlessly, or is something more disturbing and permanent under way? This issue of *Index on Censorship* looks at the country through the words of the people who know it best.

Most, though not all, of the Americans writing here are disturbed at what is going on. Michael McClintock (p88) reports on new forms of political surveillance, secrecy in immigration proceedings, the USA Patriot Act and other assaults on civil liberties that have now become part of American law and practice. Thomas R Asher (p105) is concerned by the effect that fear has had on the population since 11 September and Darryl Pinckney (p66) observes that dissenters are treated as irrelevant, out of touch. Nicholas von Hoffman (p36) believes that the absence of dissent and the self-censorship evident in the mass media's cooperation with Washington over the Iraq war was 'no deviation from past practice'.

Meanwhile, Gara LaMarche (p47) reminds us of the American right's powerful vision, nurtured by an array of think tanks and publications, and Milton Viorst's account of the place of religion in the life of George W Bush suggests a man who 'sees himself on a divine mission' (p98). Christopher Hitchens (p44) believes the promise of the new American imperialism to allow local populations to govern themselves is sincere. Salil Tripathi, meanwhile, wishes the anti-war lobby was less exclusively anti-American (p82).

With America's role in the Middle East centre stage, Joel Beinin (p51) deplores the attacks on the teaching of Middle East studies, Ahdaf Soueif (p179) puts her hope in grass-roots dissidence in Israel and America, and Amos Oz and David Grossman (p168) express some optimism as well as pessimism about the elusive peace between Israelis and Palestinians.

And how do people feel about America's extraordinary power, its patriotic fervour, its new sense of vulnerability? Patrick McGrath (p129), a new citizen, is wry about his bittersweet victory, Walter Mosley (p119) explains how hate operates and Grace Paley (p214) writes about war. But love of country is, as Richard Sennett (p32) tells us, as 'complex and hesitant as any other kind of love', and warns against Washington's language of rescue, of good triumphing over evil. ❏

WAGING A PEACE

ROHAN JAYASEKERA

IRAQ'S ALL-POWERFUL CIVILIAN CHIEF
L PAUL BREMER III SETS LIMITS TO
FREE SPEECH

To the average Iraqi, almost nothing the Americans do makes sense. Each one is a schizophrenic beast, as likely to smile and smile at a child as it is liable to club a careless driver with its rifle.

The contradiction is in the mission; the US military came to Iraq to win a war, not wage a peace. The majority of US troops believe they came to Iraq as liberators. The Iraqis tend to think differently. The US authorities think their problem is their failure to get their message across. The Iraqis already get too many different messages from the Americans. Take the message the US military sent with its seizure of 'editorial control' of Mosul City's only TV station, because of its 'predominantly non-factual/ unbalanced news coverage' – meaning the rebroadcasting of Qatari Arab satellite network al-Jazeera. 'We have every right as an occupying power to stop the broadcast of something that will incite violence,' Major General David Petraeus told reporters after being alerted to the offending broadcasts. 'Yes, what we are looking at is censorship but you can censor something that is intended to inflame passions.' According to a *Wall Street Journal* report, a US army major was relieved of her duties when she argued that the order contravened principles of free speech. After all, these are principles guaranteed by the Constitution of the United States, which every US soldier must 'solemnly swear' to 'support and defend'.

But these contradictions fly everywhere. Having invested US$20 million over three months in the rebuilding of Iraqi state TV and radio, renamed the Iraqi Media Network (IMN), the US officials in charge of the contract began baulking at the new network's news output immediately it went on air. Managers were told to drop the readings from the Qu'ran, the 'vox-pop' man-in-the-street interviews (usually critical of the US/UK invasion) and even to run their content past the wife of a US-friendly Iraqi Kurdish leader for a pre-broadcast check. The station rejected the demands and dug in their heels. 'As journalists we will not submit to censorship,' said Don North, a Canadian documentary-maker training Iraqis at the station.

US civilian administrator L Paul Bremer III, in charge of the occupying powers' Coalition Provisional Authority (CPA), was said to be infuriated by the conflicting strategies in place at the IMN, which has two TV stations, a brace of local and national radio stations and two newspapers under development. Even more annoyingly for the US chief, the country's Shia broadcasters had made much more use of much less extensive support from Iran to get their networks on air, for more hours with more news. Almost all of it was hostile to the US/British occupation forces.

A daily drip feed of increasingly embittered media coverage is turning into a flood, with every political faction in the new Iraq opening up new newspapers in Baghdad, and using them to voice popular frustration at the rising crime rate and failing public services on the American and British watch. Every day brings new allegations and abuse. The papers representing political parties hostile to the US post unattributed reports of all kinds, accusing the Western forces of gang rape, robbery and numerous 'insults to Islam'. But now the US authorities have declared 'enough'.

Bremer advocates tough new rules governing the Iraqi media to sort the mess out. According to his paperwork, all Iraqi media must be registered. Licences will be revoked and equipment confiscated from media sources that break the rules. Individual offenders 'may be detained, arrested, prosecuted and, if convicted, sentenced by relevant authorities to up to one year in prison and a US$1,000 fine'. Appeal will be to Bremer only, and his decision will be final. His nine-point list of 'prohibited activities' include incitement to racial, ethnic or religious hatred, advocating support for the banned pre-war Ba'ath party and publishing material that 'is patently false and is calculated to provoke opposition to the CPA or undermine legitimate processes towards self-government'.

Officials say the order is intended to stop 'hate speech' – the kind of hot language they say could trigger violence between Iraqis and Westerners, or possibly Iraqi Sunni and Shia or Arab and Iraqi Kurds. 'There's no room for hateful and destabilising messages that will destroy the emerging Iraqi democracy,' former IMN official Mike Furlong told the Associated Press. 'All media outlets must be responsible.' This is a long way from the stand made by Furlong's IMN colleague Don North the month before. 'This whole idea [IMN] was about starting the genesis of an open media,' he said

Opposite: Baghdad, April 2003: newspapers on sale after the fall of the city.
Credit: Rohan Jayasekera

at the time, 'so we will not accept an outside source scrutinising what we produce.'

But Bremer also wants big changes at the IMN — which he has suggested be transformed into a kind of mini-ministry to replace the old Iraqi ministry of information, made world-famous by Saddam's propagandist minister Mohammed Saeed al-Sahaf. Bremer will 'reserve the power to advise' the IMN on any aspect of its performance, 'including any matter of content' and the power to hire and fire IMN staff. Thus the man in absolute authority over the country's largest, richest and best-equipped media network could be his own regulator and the regulator of his rivals, with recourse to the US Army to enforce his rulings.

Under the direction of former Voice of America (VOA) chief Robert Reilly, the IMN was created in April 2003 by US defence technology giant Scientific Applications International Corp (SAIC) under contract to the Pentagon. SAIC's relevant speciality is what it calls 'Information Dominance/Command and Control' — a nine-point programme, according to its website, that begins with 'Battlefield Control' and ends with 'Information Warfare/Information Operations'. This kind of seamless link between military command and media management was what the Pentagon had in mind when it issued the contract to SAIC — a successor to the fuzzy TV broadcasts from USAF EC-130E 'Commando Solo' psyops (psychological operations) planes and the radio broadcasts beamed from US Army transmitters mounted on Humvee jeeps.

Reilly fell out with the VOA board of governors over his 'ideological' views on what he thought was the VOA's duty, to tell America's story to the nations it opposed. He notoriously called the fighting in Afghanistan a 'war of ideas', with the VOA 'on one side in that war'. But Reilly did not last under Bremer's regime either, and SAIC has had its contract to develop and manage the IMN cut short. It's all in Bremer's hands now.

Thus, as *Index on Censorship* goes to press, a battle for the hearts and minds of Bremer's media strategy is under way. A coalition of the free-speaking is challenging Bremer's regulatory vision for the Iraqi press. *Index on Censorship* and three other media NGOs — the Baltic Media Centre, the Institute for War & Peace Reporting and International Media Support — have published a joint report on the state of the Iraqi media, while the BBC's World Service Trust and Jordan's Arab Media Institute have produced their own assessments. A conclave of international media experts, in a meeting in Athens funded by the Greek government and the US Agency for

International Development, drafted an outline for a fairer media regime in Iraq. And some British government officials are advocating the appointment of a senior soldier/civil servant from the team that ran the media in an earlier intervention in Kosovo to do the same in Iraq. The VOA has also warned off the Pentagon. 'We are not in the psychological operation or propaganda business,' VOA Middle East chief Norm Pattiz told the *Christian Science Monitor*, citing the Pentagon initiatives. 'Without the credibility of balanced, reliable and truthful news, we would have no audience.'

These are critical days for the IMN. Reilly said before his departure that he hoped it would evolve into a 'PBS-style' responsible public broadcaster. Even the censorious paratrooper Petraeus says that Iraq needs 'something akin' to the Communications Regulatory Agency set up in Bosnia 'to establish standards and procedures for cases in which those standards are broken'. The issue is whether the IMN – a media network sired by Pentagon contract out of US Army psyops, soon to be Iraq's largest, most powerful and only truly national media corporation, topped by L Paul Bremer III, a man with absolute power over its activities and its rivals – is taking the right route to these destinations. Bremer has the power to decide. But if Iraq needs media regulation, it should be independent. If it needs media at all, it should be more independent than this. ❑

Rohan Jayasekera *is Associate Editor at* Index on Censorship. *He is presently leading a team of journalists working on training programmes for the independent press and media rights advocacy in Iraq*

For the report on the Iraqi media co-authored by *Index*
⇨ http://www.indexonline.org/pdf/iraqmedia.pdf

MAD MULLAHS AND MULLAH LITES
NILOU MOBASSER

AS US CONSERVATIVES AND
NATIONALISTS TALK UP THE THREAT
FROM IRAN, THEIR WORDS FIND
A PECULIAR ECHO IN TEHRAN

First, it was the commies and the evil empire; then, bin Laden and al-Qaida; then, Saddam Hussein and the Republican Guards; and now, most terrifying of all: the mad mullahs and the atom bomb. US statesmen hardly seem able to survive for a day without a blood-curdling enemy. But since they get more than enough airtime to scare the wits out of us all, let us now hear a word or two from the mad mullahs (and some of the 60 million or so other people who happen to be living in the same country).

When you take a closer look, you find that not all mad mullahs are quite as mad or mad in quite the same way. There are the mad mullahs who are known (at home) as the authoritarians or the conservatives. Funnily enough, they sound a lot like US statesmen. They also talk endlessly about 'the enemy' and its wicked conspiracies. They say (to the people): if you don't shut up and do as we say, 'the enemy' will come and gobble up the country. Then there are other mad mullahs (known as the reformists) who seem slightly more subtle. They say (to the other bunch of mad mullahs): unless we let people say what they like and elect who they like to run the country, then . . . 'the enemy' will come and gobble up the country. Well, yes, it does all come down to the same thing. It is not all that mad when you think about it. After all, they have been watching the events in Afghanistan and Iraq from not a million miles away. But they do seem to have come away with slightly different lessons. The conservatives say that the Taliban and Saddam Hussein are gone because they were American stooges to begin with and had outlived their usefulness for their master. They see no resemblance whatsoever between themselves and the fallen rulers in Afghanistan and Iraq. In fact, they see any criticism of themselves as an attack on Islam, equate their own interests with Iran's interests and assume that their domestic critics must be, not to put too fine a point on it, American stooges. In June 2003, the conservative daily *Jomhuri-ye Eslami* wrote: 'In the letters, statements, interviews and speeches of intimidated or servile elements, we

Tehran, June 2003: protesters demanding the release of fellow students outside the parliament. Credit: AFP / Behrouz Mehri

note their invitation to the people and the system's officials to surrender in the face of US threats and demands . . . the system's officials must confront decisively the infiltrators and intimidated elements who lay the groundwork for foreign intervention.'

The 'letters and statements' reference will become clearer below. Suffice it to say for now that the conservatives hold that US enmity stems from the fact that Iran has an Islamic state, which serves as an inspiration to Muslims everywhere. The conservative daily *Javan* wrote in June: 'By raising the issue of the Islamic Republic of Iran's nuclear activities – [the US and its Western allies] have embarked on a kind of psychological and media warfare against Iran.' US allegations that al-Qaida forces were operating from Iran, US open support for Iranian counter-revolutionary groups in Iraq, its encouragement of domestic opposition within Iran 'on the eve of the IAEA's report on Iran is particularly sensitive and pursues particular aims, such as . . . wreaking revenge on Islamic Iran because of its impact on public opinion in the world of Islam . . .'

The conservatives argue that the only answer to US threats is to close ranks and display unity; ie refrain from criticising the state and, most important, from criticising the country's top leader Ayatollah Ali Khamenei.

The reformists maintain, for their part, that strength does not lie in a unity that is based on repression and 'the silence of the graveyard', but in democracy. They argue that the US is least able to threaten Iran when it believes that Iranian officials enjoy popular support. 'The early period of Khatami's presidency and the fact that US officials fully dissociated them-selves from their past enmities against the [Iranian] nation and the revolu-tion and made efforts to establish a new contact with Iranians is a capital which is still within our grasp,' *Etemaad* newspaper wrote on 8 June.

On the same day, another reformist daily, *Yas-e Now*, wrote: 'Experience has shown that pressure on the country's international position increases when the [foreign actors and rivals] imagine and sense that the popular support of the Iranian state is wavering.'

There are also suspicions among the reformists that the conservatives are playing a double game of 'repression at home and compromise abroad'. According to this scenario, the conservatives are crushing dissent at home in order to display their power and to convince US officials – with whom they are said to be holding secret talks – that they are the only credible interlocu-tors for the Americans.

Apart from reformist newspapers, calls for greater democracy were particularly noticeable in several open letters issued in Iran in May–June 2003. The one that was the most damning for the power-holders was signed by 24 of the country's university students' unions. Although it focused on the developments in Iraq, it repeatedly urged Iranian rulers to learn a lesson from the fate of the Taliban and Saddam Hussein and dictators throughout history. It expressly rejected the idea that a country's independence can be defended in the face of foreign threats by the crushing of freedoms at home. The letter concluded: 'We therefore advise you, the rulers – now that an Alexander has pitched its camp next door and is digging in – to stop the baseless, emotional rhetoric and oratory; the inculcation of the delusions of your own power; the superficial stirring up of tension; and, possibly, the striking up of behind-the-scenes deals; and, instead, either try to win the support of the nation so that you can at least remove the [USA's] pretexts and pave the way for reform, or step aside from power so that you do not uselessly destroy the lives, property and interests of this nation.' This letter appeared on the website of Amir Kabir University's student union and was not otherwise reported in Iran.

But the missive that seemed to irritate people in high places the most was an open letter to Khamenei signed by 127 (eventually 135) of the country's 290 MPs. It was carried by two of the country's news agencies on the day it was released publicly (24 May), but an official gagging order was issued in the evening and it did not appear in any of the newspapers the following day. The signatories begin by expressing concern that President Mohammad Khatami's planned political reforms had been systematically blocked by powerful state institutions over the previous six years as if to prove 'to Iranians and the world that nothing has changed or will change in Iran and that the votes of the people whose main demand is a change of methods and approaches has no effect at all'. The signatories continue: 'The bulk of the nation is dissatisfied and disheartened; most of the elites are silent or have emigrated; material capital is fleeing and foreign forces surround the country. In these circumstances, only two possibilities are foreseeable for the country: either dictatorship and tyranny, which, on the most optimistic outcome, will lead to nothing but dependence [on foreigners] and, ultimately, collapse and disintegration [of the ruling system]; or a return to the principles of the constitution and sincere submission to the rules of democracy . . .

'Free elections and preventing violations of the constitution are two pivotal points for any democratic state. How can we prescribe a referendum for the Iraqi people and call, from Friday prayer podiums, for free elections in that country, but deprive our own people of this self-evident right?'

The MPs called on Khamenei to state clearly whether Iran was a democracy or not, even though he might find this a bit like 'drinking a cup of poison' (when Khomeini accepted the UN-sponsored ceasefire with Iraq, he said it was like 'drinking a cup of poison'). At a meeting with Iranian MPs that had been planned before the letter, Khamenei made no specific reference to it, but several of the signatories have since been prevented from speaking at public venues outside Tehran by the often-violent zealots known as the *hezbollahis*, who pride themselves on obedience to Khamenei.

In the meantime, US pressure on Iran is increasing and, although a full-scale war seems unlikely, the US and/or Israel may well hit Iran's nuclear facilities (or presumed ones) in the not too distant future and get away with it. And, while some younger Iranians unfamiliar with the history of US intervention in Iran may welcome the US pressure on 'the mad mullahs', most Iranians would probably agree with the *Etemaad* editorialist on 27 May who wrote: 'Iranians have learned that foreigners' hearts do not beat for them.' ❏

Nilou Mobasser *is an Iranian translator living in the UK*

CLOSE BUT NO CIGAR

ISABEL HILTON

AS FIDEL CASTRO GETS OLDER AND
MORE INFIRM HIS REGIME FACES ITS
FEAR BY RESORTING TO REPRESSION
– WITH WASHINGTON'S RENEWED
HOSTILITY THE EXCUSE

In the 1960s, when Cuba was still regarded by some as a place of liberty, and plane hijackings had not taken on the sinister connotation that they now have, hijacking planes to Cuba enjoyed a certain cachet. This year, however, the Cuban government has been vexed not by incoming hijackings but by a series of attempted hijackings of outbound aircraft – the most recent manifestation of the desire of many Cuban citizens to get out of the island by any means possible.

On 19 March this year, a Cuban DC-3 with 29 passengers aboard was hijacked at knifepoint by six terrorists and re-routed to Key West in Florida.

On 1 April, an An-24 aircraft en route from Nueva Gerona to Havana was hijacked by an individual carrying a fake hand grenade and demanding to be taken to the United States. When the plane landed in the US, ten of the passengers opted to stay.

On 2 April, hijackers seized a Havana Bay ferry with 50 passengers and ordered the captain to sail to the US. They ran out of fuel in international waters and were persuaded to return to the Cuban port of Mariel to refuel. There Cuban coastguards managed to take control of the vessel. Four men received life sentences and three others, judged to be the instigators of the attempt, were swiftly executed.

The day of the executions, the Cuban government announced it had foiled yet another attempted hijacking of a plane. As a sign of the regime's irritation, Fidel Castro himself appeared twice on television in April to give a long account of two of these incidents – which were, he claimed, organised and inspired by the US government. The rapidity with which the sentences were carried out caused surprise and shock on the island, where people were already reeling from the largest crackdown on dissent for years.

On 18 March, while the rest of the world was distracted by events in Iraq, there had been a wave of arrests in Cuba that netted dissidents, independent journalists, Church activists and, most poignantly, independent librarians. State security agents searched homes and confiscated fax machines, computers, books, typewriters and personal papers as official media accused the detainees of 'provocations' and 'subversive activities'. The scale and the savagery of the crackdown were a perverse tribute to the growing courage and ingenuity of Cuban civic society activists. These are not people foolish enough to try to overthrow the government. Instead, they have been working to expand the space in which Cubans can talk and think.

Since the collapse of the Soviet Union and the economic crisis that it precipitated in Cuba, the regime has been forced to take emergency measures to survive: the holding of dollars has been decriminalised and tourism hugely expanded, bringing hundreds of thousands of visitors to the island. Contact with the visitors has aroused curiosity about the outside world and brought home to the Cubans the staggering disparity in wealth between them and the tourists. Prostitution is rampant, highly skilled professionals work as hotel porters to earn dollar tips and young Cubans question, with some justice, the value of studying when the only end is a job with a salary at poverty levels.

At the same time, a relaxation in some aspects of social control has permitted a certain level of civic organisation. The Pope's visit to Cuba in January 1998, for instance, allowed Christian activists to begin to organise under the Church umbrella and in recent years civic initiatives have taken a creative turn. The most celebrated of these, the Varela Project, was one of the targets of the recent crackdown. The project – named after Felix Varela, a nineteenth-century Cuban nationalist intellectual – was the brainchild of Osvaldo Payá, a Christian democrat who took advantage of a provision in the Cuban Constitution that states that if 10,000 signatures can be collected in support of a parliamentary debate, then parliament must discuss the issue. Payá claimed to have more than 11,000 signatures in support of a petition to discuss freedom of assembly and expression, the right to own a business, electoral reform and the release of Cuba's 230 political prisoners. He presented his petition in May last year.

European countries, including Britain, urged the Cuban government to recognise the project and respond. Castro, though, said that the Varela Project did not warrant consideration. The regime organised a massive counter-movement in support of the proposition that the citizens of Cuba were happy with Communist Party rule.

Civic society, however, continued to find new outlets for its developing energies. The independent library movement had sprung from a speech made by Fidel Castro in February 1998 at the Havana Book Festival in which he said: 'There are no banned books in Cuba. It's just that there is no money to buy them.' An economist from Las Tunas, Berta del Carmen Mexidor Vázquez, took his remarks as an opportunity to launch a network of independent libraries, in which individuals share their personal collections to offer readers access to books and magazines unavailable from official sources. (Quite how restricted those can be might be guessed from the prosecution of a man last year for distributing copies of *The Universal Declaration of Human Rights*.) The first independent library was opened in October 1998 in Las Tunas. Within a year there were 15 such libraries. By the end of last year, there were 190. Now, however, the books and the libraries are banned. Several independent librarians were among those arrested, others were threatened and their books confiscated.

The independent journalists are men and women who publish, largely on the internet, independent news from Cuba. Among the best known is Raul Rivero, founder and editor of the independent news service Cuba Press. Rivero had worked for Prensa Latina, the official news agency, but in 1991 he abandoned official journalism, calling it a 'fiction about a country that does not exist'.

In October last year, an assortment of grass-roots political groups, human rights activists, 190 independent libraries and more than 30 dissident press services launched the Assembly to Promote Civil Society – a movement that aimed to build up alternative institutions to the party state in preparation for a post-Castro Cuba. Their purpose, they said, was 'the peaceful struggle for the rebirth of civil society'. Marta Beatriz Roque Cabello, the group's spokesperson, an independent economist who had already served a three-year prison term after publishing a paper calling for political reform, said she had concluded that Fidel would never concede political reform, but that the group was working for the longer term.

Marta Beatriz Roque was among the detainees; she was sentenced to 20 years in prison. Other well-known victims of the crackdown included Dr Oscar Elias Biscet Gonzalez, a lawyer, and Hector Palacios Ruiz, a dissident and founder of the Democratic Solidarity Party, who was involved with the Varela Project.

Havana, Cuba, March 2003: Marta Beatriz Roque Cabello during a news conference.
Credit: AP Photo / José Goitia

At the trials, which were held across the country in the first week of April and were closed to all outsiders, the 75 defendants were convicted of working with the United States to undermine the Cuban government and damage Cuba's national interests. They were, according to the government, 'mercenaries in the pay of the United States'. The sentences ranged from six to 28 years, with an average of more than 19. Raul Rivero was sentenced to 20 years; Hector Palacios Ruiz, who was accused of receiving large sums of money from the US government, to 25.

Why them and why now? It's a question with no simple answer. None of the initiatives was aimed at overthrowing the government but, as Castro gets older and visibly more infirm, the regime, faced with obvious questions about its future, has fallen back on repression, with an increased level of hostility from the Bush administration as its excuse. Bush's appointee as Under Secretary of State for the Americas, Otto Reich, is a notorious hard-liner and Cold Warrior who is associated with several anti-Castro organisa-tions. While support has been growing in the US Congress for a liberalisation of relations with Cuba, the administration has set a more confrontational course. In 2001, five Cuban nationals received long prison terms in Florida after being convicted of espionage; in May 2002, the US

Under Secretary of State for Arms Control, John R Bolton, accused Cuba of developing a 'limited capacity for germ warfare research' 'intent on acquiring weapons of mass destruction, particularly biological weapons' – a statement that should be read in the context of the new US doctrine of pre-emptive war against targets that it deems might be a future threat.

In the same month, in a speech in Florida, George W Bush proposed increased US government aid to dissidents. In September last year, the new head of the US Interest Section in Havana, James Cason, began a high-profile policy of public support for Cuba's dissidents. Cason reportedly helped launch the youth wing of the dissident Partido Liberal Cubano and, in October 2002, invited a group of dissidents to meet US newspaper editors at his residence in Havana. On 24 February 2003, he participated in a meeting of the dissident Assembly for the Promotion of Civil Society at the home of Marta Beatriz Roque, a meeting at which Cason criticised the Castro government and reiterated US support for the dissidents. Complaints from the Cuban Foreign Ministry did not prevent Cason from organising two other such meetings at his residence in March. Cason's activities were cited by the Castro regime as evidence that the detainees were involved in a CIA-sponsored plot against the government.

But Osvaldo Payá, founder of the Varela Project, was not arrested. Payá had been allowed to leave Cuba in January to accept the Sakharov Prize, the European Union's top human rights prize. He toured eight countries and was received by Pope John Paul, by US Secretary of State Colin Powell and by the heads of government of Spain, Mexico and the Czech Republic. Now his supporters in Europe have begun to lobby for his nomination for the Nobel Peace Prize, a prospect unlikely to give Castro any pleasure. Though Payá remains free, his associates have received savage prison sentences.

The crackdown has alienated groups in the US that have been agitating, with increasing effect, for greater contact and a relaxation of the embargo against trade and travel to Cuba; it has severely damaged relations with the European Union, the source of most of Castro's investment and foreign aid. The EU decided last week to limit high-level government visits and reduce participation in cultural events in Cuba. Castro responded by organising protests at the Spanish and Italian embassies in Havana and has warned of further action if the EU maintains support for Cuban dissidents. ❏

Isabel Hilton *is a London-based writer and broadcaster*

NEVER DARKEN MY DOOR AGAIN

ALI A ALLAWI

RACIST, INTELLECTUALLY SUSPECT AND
VULGAR, THE BA'ATH PARTY IS ALL BUT
EXPIRED. AND GOOD RIDDANCE TOO

Somewhere in the 1920s, the Arab National idea, which had hitherto been a reformist and even liberal notion allied to a moderate Islam, well integrated into the sociocultural map of the Middle East, took a wrong turn. It began to develop definite racist overtones, hegemonistic values and an exclusivist and intolerant perspective on politics and society.

The architect of this suicidal turn was that fastidious Ottoman intellectual dandy Sati' al-Husri, with his broken Arabic and borrowed philosophy from Henri Bergson and German idealism. He imposed his ideas on an entire generation of Iraqis through his control of the educational system and his cultivation of ever more extreme political ideologues, who used his vulgarisation of Arab nationalism as a tool of control over an ethnically and religiously diverse people.

In the 1950s, this sorry experiment in Iraq became the norm elsewhere in the Middle East. One regime after another tottered and fell to Arab nationalists, those exemplars of Arab 'democracy' who gave us the unlamented regime of South Yemen, the Nasserist apologists and their apotheosis, the Ba'ath Party, in both Iraqi and Syrian varieties. Kurds and Berbers became 'mountain Arabs', Islam was a folk identity, and there were no ethnic or religious minorities to clutter this pristine vision of an indivisible Arab nation with an (undefined) historic mission. The Iraqi Ba'ath Party, riding high on massive oil wealth in the 1970s, underpinned its vicious racist and sectarian policies by reference to these absurd theories.

Such was the power of these ideas that there was not a peep from the Arab nationalists when Iraq was ethnically cleansed of its 500,000 Fayli Kurds; when the majority Shia, always suspect in nationalist lore, were reduced to cannon fodder in the regime's wars of aggression; when Kurds were forcibly relocated, gassed and Arabised, all in the name of some homicidal fantasy about the Arab nation guarding its eastern gateways from the Persian invader. Saddam Hussein rode to power on a tank, but he was served by an army of grovelling intellectuals who betrayed every principle of their trade. Only Kenan Makiya, to his everlasting credit, dared to rise to the challenge in his moving book, *Cruelty and Silence*.

The cowardly Arab intellectuals who theorised and justified the murderous regime of the Ba'ath, and who continued to view Saddam Hussein as a champion of their cause on the grounds of a phantom Arab 'solidarity', are directly responsible for the tragedies that have befallen Iraq and its people. They have crashed against the harsh realities of an Arab decay caused mainly by the grotesque ideas that these wreckers have forced on Arab society, in alliance with the military and secret police thugs who still cling to power.

The debacle in Iraq will not have any serious effect on the policies and practices of these regimes. It is being met by denial and by the reaffirmation of the old verities. The Arab regimes, led by Syria, are quaking in their shoes after the fall of Ba'athism in Iraq – for that is what it really is, the abject and final failure of an ideological system whose champions blithely presided over one disaster after another.

Can a leopard change its spots? I doubt it, although what needs to be done is as clear as daylight. Reform of decrepit state structures, economic liberalisation, jettisoning of a spent ideology, dissolution of security apparatuses, demilitarisation, intellectual and political freedoms, openness and tolerance – in fact, everything that the nationalist ideologues abhor.

That is why de-Ba'athification in Iraq is so important. The cult of violence, aggression and hatred, which the Ba'ath has so assiduously cultivated, must be uprooted from society and its scars have to heal. The legacy of Sati' al-Husri, realised by the Ba'ath and by Saddam Hussein, is the ruin of Iraq. It brought the brutalisation of societies, the pauperisation of nations, rampant theft and corruption, sectarian and tribal divisiveness and, now, cowardly cringing under a hyperpower whose goals are uncertain but which has taken an intense dislike to these regimes.

Where will this end? I cannot say for sure, but Ba'athism, Arab nationalism – in fact, any totalitarian thought system – cannot survive in the Middle East any more. They deserve to be junked in the scrapyard of failed systems. Good riddance, I say. ❏

Ali A Allawi *is an Iraqi economist in London, who has been active in the Iraqi opposition*

NO PEACE FOR THE WICKED

MICHAEL WALSH

'FOR NEVINSON THERE IS NO
ARMISTICE. HE IS ALWAYS AT WAR'

CRW Nevinson was openly declared to be *the* painter of the Great War. Not only was he young, uniformed and daring, but he also was seen as an uncompromising truth-teller who could bring the public the art from the Western front that they wanted to see. Both intelligent and pertinent, he was nationally recognised as being the greatest modern artist of war, and indeed the greatest artist of modern war.

By the outbreak of the Great War in August 1914 CRW Nevinson, the child of radical journalist Henry Nevinson and Margaret Nevinson, a campaigner for women's rights, was already regarded as one of London's most infamous rebels and prominent avant-garde artists. A conscientious objector, he did not initially shy from the front, serving with an ambulance unit during the first battles at the Ypres Salient.

By 1916, there was no artist in Britain who could compete with him in sales, attendance figures for exhibitions and high-profile daily appearances in the major newspapers. This brought him to the attention of the Department of Information, who commissioned him as an Official War Artist.

His works were not quite what the department had in mind. The rebel artist was difficult to harness. He visited parts of the front before Passchendaele – a trip that got him sent home – and when his works *A Group of Soldiers* and *Paths of Glory* were to be exhibited in London the censor clamped down and forbade both. Nevinson argued in the press and got one of the bans lifted. The other he exhibited anyway with the word 'Censored' pasted across it, which infuriated officials even more. He finally wrote an article entitled 'When the Censors Censored "Censored"'.

The public, needless to say, felt that, yet again, he was the truth-teller, the David fighting the Goliath of the British government. But did Nevinson knowingly manipulate the censorship issue? Though claiming he had no direct aesthetic, political or theoretical drum to beat, merely self-invented virtue and rabid individualism, he nevertheless courted censorship and used it to his own advantage. ❏

Michael Walsh is an Assistant Professor in the Department of Art History and Archaeology, Eastern Mediterranean University in Northern Cyprus, and the author of CRW Nevinson: This Cult of Violence *(Yale University Press, 2002)*

For Michael Walsh's analysis of Nevinson's battles with the censor ⇨
http://www.indexoncensorship.org in August

Opposite: A Group of Soldiers, *1917. Credit: Imperial War Museum, London*

Returning to the Trenches, *1914. Credit: National Gallery of Canada, Ottawa*

Night Arrival of the Wounded, *1915. Credit: Private collection*

CRW Nevinson as a medical orderly during World War I. Credit: Private collection

Road from Arras to Bapaume, *1917. Credit: Imperial War Museum, London*

Above: Paths of Glory,
*1917. Credit: Imperial
War Museum, London*

Right: Paths of Glory
*'censored', 1918.
Credit:* Daily Mail,
2 March 1918

La Patrie, *1916. Credit: Birmingham Museums & Art Gallery*

Harvest of Battle, *1919. Credit: Imperial War Museum, London*

REWRITING AMERICA

'ONE NATION UNDER GOD, INDIVISIBLE,
WITH LIBERTY AND JUSTICE FOR ALL.'
WHERE IS THE COUNTRY GOING? AMERICANS
REPORT ON THE STATE THEY'RE IN

New York City, 2003: store window on 23rd Street.
Credit: Thomas Hoepker / Magnum Photos

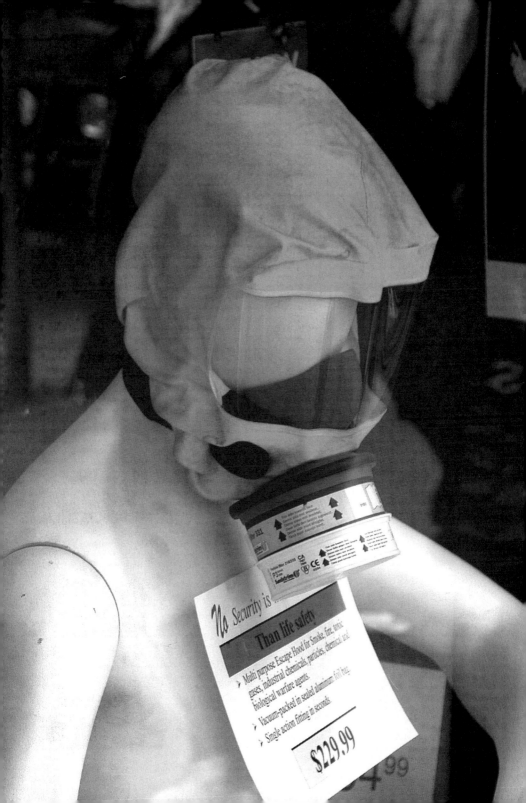

A NATION'S NARRATIVE

RICHARD SENNETT

BOTH THE VIRTUES AND DANGERS
OF PATRIOTISM DEPEND ON HOW
THE STORY IS TOLD

Dr Johnson's declaration that patriotism is the last refuge of a scoundrel in a way cheapens one of the most explosive of human sentiments. The declaration supposes that a cunning president or prime minister could manipulate love of country to achieve his or her own selfish ends. Or again, that the masses are so ignorant, such blind believers, that all the scoundrel need do is wave the flag, speak of blood and soil, and the patriotic sheep will follow where he wills.

If only patriotism were so simple. Patriotic sentiment is a compound of many elements, and love of country is as complex and as hesitant as any other kind of love. It creates a narrative of collective life. It tells a story of what binds disparate people together, and both the virtues and dangers of patriotism depend on how the story is told. That is to say, it's not merely a representation of a nation or a particular culture, it's a representation that is achieved through narrative. The destructive elements of patriotism come in imagining that there's a dénouement, a cathartic climax to the story of the people or a culture – that is, a moment when a decisive act will finally fulfil their destiny. And the danger history shows us is that this narrative dénouement too often involves denying or destroying another people in order to experience catharsis.

The narratives of patriotism that are destructive, the kinds of dénouement that both aggress against others and seem to fulfil something in this narrative, hold up, in particular, a strong promise to human groups who are internally divided or disorientated by forces beyond their control. For them, patriotism is the last refuge of the confused.

The notion that somehow the ongoing, shared history of dissonance might be resolved by a cathartic destructive act seems to me a real danger in patriotic experience, and marks the modern social experience of patriotism today.

A great patriotic crisis of my own youth arose among people like myself who resisted the American war in Vietnam, in the 1960s and the 1970s. Then, as now, the US was not the well-oiled internal machine that foreigners often imagine. Then, the country was in the midst of a racial explosion, the boom after World War II had come to a temporary halt, and the white working classes were beginning to suffer. American affluence then, as now, was affluence for an elite.

When America decisively entered Vietnam, in the mid-1960s, our country did have a long-standing patriotic narrative: America appeared in the guise of a rescuer, saving foreigners from destroying each other. That patriotic narrative had shaped fighting in the two world wars, and justified the enormous costs of pursuing the Cold War. Vietnam looked to be just one more chapter in this established story. When soldiers such as the young Colin Powell entered Vietnam, they quickly saw that this story of rescue did not apply. The enemy turned out to be a resolute, committed people. The allies for whom the troops were fighting turned out to be a corrupt, locally unloved bureaucracy, and American strategy itself proved unable to deliver on the promise of rescue.

This patriotic narrative, frustrated by a foreign adventure, now swerved. It swerved against those at home who protested against the war. The American troops were drawn mostly from the ranks of poor blacks and poor Southern whites. Middle-class young men in universities largely avoided military service. The middle-class young, however, were the strongest anti-war voices. They were, in principle, the friends, the spokesmen for troops suffering abroad. But the practice of patriotism proved different.

We know from the researches of people such as Robert Jay Lifton and Robert Howard, among many others, that the troops felt themselves besieged on two fronts: locally on the ground by the Vietnamese and symbolically at home by these protesting friends. The Vietnamese were considered to be patriotic enemies, and the protestors protesting against the situation in which the troops were placed were accused of being unpatriotic. As a decisive victory on the ground receded, a consuming victory against enemies at home became ever more vivid as a desire. In 1968, Howard recounts, at the height of the anti-war protests, thousands of American troops wore the sign on their helmets: 'America – Love it or Leave it.'

The sense of betrayal from within stiffened a kind of resolve, a kind of 'fantasy', as Lifton puts it. The government should do something decisive to shut up these enemies within, in order to validate the patriotic project. And in the States the public's desire that politicians do something decisive to quell internal disorder and protest brought into power the right-wing Richard Nixon.

I recount this history in part because it illuminates the complex ingredients of patriotic sentiment. These American troops and the working classes at home were not scoundrels. They were deeply confused. Within the shell of war against an internal enemy, these people imagined another war occurring in their own society, waged against those traitors who were posing as friends. The consuming act in this internal struggle to validate the patriotic narrative would be to silence dissent.

I recall this past also because it may help you in understanding something of the dynamics of American society today. The language spoken in Washington now is still this classical language of rescue, of redemption, of good triumphing over evil, and as in the past the scenario for this narrative, the strategic scenario, is lacking in clarity or in purpose. But consider the domestic condition of the American superpower. Here is a country even more internally fragmented and disjointed than it was 40 years ago. Confused, of course, and much angered now by terrorist attacks on it. A country whose internal divisions of class have grown greater and whose racial divisions and ethnic conflicts have not healed.

Unlike Britain – and it's something I'm struck by as a point of Anglo-European misunderstanding – the American left lacks the traditional role of a loyal opposition. And I've come to feel that some elements of the American left have learned too well the lesson that I sketched from Vietnam. They've silenced themselves, fearing that opposition will prove them to be not good Americans. That's how this syndrome gets internalised.

Thinking in stories is, of course, a basic element in interpreting the everyday world as well as the world of art. And narratives in the everyday world do not, any more than narratives in art, invariably follow a single set of rules. As in fiction, shared histories in everyday life need not end in cathartic acts that are repressive or destructive. And no longer, I think, need patriotism follow a single course. If the strategic defects of current American strategy are as great as those of the Vietnam War – and I think they are – then the challenge to our people, that is to the American people, will lie in avoiding what happened in Vietnam, avoiding the search for a narrative catharsis, when we turn to one another to find a resolution, a solution, a defining moment. ❏

Richard Sennett *is Professor of Sociology at the London School of Economics and New York University. This is an edited version of a talk given at the* Index/Orange *debate, Oxford, 2003*

Radio Free Maine

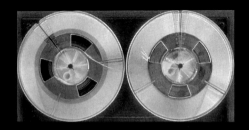

VOICES OF THE LEFT
UNEDITED & UNCENSORED

Radio Free Maine is an unparalleled living archive
of audio and video tapes featuring some of the
United States' most critical and dissenting voices.
NOAM CHOMSKY, HOWARD ZINN and **RALPH NADER**
recorded live at conferences and public appearances.

AUDIO TAPES
$11 each post paid to US
Canada and Mexico, add $1 postage per tape; all other countries, add $3

VIDEO TAPES
$20 each post paid to US
Canada and Mexico, add $2 postage per tape; all other countries, add $5

Payment in US funds must accompany order
Allow two weeks for delivery
Free catalog with every order

For a catalog of **Radio Free Maine** audio and video tapes, please send
a self-addressed envelope, stamped with $1 postage

Please make check/money order payable to ROGER LEISNER and send to
RADIO FREE MAINE, P.O. BOX 2705, AUGUSTA, MAINE 04338

For more information go to www.radiofreemaine.com

IN THE WAR WHOREHOUSE

NICHOLAS VON HOFFMAN

IN PEACETIME THE MASS MEDIA INCULCATE THE
NORMS AND OPINIONS THAT A NATION WANTS
IN ITS PEOPLE. IN WARTIME THEY BECOME THE
MEANS BY WHICH THE GOVERNMENT INSTRUCTS
THE POPULACE

On 24 June 1876, elements of the United States Army's 7th Cavalry Division, commanded by George Armstrong Custer, engaged a group of Sioux and Cheyenne braves led by Chief Sitting Bull at Little Big Horn, Montana. The skirmish that ensued resulted in the death of Custer and all of his 250 men – twice the number of fatalities so far sustained by the United States 127 years later in its 'war' with Iraq.

Like many a sight seen in the deserts through which the US military's Humvee jeeps drove this winter, the war was mostly mirage, something that evidently escaped the notice of the hundreds of correspondents sent to cover it. What one overheated television reporter compared to the Battle of the Somme was little more than what in Los Angeles they call a drive-by shooting. It is only a mild exaggeration to say that American service personnel in Iraq were in greater danger from absent-mindedly-driven Coca-Cola trucks than from the opposing army, which had less firepower than that deployed by the police department in Milwaukee, Wisconsin.

Conquering by bribing people on the other side is an ancient and civilised form of warfare and if it was practised by the United States in Iraq it would explain the absence of anything that can remotely be called a battle. Evidence supporting the great non-conflict hypothesis surfaced in an article by Vago Muradian in the 19 May edition of *Defense News*, an arms industry publication living on the best of terms with the Pentagon brass. The article quotes General Tommy Franks, the man who ran the alleged war, as saying – by way of an explanation for the absurdly easy American victory – 'I had letters from Iraqi Generals saying, "I now work for you."' Another Pentagon official told the reporter, '. . . we knew how many of these [Iraqi generals] were going to call in sick.' And finally there is this quotation: 'What is the effect you want? How much does a cruise missile cost? Between US$1 and $2½ million. Well, a bribe is a PGM, a much cheaper precision-guided munition – it achieves the aim but it's bloodless and there is zero collateral damage.'

The news that there was no war because the other side was paid to take a family leave day was picked up by Fred Kaplan, one of the best military journalists about, who published these good tidings on the internet in *Slate* magazine on 20 May – and there the story died.

None the less, the proposition that the Iraqi military had been paid to take a dive was supported by occasional puzzled dispatches filed out of Baghdad in the days immediately prior to the commencement of the bombing, reporting that no preparations for war were visible. No sandbagging, no evacuations, no mobilisation of air-raid wardens or medical personnel were evident. Here was a capital city of 5 million people under threat of imminent invasion and bombardment and it was business as usual.

If it wasn't a war, then what was it? Probably something akin to a turkey shoot. The press duly and diligently reported on the tens of thousands of bombs dropped on the Iraqi military. What got skipped over was that the turkeys could not or would not shoot back. It is the tales of heroic derring-do in the face of a completely defenceless opponent that cause the cynical to cock a suspicious eyebrow.

We can only speculate as to why so little was made of the battle-free nature of the conflict. At least three reasons suggest themselves. 1) The lazy intellectual torpor afflicting not a few American journalists. 2) The embarrassment print and broadcast media would face if they were to tell their publics: 'Whoops! That war, those heroes, those bloodcurdling, tear-jerking scenes we have been entertaining you with for weeks on end – well, it didn't happen.' 3) Although you might conclude that the United States government would have a motive to step forward and claim for itself a humane, non-lethal, non-destructive kind of warfare, that's not the reputation which the fire-eating, Israelised bellicists in the Pentagon want. The public relations policy pursued in those precincts is the old Roman one of *oderint dum metuant*. In short it's fear, not love, they seek to inspire.

In that spirit Rachel Corrie, a young American woman making her non-violent protest by being killed standing in front of a rampaging Israeli bulldozer in Gaza, was a one-day story. She might as well have been a suicide bomber. In contrast there is Private Jessica Lynch, the wounded soldier rescued from her fiendish Iraqi captors by the derring-do of the night-raiding US Army Rangers who braved death to snatch this young woman to safety. Thanks to the foresight of the military, an army TV cameraman was

Baghdad, April 2003: satellite dishes allowing international TV networks to send live broadcasts anywhere in the world. Credit: courtesy Anthony Borden, IWPR

brought along lest these heroic doings go unrecorded. For several days afterwards Jessica and her friends dominated all the US news channels.

It remained for Canada's *Toronto Star* to discover that there were no guards preventing Private Lynch from leaving the hospital, only a group of non-fiendish Iraqi medics doing their best to heal her wounds. The paper wrote that 'the so-called daring rescue was essentially a Hollywood-style stunt'. A few weeks later the BBC did a full exposé of the whole mendacious episode, but apart from a quick mention on CNN, a story in the *Washington Post* and an indignant column in the *Los Angeles Times*, the business was ignored by the mass media. The Potemkin war raged on, if not in Iraq, then on televisions and front pages across America.

With literally hundreds of journalists 'embedded', as we learned to say, in American military units, how could they have failed to see that – whatever might be going on around them – it wasn't a war in the ordinary meaning of the word? For a full answer we will have to wait for Phillip Knightley to revise his classic study of the history of war and journalism, *The First Casualty*. Until then we do know that many of the reporters sent to war by their assignment editors were neither well enough read nor well enough trained to resist co-option. Judging from their copy, they simply enlisted and out-gunghoed the Marines.

Many were the fairest-looking but least conscientious people in American journalism – men and women aptly described as war whores. They were the on-camera personalities, their American flag lapel pins glittering, who whooped and hollered as they and the military went a-romping through the Iraqi desert. Day in and day out, hour after hour, they tingled with happy excitement as they strained to infect their viewers with their enthusiasm for this strange adventure on the sands of Araby. Whether or not war is truly the health of the state, it can do wonders for one's own career. These were not the people to so much as whisper that it was all a charade.

However much war may depress advertising and ruin the news budgets of the big media corporations, it gooses the ratings and it makes stars of the on-air performers. And heroes, too. HBO ran the movie *Live from Baghdad*, a full-length docudrama glorifying war whoredom. War packaged as a reality show played around the clock on the news channels as the journalistic war profiteers promoted themselves and their careers. You could see the giddy emotional state of these men and women, clutching their microphones as their adrenalin-hyped voices reported from Washington, Baghdad, London, Amman or, better yet, from the deck of an aircraft carrier. These handsome men and attractive women in their soignée rumple had all the swash and all the buckle of the glamour-perfected pre-Technicolor movie stars. Seldom has ambition revealed itself as vividly as it did in the glistening eyes of the reporters, their happily agitated voices, their perturbed, gulping deliveries, the stagy bathos concealing their erotic delight in the cannon's comforting boom and the machine gun's reassuring chatter.

Simply put, the American mass media put itself at the service of the state. Any space between the two, often not very wide in times of peace, vanished. The right and the wrong of that cooperation depends on whether or not you were for or against the invasion of Iraq.

History tells us that when the United States went to war in the twentieth century, American journalism was among the first to enlist. The mass media's obedience to the Washington party line represents no deviation from past practice. In 1917 the government padlocked a small number of anti-war publications and since then wartime deviation from government policy has been rare indeed. A belief persists that the mass media parted company with the government over the Vietnam War, but it didn't. From the start the media backed the Vietnam War to the hilt, only occasionally arguing with the government over the best way to win it. Whether you regard it as jingoism or patriotism, the mass media reaction to the Iraqi war was on time and on track. If George Bush said 'it's a war' or said 'it's a dinosaur', that's what the media saw and that's what the media said.

A minority of Americans, doubtless influenced by too much study of eighteenth-century political philosophy, believe in a press whose responsibilities do not include helping the government to win a war. These are the people who talk of objectivity, telling it like it is, etc, etc. Such opinions would have long since been relegated to Unitarian Church seminars were it not for the news industry using these slogans as the basis of a never-ceasing advertising campaign for itself, one similar to automobile advertisements in being a mishmash of truths, lies and in-betweenies. If people believe that the media are supposed to be free, non-partisan, fearless, objective and independent, it is in no small measure because the industry never stops telling the populace that is what they are. The mass media's description of the role they play is a haphazard reflection of the actualities.

Most American mass media most of the time contain little or no foreign news. All but a couple of hundred of the nation's thousands of radio stations broadcast no news at all, literally not a word. In peacetime, television stations and newspapers, with perhaps 25 exceptions, skip coverage of events abroad. Partly this situation is owing to the conservatism of the score or so of corporations that own virtually all of the mass media. Regardless of who is in the White House, it is their government and why should they ping it? But from time to time one or the other will break ranks and attempt to present current affairs to its public. It will soon give the idea up after it relearns the home truth that the vast majority of Americans will not watch or read news, unless it's local news, sports or gossip. Anyone who thinks otherwise will go broke trying. Those who doubt this observation might want to compare and contrast the international news service offered by CNN with the entirely different service presented to its American audience. American CNN is bubble-head news. It is an unwatchable gallimaufry of crime, scandal, tear-jerker reunions and the like.

In peacetime the functions of mass media are advertising, entertainment and inculcating the norms and opinions that a nation, terrified of disunity, wants in its people. Even seemingly centrifugal ideas such as 'diversity' are reconfigured by the mass media and used to enforce the conformity that may presently be among America's strongest characteristics. In wartime such institutions have no capacity to be other than the means by which the central government instructs the populace.

This could even be said of such top-notch media as the *New York Times*, which often functions as an American *Osservatore Romano*, the semi-official publication of the government and the leading elites and power groups outside government. To the practised reader there are days when the *Times*'s front page looks more like a bulletin board of leaks and announcements from major private and public institutions than a newspaper printing independently gathered information.

Of late the *Times* has run into trouble. One of its reporters was revealed to be a cocaine-using wingnut who for months found it more convenient to invent the content of his news dispatches than to get on a plane and report them. It turned out that the newspaper's internal controls were too feeble to recognise what was fact and what was creative writing. That scandal had no sooner subsided than it was learned that Rick Bragg, a senior reporter, had been claiming an unpaid intern's legwork as his own. These incidents merely confirmed what perspicacious readers have known for some years, which is that one cannot rely on the paper's accuracy as one once could.

The noise attendant on these events was deafening, although their significance is not great. The *New York Times* has no plausible competition as the prestige national newspaper, so its readers will put up with an awful lot before they begin grubbing around for a substitute. It is the third, less widely reported uproar involving Judith Miller, a star foreign correspondent, that is causing consternation. In the lead-up to the invasion and afterwards, Miller was the principal *Times* correspondent writing about weapons of mass destruction. Her copy has been an unending warning that the Iraqis were ready, willing and able to let loose a nightmare of carnage on an innocent world. Since other, less prestigious publications and much, if not most, of television take their cue from the *Times*, her stories solidified the conviction that these weapons existed and were aimed at the American heartland. It is reasonable to assume Miller's work played no small part in building popular support for the war in the face of scepticism almost everywhere else.

Long before her weapons of mass destruction hit the page, Miller's critics, mostly other foreign correspondents and think-tankers, had come to believe that she is less of a reporter than a conduit through which powerful people and institutions get their side of the story out. Their suspicions about Miller were confirmed when it popped out that her main source for her weapons stories is Ahmad Chalabi, the Iraqi exile with a troubled past whom the White House and the Pentagon once hoped to govern their newly conquered territory. It also came out that at least one of her stories

*Ramaila Oilfield, Iraq, 27 March 2003:
Brigadier General Robert Crear talks to the
international media. Credit: US Army /
Pfc Mary Rose Xenikakis*

concerning WMDs had been all but dictated and edited by the army before Miller sent it to the *Times*, which put it on its front page.

The Miller episode provides a glimpse of some of the processes and manipulations by which the United States is governed, but it does not describe the completeness and uniformity of their effect on the population. No major news organisation evinced doubts that the famous 'smoking gun' would be found, and now that it is turning out to be a dribbling water pistol, the subject is passed over everywhere in near silence. The diminished and almost furtive forces of dissent blame the concentration of media ownership for the shrinkage of public dialogue into public monologue, but this may be wishful thinking. When Americans do have a podium on which to stand and freely express themselves, they rarely have much to say. And when they do, few of their fellow citizens are inclined to listen. Published organs representing dissenting points of view are few in numbers and readers. Only one United States senator, Robert Byrd of West Virginia, fully, completely and unqualifiedly opposed the invasion of Iraq.

The entertainment media are as important in the provision of information and the shaping of opinion as journalism. For the past ten or 15 years, movies, theatrical and made for TV, have presented a diet of shows glorifying American military might and how that might was used by the United States to save weak, incompetent, inferior democracies such as Great Britain. Ham-handed propaganda movies like the odious *Saving Private Ryan* are taken to be historical truth by the great unwashed and by the editorial writers. The country is soaked in false, inaccurate, distorted and self-adulatory histories. Thanks to these media, America is coming to see itself as the dissed democracy of generosity, goodness and valour which is met by ingratitude, spite and envious hatred, the natural consequence of being better than everyone else. The secondary message is that America is alone in a hostile world in which friends are few and unreliable.

At the same time political semiotics have been changed. American flag idolatry is practised all over; the flag lapel button or brooch for women is nigh on mandatory in certain occupations; the yellow ribbon is universally hung from trees, mailboxes, porches and all manner of public places. George W Bush has a four-person team doing for him what the 1930s movie maker Leni Riefenstahl did for Adolf Hitler, that is prepare backdrops heavy with symbolic meaning for presidential appearances. The pledge of allegiance has become a tool of social intimidation. One is pressured to recite it in the classroom, on the athletic field, at theatrical events and at the commencement of every kind of meeting. The singing of the national anthem is incessant. Athletic events begin with an 'Oh, say can you see' and are interrupted midway for a rousing chorus of 'God Bless America'. The country is taking on a hue and tone reminiscent of the authoritarian state.

As it does so, the distinction between patriotism and militarism is getting blurred. Even before 11 September the public was being schooled to believe in a version of *dulce et decorum est pro patria mori* which to a non–American might sound not unlike the creed of the suicide bomber. As the first mass sybaritic society, one that has perfected vicarious warfare in which only the other side falls down dead, few acts of self-immolation are to be anticipated, but others are sure to die. ❏

Nicholas von Hoffman is a journalist and author of several books including We are the People our Parents Warned us Against *(Ivan R Dee, 1989). He has written the libretto for a new opera,* Nicholas and Alexandra, *which opens in Los Angeles in September 2003*

SINCERE PROMISES

CHRISTOPHER HITCHENS

THE WORD 'UNILATERALISM' IS DOING
IDIOMATIC DUTY FOR THE WORD 'IMPERIALISM',
SIGNIFYING A HYPERPOWER THAT WANTS TO BE
EXEMPTED FROM THE RULES BECAUSE — WELL,
BECAUSE IT WROTE MOST OF THEM

In the lexicon of euphemism, the word 'superpower' was always useful because it did little more than recognise the obvious. The United States of America was a potentate in itself and on a global scale. It had only one rival, which was its obvious inferior, at least in point of prosperity and sophistication (as well as a couple of other things). So both were 'empires', in point of intervening in some countries whether those other countries liked it or not, and in arranging the governments of other countries to suit them. Still, only a few Trotskyists like my then-self were so rash as to describe the Cold War as, among other things, an inter-imperial rivalry.

The United States is not supposed, in its own self-image, to be an empire. (Nor is it supposed, in its own self-image, to have a class system — but there you go again.) It began life as a rebel colony and was in fact the first colony to depose British rule. When founders like Alexander Hamilton spoke of a coming American 'empire', they arguably employed the word in a classical and metaphorical sense, speaking of the future dominion over the rest of the continent. By that standard, Lewis and Clark were the originators of American 'imperialism'. Anti-imperialists of the colonial era would not count as such today. That old radical Thomas Paine was forever at Jefferson's elbow, urging that the United States become a superpower for democracy. He hoped that America would destroy the old European empires.

This perhaps shows that one should beware of what one wishes for because, starting in 1898, the United States *did* destroy or subvert all of the European empires. It took over Cuba and the Philippines from Spain (we still hold Puerto Rico as a 'colony' in consequence) and after 1918 decided that if Europe was going to be quarrelsome and destabilising, a large American navy ought to be built on the model of the British one. Franklin D

Roosevelt spent the years 1939 to 1945 steadily extracting British bases and colonies from Winston Churchill, from the Caribbean to West Africa, in exchange for wartime assistance. Within a few years of the end of World War II, the United States was the regnant or decisive power in what had been the Belgian Congo, the British Suez Canal Zone, and – most ominously of all – French Indochina. Dutch Indonesia and Portuguese Angola joined the list in due course. Meanwhile, under the ostensibly anti-imperial Monroe Doctrine, Washington considered the isthmus of Central America and everything due south of it to be its special province in any case.

In the course of all this – and the course of it involved some episodes of unforgettable arrogance and cruelty – some American officers and diplomats did achieve an almost proconsular status, which is why *Apocalypse Now* is based on Joseph Conrad's *Heart of Darkness*. But in general, what was created was a system of proxy rule, by way of client states and dependent regimes. And few dared call it imperialism. Indeed, the most militant defenders of the policy greatly resented the term, which seemed to echo leftist propaganda.

But nowadays, if you consult the writings of the conservative and neo-conservative *penseurs*, you will see that they are beginning to relish that very word. 'Empire – sure! Why not?' A good deal of this obviously comes from the sense of moral exaltation that followed 11 September. There's nothing like the feeling of being in the right and of proclaiming firmness of purpose. And a revulsion from atrocity and nihilism seems to provide all the moral back-up that is required. It was precisely this set of emotions that Rudyard Kipling set out not to celebrate, as some people imagine, but to oppose. He thought it was hubris, and he thought it would end in tears. Of course, there is always some massacre somewhere or some hostage in vile captivity with which to arouse opinion. And of course it's often true that the language of blunt force is the only intelligible one. But self-righteousness in history usually supplies its own punishment, and a nation forgets this at its own peril.

Unlike the Romans or the British, Americans are simultaneously the supposed guarantors of a system of international law and doctrine. It was on American initiative that every member nation of the United Nations was obliged to subscribe to the Universal Declaration of Human Rights. Innumerable treaties and instruments, descending and ramifying from this, are still binding legally and morally. Thus, for the moment, the word 'unilateralism' is doing idiomatic duty for the word 'imperialism', as signifying a hyperpower or ultra-power that wants to be exempted from the rules because – well, because it wrote most of them.

However, the plain fact remains that when the rest of the world wants anything done in a hurry, it applies to American power. If the 'Europeans' or the United Nations had been left with the task, the European provinces of Bosnia–Herzegovina and Kosovo would now be howling wildernesses, Kuwait would be the nineteenth province of a Greater Iraq, and Afghanistan might still be under Taliban rule. In at least the first two of the above cases, it can't even be argued that American imperialism was the problem in the first place. This makes many of the critics of this imposing new order sound like the whimpering, resentful Judean subversives in *The Life of Brian*, squabbling among themselves about 'What have the Romans ever done for us?'

I fervently wish that as much energy was being expended on the coming Ethiopian famine or the coming Central Asian drought as on the pestilence of Saddam Hussein. But, if ever we can leave the Saddams and Milosevics and Kim Jong-ils behind and turn to greater questions, you can bet that the bulk of the airlifting and distribution and innovation and construction will be done by Americans, including the new nexus of human rights and humanitarian NGOs who play rather the same role in this imperium that the missionaries did in the British one (though to far more creditable effect).

A condition of the new imperialism will be the specific promise that while troops will come, they will not stay too long. An associated promise is that the era of the client state is gone and that the aim is to enable local populations to govern themselves. This promise is sincere. A new standard is being proposed, and one to which our rulers can and must be held. In other words, if the United States will dare to declare out loud for empire, it had better be in its capacity as a Thomas Paine arsenal, or at the very least a Jeffersonian one. And we may also need a new word for it. ❏

Christopher Hitchens *is a contributing editor to* Vanity Fair *and lives in Washington, DC. He is the author of many books including* Orwell's Victory *and* Letters to a Young Contrarian. *This is an extract from* Regime Change *(Penguin, 2003)*

BRIDGING THE GAP

GARA LAMARCHE

WHERE ARE THE STRONG ALTERNATIVE
VISIONS AND THE INSTITUTIONS NEEDED
TO CHALLENGE THE RIGHT'S NEAR
DOMINANCE OF AMERICAN POLITICS?

Franklin D Roosevelt, the great president so firmly established in the American pantheon that even those who seek to lay waste to his achievements must pay him homage, left two powerful legacies that changed the course of US history. The first was the acknowledgement of state responsibility for the social security of citizens; the second the creation of global institutions built on the recognition that the path to world security lies in the rule of law, the protection of human rights, and the interdependence and cooperation of states.

The first two Republican presidents in the post-Roosevelt era, Eisenhower and Nixon, were staunch internationalists who largely accepted the framework for the modest welfare state that Roosevelt built and Truman enlarged. Ronald Reagan took a more confrontational stance with both the Soviet Union and the welfare state; George HW Bush (or '41', as his son likes to call him) was a fairly traditional conservative more interested in diplomacy than in domestic issues. None of them took the axe to the Roosevelt legacy that George W Bush is now wielding, with the support of the leadership of both houses of Congress.

I was among those who failed to predict just how radical this second Bush administration would be. Bush had been governor of Texas, where he enjoyed a reputation for bipartisanship (easier to achieve in a state where most Democrats are so conservative they would be Republicans almost anywhere else) and on a few occasions he had been known to go against the wishes of the fundamentalist right. It seemed to many in 2000 that the narrowness of his victory would require Bush to govern more from the centre.

We were wrong. Not only has Bush acted as if he had been elected in a landslide, with a strong mandate, but virtually without exception he has opted for extremist policies.

A simple exercise will illustrate. Taking just two days in June, there were items in the *New York Times* about efforts by the Bush Administration to:

- change the funding formula for Head Start, threatening a programme that provides early childhood education for millions of poor children;
- deport Muslim immigrants with no suspected involvement in terrorism for technical violations of their residency status;
- weaken already lax enforcement of gun laws;
- take the first steps to privatise the Medicare programme, which ensures health care for senior citizens;
- extend the latest Bush tax cut – in which the lion's share of benefits already goes to the richest Americans – while making deep cuts in services such as after-school programmes, and ballooning the national debt to a record-breaking US$400 billion;
- confirm as a life-tenured federal judge the Attorney General of Alabama best known for fighting to install the Ten Commandments on the wall of every courtroom;
- open up coastal preserves to offshore oil drilling;
- ban the annual Gay Pride Celebration by Justice Department employees.

The way the US went to war with Iraq, of a piece with its rejection of the Kyoto Treaty and the International Criminal Court as a sign of the administration's contempt for a multilateral approach to global security, justice, environmental and economic concerns, is well known to much of the world – better known, in fact, than it is to most Americans.

Since the United States dominates the world to a greater extent than any nation has dominated the world before, many want to know how we arrived at the state of affairs where power is exalted over law, and the poor are made poorer in order for the rich to become richer. They are hopeful for any signs that it might change. To give a comprehensive answer as to why this should be is beyond the scope of this short essay. But what is most missing from civil society in early twenty-first-century America, 'land of the free', is any significant opposition or dissent. This is not accidental; it is very nearly structural, and the result of a concerted effort by the right to control the institutions that might provide opposing voices.

The steady deregulation of the electronic media, which took a giant step backwards in June with the Federal Communication Commission's 3–2 vote to relax the rules on media concentration, has increasingly made the airwaves look like the shrillest British tabloids, combining sex and sensation-

Head Start programme, one of the most successful campaigns of the 1960s.
Credit: Eli Reed / Magnum Photos

alism with heated rightwing diatribes and slanted news coverage. Fox News, which has overtaken CNN in the ratings, is the paradigm of this trend. And the conglomeration of media is also troubling for what is left off: Clear Channel Radio, which owns an ever growing share of the local radio market, not only banned the Dixie Chicks band over one of its singers view of her president, it exhorted listeners to burn the band's CDs.

The blueprint for Bush's policies has been carefully developed for years by a small network of conservative foundations and think tanks. For more than 20 years they have been promoting a simple approach that markets and power, at home and abroad, should be freed of the inconvenient constraints of law. They've fed a generation of writers and policy specialists, supported and promoted their research, put them on television, and installed them in government positions and judgeships.

Meanwhile, the story goes, the progressive side (one of the many dilemmas of 'progressives' has been to find a label less politically toxic than 'liberal' or 'left') has been tripping over the complexity of its multiple, nuanced messages, unwilling to play the hardball game of its opponents. When you consider the defensiveness and timidity of those who might be expected to exercise moral leadership at a time when their deepest values and institutions are under attack – university and foundation presidents, officials of both political parties – the picture grows even worse.

But there are hopeful signs. From the grass roots, www.moveon.org has followed up its internet-based 'viral' campaign to foster anti-war protest with a massive effort against the FCC's broadcast deregulation plans. The FCC went ahead anyway, but the mobilising ability of this new force has not gone unnoticed. Other institutions are emerging to counter the right's influence over policy and law. These organisations, which aim to bridge the worlds of politics, the academy and mobilised constituencies such as labour and students, include the American Majority Institute, aiming to provide both a coherent message and a timely public response to key issues, and the American Constitution Society, a forum for those who still see the law as a force for justice and equality and an ally of social change.

But the right's near dominance of US politics, government and media will not be reversed without a strong alternative vision and the institutions to promote it. Do those who are taking steps in this direction have the determination and strength to stay the course? Whether Roosevelt's trans-formation of America and its role in the world endures and adapts in any meaningful form will depend on the answer to that question. ❏

Gara LaMarche is Vice-President and Director of US Programs for the Open Society Institute

WISE WORDS ON DEAF EARS

JOEL BEININ

11 SEPTEMBER SHOULD HAVE CONVINCED
AMERICAN POLICYMAKERS OF THE
FOOLISHNESS — DANGERS, EVEN — OF
ALLOWING THE US ACADEMIC STUDY OF
THE MIDDLE EAST TO BE CONSTRAINED BY
THE SENSITIVITIES OF A FEW. IT DIDN'T

To paraphrase Mark Twain, reports of the death of Middle East area studies have been greatly exaggerated. During the 1990s, many manifestos proclaimed that area studies, as a product of the Cold War, were shaped by the political discourse of a bygone era and mired in overly descriptive and untheoretical particularism. Hence we were advised to cast our lot with our individual disciplines, which had a more universalist outlook. The critique of the insularity of Middle East studies was appropriate, though I am not convinced that Middle East studies was or is any more insular than Chinese or Russian studies, or American studies for that matter.

The critique of area studies was also based on a misperception of its history. Middle East area studies began to emerge during the interwar period, not during the Cold War. That is to say that Middle East studies was emerging with an autonomous intellectual agenda before the Cold War and the concerted intervention of the US government. That agenda was shaped by missionary and petroleum projects distinct from, although allied with, the interests of the state and whose success required empathic understanding of Middle Eastern peoples. For this reason, those with Middle East expertise were regarded with suspicion in some circles, including parts of the academy. The National Defense Education Act of 1958 provided financial support and public sanction for the growth of Middle East area studies and simultaneously attempted to mobilise academic knowledge for the purposes of the state.

From these revised understandings of the relationship of area studies to disciplines and the history of Middle East studies we can learn several things. First, while situating our research and teaching in relation to existing bodies of knowledge and intellectual conversations remains imperative as ever, we need not feel overly inferior about the marginality of the Middle East in the structure of disciplinary knowledge. As 11 September made painfully clear, it is those who did not think that the Middle East or Islam were worthy of study who were insular, if not myopic.

Islamic social movements are a major phenomenon of global modernity, and the contemporary world cannot be understood without giving them a prominent place. Islamic social movements were also a prominent feature of an earlier phase of globalisation – the era of the new imperialism from the 1870s to 1914. It, too, cannot be adequately understood without accounting for them. And, as Janet Abu-Lughod has argued, Islam was the cultural cement of the fourteenth-century Eurasian commercial system. A very strong case can be made that for most of the past two thousand years, China and the Islamic world – not North America and Western Europe – have been the dominant centres of global economic and cultural power.

In several different historical eras, Middle East studies can play an important role in implementing Dipesh Chakrabarty's call to provincialise Europe, and along with it the categories of knowledge that emerged with the global dominance of Europe and North America. This is a worthy project, not because Euro-American culture deserves to be regarded with more suspicion and hostility than any other culture, but because, powerful as the United States now is in relation to the rest of the world, that power is situated in contingent historical conditions, whether we like it or not. Historically informed and self-critical awareness of the categories of our knowledge and the sources of our power is a good antidote to imperial hubris.

The early history of Middle East studies also teaches us that our project has always involved the collaboration of scholars of Middle Eastern origins with those based in North America and Europe. Middle East studies as we know them are inconceivable without institutions such as the American University of Beirut, the American University in Cairo and Robert College; publications such as *L'Egypte Contemporaine* and *Revue du Monde Musulman*; and individuals such as Philip Hitti, Albert Hourani and Charles Issawi. American Middle East studies are a cosmopolitan product. This has always been a source of anxiety, and in some cases outright panic, for those dedicated to policing the boundaries of knowledge and public discourse and enforcing a narrow view of American interests. We should embrace it as a reason for pride.

Middle East studies have had a shifting relationship with the US government and its adventures in the region. During the 1950s and 1960s, modernisation theory was the dominant social science orthodoxy. It was fully compatible with the project of expanding the post-World War II informal US imperium. In those decades, many scholarly studies praised US allies in the Middle East – Turkey, Lebanon, Tunisia and Iran – as successful examples of modernisation.

The 1967 Arab–Israeli war, the second Lebanese civil war and the Iranian revolution undermined the appeal of modernisation theory and stimulated critical intellectual projects that were directly or indirectly inspired by the global upsurge of 1968. Among the most enduring of them is the Middle East Research and Information Project, with which I have been associated for nearly 25 years.

Some have suggested that scholars of the Middle East have been especially prone to adopt approaches critical of US government policy in the region. But even a cursory look at the literature of Latin American studies or scholarship on any other area of the world, including the United States, reveals that this was a broad intellectual tendency that was especially strong in history, sociology and literary studies.

After the collapse of the Soviet bloc, much of American international studies became enthused by the concept of civil society because it seemed to have played a prominent role in the liberation of Eastern Europe. In the Middle Eastern context, this often involved investigating the extent to which Islam is compatible with democracy. This research agenda was not a conspiracy of anti-American radicals who wished to obfuscate the true character of Islam; it was encouraged by circles in and close to the US government.

Several other conceptual approaches and research agendas have mobilised varying degrees of enthusiasm among scholars of the Middle East over the years. This is not the place to evaluate them. I simply wish to point out that some of them have been compatible with the outlook of successive US governments and American interests as they define them, while others are rooted in competing views of what American interests should be. Moreover, while there certainly have been intellectual fashions and dominant tendencies, there have always been oppositional views of various kinds.

Does anyone doubt that this is the normal state of affairs in a democratic society? Humanistic scholarly life proceeds through a process of argumentation. While there is no final and absolute truth, disputation and debate, intemperate and infused with egoism as it may sometimes be, is the only vehicle we have to challenge received wisdom and open new intellectual horizons.

The holders of state power have always tried to impose an intellectual agenda compatible with their interests, as students of Middle East history know from the attempts of the 'Abbasid Caliphs al-Ma'mun (813–33) and al-Mu'tasim (833–42) to impose the rationalist *mu'tazili* doctrine on their subjects. And there have always been those who have struggled against the imposition of doctrines associated with state power, as we know from the ardent resistance of Ahmad ibn Hanbal (780–855) to the *mu'tazili* doctrine. As some would have it, the victory of ibn Hanbal in this confrontation is part of 'what went wrong' in Islamic societies. We could just as easily draw a different lesson: that when states attempt to impose an intellectual ortho-doxy – even an 'enlightened' one such as rationalism, secularism, moderni-sation, Arab socialism, Marxism-Leninism or neo-liberal economics and 'freedom' – they inevitably generate a resistance, which may or may not itself be enlightened. And in combating that resistance they may very likely adopt cruel and authoritarian measures that will undermine the legitimacy of whatever 'enlightened' ideas they espoused. The recent histories of Iraq, Syria, Egypt, Tunisia, Algeria, Iran and Turkey offer volumes of evidence for this proposition.

Governments ought to keep a certain distance from the academy. There will usually be plenty of scholars who will, of their own free will, choose to serve the interests of established power if given even modest incentives. If not, then perhaps they do not deserve to be served.

Let me conclude by saying something about the scurrilous attacks that have been levelled against the Middle East Studies Association of North America (MESA) collectively and several of our members individually during the course of the past year. The gist of these attacks is that MESA has been taken over by a crowd of post-colonial studies/post-modernist radicals inspired by Edward Said and that this takeover has been facilitated because half of our membership is composed of people of Middle Eastern origins. MESA is, therefore, an unpatriotic and not truly American organisation. Consequently, MESA and its members have been uninterested in warning the US about the dangers of radical Islam. Against the prevailing opinions in Washington, our members persist in opposing US policy on the Arab–Israeli conflict, on the pre-emptive war against Iraq and other such issues.

Anyone familiar with MESA and its members will know that these claims are an amalgam of outright mendacity and tendentious readings of the

San Francisco State University, August 2002: student of Middle East studies.
Credit: AP Photo / Eric Risberg

scholarship and popular writings of some MESA members by a highly selective body. Neither the board nor the Program Committee, which is primarily responsible for the content of the annual meetings, has any interest in
imposing an intellectual or political orthodoxy on the MESA membership.
This would, in any case, be impossible; and that is a good thing. The board,
and especially its Committee on Academic Freedom on the Middle East and
North Africa, has consistently defended human rights and academic
freedom. The board has also taken the position that it is in the national

SIGNED: ANGRY OF PHILADELPHIA

Campus Watch is a project of the Middle East Forum – a private, Philadelphia-based think tank – which has chosen to set itself the task of reviewing and critiquing Middle East studies in North America 'with an aim to improving them'. It accuses their targets of 'admitting only certain viewpoints and doing their best to close off alternate views', avoiding selected topics such as militant Islamic violence and 'presenting an activist propaganda in the classroom'.

The group, led by director Daniel Pipes and managing editor Jonathan Calt Harris, routinely single out US academics who have rejected what they describe as 'the views of most Americans and the enduring policies of the US government about the Middle East'. And in a strategy that has earned it the nickname 'the Campus Stasi', Campus Watch is setting about 'to monitor and gather information on professors who fan the flames of disinformation, incitement and ignorance'.

Among the 'examples' they cite on their website (www.campus-watch.org):

'There may be a war on terrorism under way, but the [offending] scholars downplay the dangers posed by militant Islam, seeing it as a benign and even democratising force.

'With only one exception, every American president since 1948 has spoken forcefully about the benefits to the United States from strong and deep relations with Israel. In contrast, American scholars often propagate a view of Middle Eastern affairs that sees Zionism as a racist offshoot of imperialism and blames Israel alone for the origin and persistence of the Palestinian problem.

'While Americans overwhelmingly supported the war to liberate Kuwait in 1991, the Middle East specialists just as overwhelmingly rejected that use of force; and the same divide has recurred in 2002 . . . [over the] military campaign against Iraq.

'Scholarly offerings frequently present in a benign light such hostile actors as the Islamic Republic of Iran, the Syrian Ba'ath regime, and other Middle East despotisms. In contrast, they emphasise and often exaggerate the faults of Israel, Turkey, Egypt and Kuwait. They blame Washington, not Tehran, for the hostile relations between these two states.'

Such attitudes, it claims, 'denigrate US interests' on campus. And those US interests, it explains, 'include strong ties with Israel, Turkey and other democracies as they emerge; human rights throughout the region; a stable supply and a low price of oil; and the peaceful settlement of regional and international disputes'. ❑

interest as well as the interest of advancing scholarship that there be an administrative separation between academic life and the United States government. Reasonable people might disagree about that, but I do not believe that holding one view or another on this matter is evidence of lack of patriotism.

In contrast to the fanciful notions of those who have attacked MESA, the history of the association since it was founded demonstrates that the range of intellectual opinion and topics open to discussion has broadened considerably over time. For example, the first annual meeting was held six months after the 1967 Arab–Israeli war. The board prevented formal discussion of that event at the meeting and even asked a graduate student to withdraw a proposed paper on the Arab–Israeli conflict 'due to the sensitivity of the subject'.

This was an expression of the gentlemen's agreement – and the founders of MESA were overwhelmingly gentlemen – which facilitated the establishment of MESA: discussion of the Arab–Israeli conflict would be avoided because it would generate too much controversy and undermine the collegiality of the organisation. Most importantly, as Timothy Mitchell has argued, airing of controversy on topics such as the Arab–Israeli conflict would undermine the claim of Middle East studies to objective and scientific knowledge. Consequently, for years there was no discussion of the Arab–Israeli conflict at MESA.

We have come a long way since then. No one would dare to propose that the Arab–Israeli conflict, or the mass murder of Armenians in the late Ottoman period, or the CIA's involvement in attempts at regime change in Iran, Syria, Lebanon and elsewhere, to name only a few controversial topics, should be excluded from discussion at MESA meetings.

We have three basic options before us in dealing with such controversial issues: 1) to ignore them; 2) to try to impose conformity; or 3) to encourage free and open discussion. I am sure that the consensus of MESA members is that the third option is the only one a scholarly organisation can consider.

The free and open discussion that has occurred within and beyond MESA has led to a significant expansion of the range of what are considered legitimate topics of enquiry and to a liberation of some space for articulating previously repressed opinions. For example, when I was an undergraduate at Princeton, I was not permitted to write my senior honours thesis on the post-1948 Palestinian national movement, on the grounds that the topic was less than 50 years old. Professors in Princeton's Department of Near Eastern

Studies who were critical of Israel rarely expressed their views to students. There was no class on the Arab–Israeli conflict. This was not a subject for public discussion. The topic was covered in a single lecture in the survey course on modern Middle East history. Most of us were not fully aware of the differences of opinion among our teachers, even as we saw some of them manoeuvring to reshape the political and intellectual tone of the department.

As a doctoral student at the University of Michigan I was told by my adviser, the late Richard P Mitchell, that he would support me if I wrote a PhD thesis on the formation of the Arab working class in Palestine, but that if I wrote a dissertation about Israel or Palestine I would likely have difficulty getting an academic job. That was the origin of my engagement with Egypt. While this has been an entirely positive experience, it was originally motivated by fear that those who held the then dominant views in the field of Middle East studies would use their power to restrict debate and impede the advancement of those with unorthodox views. I did not need much convincing that Dick Mitchell's advice was wise, as I had already witnessed the misuse of academic power on matters relating to the Arab–Israeli conflict while pursuing an MA at Harvard.

The intellectual boundaries of Middle East studies have been substantially redrawn since the time of my undergraduate and graduate training. This is what the self-proclaimed enforcers of academic propriety object to. Opinions that previously could barely be articulated at all now circulate relatively freely on campuses.

That freedom is now under attack and we must vigorously defend it. For example, Harvard President Lawrence Summers has clumsily attempted to police the limits of acceptable opinion on Middle Eastern topics by suggesting that calling for divestment from corporations doing business with Israel is 'anti-Semitic in . . . effect if not . . . intent'. One need not support the substance of the demand for divestment in order to discern the difference between even the most vehement criticism of Israel and its policies and anti-Semitism. We must resist such attempts to delegitimise dissenting opinion. They are grave threats to academic freedom and intelligent public discourse.

The administration and faculty of the University of North Carolina acted much more wisely and bravely in refusing to capitulate to attacks from the Christian right Family Policy Network and others in choosing as the summer reading assignment for incoming freshmen Michael Sells's translation and interpretation of the early verses of the Qur'an, *Approaching the Qur'an: The Early Revelations.*

Those who have attacked MESA are, in the main, neo-conservative true believers with links to the Israeli right. They tend to think that phrases such as 'war on terrorism', 'clash of civilisations' and 'axis of evil' are serious explanations for what is happening in the contemporary Middle East. They are welcome to their opinions; and they certainly have no dearth of outlets for expressing them.

Many of us may feel that because the attacks on MESA are intellectually vacuous, there is no need for us to respond. In my opinion, it would be a mistake for us to dismiss such slogans as arrant nonsense, simplistic and ahistorical as they may be. If we believe so, we must marshal the appropriate arguments to demonstrate the case. We should expose students to this material and teach them to understand the debate. And we should make our case to the broader public in whatever venues are available to us. Moreover, we cannot ignore the fact that these notions are being propagated by circles close to the government of the most powerful country in human history in concert with unprecedented assertions of a right to make and unmake regimes throughout the world, especially in the Middle East. It is a dangerous moment when a state accustomed to thinking its dominion is absolute confronts the limits of its power, as was the case on 11 September 2001. ❏

Joel Beinin is Professor of Middle East History at Stanford University and Past President of the Middle East Studies Association of North America

The full version of this text, the Presidential address at the 2002 annual meeting of the Middle East Studies Association of North America, is published in the MESA Bulletin, *vol 37, no 1 (July 2003)*

PULLING THE PLUG ON FREE SPEECH
CHRIS HEDGES

The New York Times *Pulitzer prize-winning war correspondent was only three minutes into his speech to new graduates at Rockford College in Illinois when some students – angered by his critique of US strategy in Iraq and the Middle East – rushed the stage and tried to drown him out with shouts and foghorns. Some students staged a silent protest at the back of the hall. Another student threw her graduation cap and gown at the stage in anger. Hedges' microphone was twice cut off and he had to be escorted from the building by security before the event finished. Rockford College was once famous for its liberal traditions; its most famous alumni was Jane Addams, pacifist and 1931 Nobel Peace Prize-winner.*

Fear engenders cruelty; cruelty fear, insanity and then paralysis. In the centre of Dante's circle the damned remained motionless. We have blundered into a nation we know little about and are caught between bitter rivalries and competing ethnic groups and leaders we do not understand. We are trying to transplant a modern system of politics invented in Europe characterised, among other things, by the division of earth into independent secular states based on national citizenship into a land where the belief in a secular civil government is an alien creed. Iraq was a cesspool for the British when they occupied it in 1917; it will be a cesspool for us as well – the curfews, the armed clashes with angry crowds that leave scores of Iraqi dead, the military governor, the Christian Evangelical groups who are being allowed to follow on the heels of our occupying troops to try and teach Muslims about Jesus.

At this point Hedges stopped speaking because of a disturbance in the audience. Rockford College President Paul Pribbenow took the microphone: 'My friends, one of the wonders of a liberal arts college is its ability and its deeply held commitment to academic freedom and the decision to listen to each other's opinions. If you wish to protest the speaker's remarks, I ask that you do it in silence, as some of you are doing in the back. That is perfectly appropriate but he has the right to offer his opinion here and we would like him to continue his remarks.' Hedges then continued . . .

The occupation of the oilfields, the notion that the Kurds and the Shi'ites will listen to the demands of a centralised government in Baghdad, the same Kurds and Shi'ites who died by the tens of thousands in defiance of Saddam Hussein, a man who happily butchered all of those who challenged him, and this ethnic rivalry has not gone away. The looting of Baghdad, or let me say the looting of Baghdad with the exception of the oil ministry and the interior ministry – the only two ministries we bothered protecting – is self-immolation.

As someone who knows Iraq, speaks Arabic, and spent seven years in the Middle East, if the Iraqis believe rightly or wrongly that we come only for oil and occupation, that will begin a long bloody war of attrition; it is how they drove the British out and remember that, when the Israelis invaded southern Lebanon in 1982, they were greeted by the dispossessed Shi'ites as liberators. But within a few months, when the Shi'ites saw that the Israelis had come not as liberators but occupiers, they began to kill them. It was Israel who created Hezbollah and it was Hezbollah that pushed Israel out of southern Lebanon.

As William Butler Yeats wrote in 'Meditations in Time of Civil War', 'We had fed the heart on fantasies / The heart's grown brutal from the fare.'

This is a war of liberation in Iraq, but it is a war now of liberation by Iraqis from American occupation. And if you watch closely what is happening in Iraq, if you can see it through the abysmal coverage, you can see it in the lashing out of the terrorist death squads, the murder of Shi'ite leaders in mosques, and the assassination of our young soldiers in the streets. It is one that will soon be joined by Islamic radicals and we are far less secure today than we were before we bumbled into Iraq.

We will pay for this, but what saddens me most is that those who will by and large pay the highest price are poor kids from Mississippi or Alabama or Texas who could not get a decent job or health insurance and joined the army because it was all we offered them. For war in the end is always about betrayal, betrayal of the young by the old, of soldiers by politicians, and of idealists by cynics. Read *Antigone*, when the king imposes his will without listening to those he rules or to Thucydides' history. Read how Athens' expanding empire saw it become a tyrant abroad and then a tyrant at home. How the tyranny the Athenian leadership imposed on others it finally imposed on itself.

This, Thucydides wrote, is what doomed Athenian democracy; Athens destroyed itself. For the instrument of empire is war and war is a poison, a poison which at times we must ingest just as a cancer patient must ingest a poison to survive. But if we do not understand the poison of war – if we do not understand how deadly that poison is – it can kill us just as surely as the disease.

We have lost touch with the essence of war. Following our defeat in Vietnam we became a better nation. We were humbled, even humiliated. We asked questions about ourselves we had not asked before. We were forced to see ourselves as others saw us and the sight was not always a pretty one. We were forced to confront our own capacity for atrocity – for evil – and in this we understood not only war but more about ourselves. But that humility is gone.

War, we have come to believe, is a spectator sport. The military and the press – remember, in wartime the press is always part of the problem – have turned war into a vast video arcade game. Its very essence – death – is hidden from public view. ❏

Chris Hedges *is a journalist. His new book,* What Every Person Should Know About War, *is published by Free Press in the United States*

Excerpted from the transcript of his speech as published by the Rockford Register Star *(http://www.rrstar.com)*

STERN LESSONS

AFTER 11 SEPTEMBER 2001, SOME
PEOPLE IN UNIVERSITIES IN AMERICA
BECAME A LITTLE LESS FREE

• In December 2001, Janis Besler Heaphy, publisher of the *Sacramento Bee* newspaper, was booed off stage at California State University after asking: 'To what degree are we willing to compromise our civil liberties in the name of security?'

• The same month, Duke University professor Gary Hull had his college website shut down after he posted an article entitled 'Terrorism and its Appeasement' calling on Congress to declare war 'on secular grounds and name the terrorist-sponsoring nations to be obliterated'. He was later instructed to add a disclaimer disassociating the university from his views.

'The general feeling in post September 11 America seems to be that "No one should have to listen to ideas or even acts that upset them."'
—Chronicle of Higher Education

• Saint Xavier University professor Peter Kirstein responded angrily to Cadet Robert Kurpiel's request for permission to promote the US Air Force Academy at the school. 'I am furious you would even think I would support you and your baby-killing tactics,' he told Kurpiel. 'You are unworthy of my support.' On 15 November 2002 Kirstein was suspended.

• Professor Kenneth Hearlson of Orange Coast Community College was suspended for 11 weeks after Muslim students accused him of calling them 'terrorists', a claim he denied. A lobby group, Foundation for Individual Rights in Education (FIRE), used audiotapes to win his reinstatement. Hearlson had asked students on 18 September 2001 why Muslims condemned terrorist attacks in New York but not attacks in Israel.

'I probably do feel a little less free in my classes each year. But that seems to me an appropriate acknowledgement both of the increasing diversity of our society and the likelihood that I will have more and more people of different faiths and backgrounds in my classes.'

—*Law professor Robert O'Neil, Virginia University*

• On 12 September 2001, University of California library assistant Jonnie Hargis emailed a message disputing the use of US taxpayers' money to fund the Israeli military and asking, 'Who are the terrorists anyway?' The university suspended him for a week, claiming that he had created 'a hostile environment' for his colleagues with his views. The university was later advised to clarify its policies on alleged email abuse.

• When history professor Richard Berthold told his class on 11 September 2001, 'Anyone who can blow up the Pentagon has my vote,' state legislators threatened to cut the University of New Mexico's funding unless he was fired. Initially dismissed, he was reprimanded after apologising, but barred from teaching freshmen for a year.

'The ability of an administration to control the content of college newspapers is worrying to us who believe the college press should be free and independent.'

—*Trevor Brown, Dean of the University of Indiana*

• A front-page story, a cartoon and an editorial intended for the 15 March 2003 issue of *The Arrow*, a student paper at Utica High School in Michigan, were removed from the publication on the order of the school's principal. The reports described a pending lawsuit brought by a local resident who claimed that school bus exhaust fumes had made him ill; the principal claimed they contained 'factual errors'.

• *The Rearguard*, a student paper at Portland State University, was closed on 23 February 2001, after officials discovered that the students were investigating six-year-old confidential school files labelled 'to be destroyed' found outside the paper's offices. The paper was reopened only after its student editor promised to return the files and promised to drop such investigations.

• The Hudson Valley Community College student newspaper's staff were officially locked out of their office for eight days in February 2000 after they published a 'help wanted' advertisement from a local strip club that featured a picture of a woman in a bikini. The paper could be reopened only after staff had promised not to run such adverts again.

'We want to be able to tell people who use the library that records are confidential, and they can use materials without fear of intimidation. That's being now usurped by federal agents.'
—Barbara Dimick, Madison Public Library director

• The Federal Bureau of Investigation was reported to have visited 545 US libraries between September 2001 and October 2002 requesting details of readers' records, specifically the kind of books they chose. Legal powers provided by the US Patriot Act allow the FBI to right to request such information 'to protect against international terrorism or clandestine activities' – and ban the librarians and booksellers from even mentioning the FBI's inquiry to others.

• During the US anthrax scare, Temple University computer centre chief librarian complained that two FBI agents ordered two staff secretly to copy the contents of a library employee's computer hard drive – the employee had been detected to have received an email containing the word 'anthrax'.

'Ever since their founding, American colleges have punished students for words and actions deemed offensive, immoral or seditious.'
—John K Wilson, State of Academic Freedom ❏

Compiled by **Ioli Delivani**

Sources: cnn.com, College Freedom, Common Dreams News, FIRE, Indiana Daily Student, *Intermarket Forecasting*, International Herald Tribune, Saint Xavier University Chicago: News and Events, *Student Press Law Center*, Daily Californian, Village Voice

LETTER FROM DAY 21

DARRYL PINCKNEY

WANT TO UNDERSTAND THE NEW
AMERICA? LIE DOWN IN FRONT OF
THE TELEVISION AND SUBMIT TO ITS
SATURATION 'NATIONAL NARRATIVES'

On Day 14 of the war, I was on the Queensboro Bridge en route to
La Guardia airport, trying to count the American flags and poles spaced
along the construction and road work in the lane to my right. Workmen's
booths had union signs in support of our troops, Bush and America. I was
on my way to my home town, Indianapolis, Indiana, the place in which I
experienced America in a way I did not when in New York. Since my
childhood the US population has shifted steadily westward, so much so that
any place east of the Mississippi River is spoken of as being the East. But
when I was growing up, Indiana was considered a part of the Midwest, the
American heartland. As my father turned the car into the old neighbourhood, the yellow ribbons on maple and oak trees as well as the flags
presiding over manicured lawns told me where I was.

I first encountered the war on terror's 'racial profiling' in Indianapolis.
Back in December 2001, the first Christmas after the attack on the World
Trade Centre, I was leaving Indianapolis for New York. Indianapolis
airport, like all US airports, had been placed under federal control. Heavily
armed National Guardsmen were stationed inside and outside the terminal.
The white, middle-aged women at the check-in counter told me my suit-
case would go through a new security procedure. After I received my
boarding pass, a security type requested that I follow him and my bag. He
put my bag through a special, large X-ray machine, a high-tech one that
because of its size nevertheless put me in mind of the clumsy, low-tech
equipment the East German border guards manned at Checkpoint Charlie
in the last decade of the Cold War. A young, neatly dressed white couple
also had to stand on a designated, roped-off mat as they, too, watched their
bags ride the conveyor belt into the X-ray machine. Then I was free to go
through the metal detector and head towards the departure gates. I was
thinking that the new security arrangements weren't so bad. But just as I
was boarding the plane, I was asked to step out of the line.

I found myself together with two other black guys behind a desk set up to the side of the departure gate. The two black guys were tall, huge, young, built like prison inmates and dressed like hip-hop stars – head rags, construction boots, jeans falling off their hips. The white security guards asked them to empty their pockets, to surrender their carry-on items, boots and belts. By the time it was my turn to step up to the desk, the young white guy running the electronic wand over my arms, legs and socks was trembling. Clearly he had never been a part of a security operation based on race. And the young white couple whose bags had gone through the special X-ray machine were shaking as they waited their turn. Clearly, they'd never been stuck with blacks before, left feeling accused by the dark side of the authority.

As I got on the plane, the two huge hip-hop dudes were already seated in first class. One whose lungs were big enough for the whole plane to hear him when he talked normally observed as I passed, 'They checked you, too, huh? Just us, right? Well, if it makes them feel more secure, hell, I'm all for it.' In economy, I noticed a smartly dressed black guy seated with a similarly GQ white guy. When the plane made it to the New York area, I asked the black guy travelling with the white guy if he'd been pulled aside at the gate in Indianapolis for a security check. He hadn't. I went up to the two hip-hop dudes in the luggage claim area and said not only had a young white couple also been stopped, one black guy hadn't. 'Yeah, but you know what? I'm an actor. I travel a lot. One thing I've noticed is that they never stop the gay guys. Only us guys with beards,' he said, thumping me and then himself. He thought it might be good for white people to see racial profiling in action every time they took a plane. He said it was important for people to witness such things in a country where we were allowed to see less and less of what was really happening.

But a year later, Operation Iraqi Freedom was being covered in a way no war had been before. Coverage of the Iraqi invasion was around-the-clock. My parents have reached the age at which the television is not only on all the time, as if for companionship, it is usually tuned to the same terrestrial network all day long, the station that runs the ads of most interest to senior citizens. My parents sit with local and big-city newspapers, with the *Nation* and the *New York Review of Books* – they who were appalled when I told them that the al-Jazeera news network had received a prize from *Index on Censorship,* they who weren't surprised to learn that the al-Jazeera online service was mysteriously hacked, blocked, in the US – but in spite of their stacks of reading material, they absolutely had to get the pictures and the sounds, had to have television, had to have their habitual station. Suburban homes often have as many televisions as they do telephones. If I wanted to escape my parents' channel, I had much to choose from. Anyone who wanted to could have a report of some kind at any hour: the national commentators were suitably grave; the local news anchor people came across as comfortingly upbeat; CNN was mercilessly repetitious; and the Murdoch affiliate in town was as gung-ho about the troop advance as a sportscast.

Living away from the US is no longer as far away as it was 50 years ago, in Wright and Baldwin's day, but you don't know what the US is like, what people in the US are going through, until you have submitted to its saturation reporting, to the 'national narratives' thousands collaborate on turning the news into. And people in the US don't get news from any non-American sources unless they hunt for it. My ability to filter the American national narrative diminished when my source of news included lots of television. But then overnight the news itself changed: success for our troops, toppled statues, cheering crowds of the liberated. Television magazines and morning interview programmes went solemn with relief, with humility about the victors' responsibilities. Entertainment programmes ran features on which reporter would emerge from the war a superstar of reporting. They all picked the young NBC reporter who then died of a heart embolism.

Television is not a window on to America; if anything, television masks America. Peter Bart, writing in *Variety*, the entertainment weekly, the hallowed trade publication of Broadway, recognised this when he reviewed the Iraqi war and its coverage, saying that it was 'a winner, as expertly executed as it was scripted'. He went on to ask, 'So if it played so well, why did the whole exercise feel so surreal? Why was it discomforting to watch history cosy up to showbiz? To start with, were we really watching war or a sort of sprawling trailer about war?' Bart contended that even though this was 'history's first mega high-tech war', the hunkered-down, embedded reporters gave very little sense of the weaponry, the place, the conflict. He claimed that the total access and constant coverage were part of a carefully constructed illusion. The viewers were kept at a distance. The cameras didn't really tell us where they were and the embedded journalists were engaged in what Bart called 'advocacy', rather than reporting. These days they won't get the story unless they're close to the sources of power and the

America, November 1948: a new addition to the family. Credit: AP Photo

only way to be close to the sources of power is to agree with them, to repeat what they say, to broadcast what the powerful feed the press. We watched as one nation and didn't see too many corpses, which was somehow proper in a country where, according to the polls, most people believed that Saddam had something to do with al-Qaida or soon would have.

I came back to New York in a snowstorm, on Day 21 of the 'regime change' mission. I took a break from the newspapers, didn't look at television or the computer screen, didn't go to Times Square to watch a statue of Saddam fall on the big screen. I wanted to avoid the paradox of my position – outwardly glum, but secretly pleased when things looked rough for Bush, Rumsfeld, Wolfowitz and Rove; outwardly pleased for the soldiers, for the Iraqi survivors, Great Britain's Channel 4 News diplomatic correspondent, Lindsey Hilsum, filing from the Palestine Hotel in Baghdad, but inwardly glum as Baghdad airport was conquered.

But I answered the phone. After the fall of Baghdad, a rumour flew out of the Kennedy Centere to my phone to the effect that Israel was preparing a strike on Syria. They want Syria out of Lebanon; they want Syria to stop backing Hezbollah; they will say that Saddam's illegal arsenal was moved to Syria. That same day a rumour flew out of a Washington restaurant to my phone to the effect that Condoleezza Rice said that the administration was going to get serious about a Palestinian settlement. The truth is that few know and those few who do know are not friends of my beliefs. A high school classmate of mine serves in the Bush Administration. It's as though every frat boy and yahoo I was ever rude to now runs the world.

The war was not the problem that the occupation of Iraq will be. This war we can't pay for and probably won't pay for may mean liberation for Iraqis, but little control over their own assets or natural resources for a good long while. The National Debt Clock on Sixth Avenue will soon reach four and a half trillion. What happened to the Clinton surplus? Answer: arms. The early signs are that US policy is likely to be a mixture of inadvertently infantilising the Iraqis while at the same time rushing to create a new Iraqi middle class. Whatever the policy, it will be derived from an overriding assumption that desperate regions want what we have. There is a reason everybody on the planet is longing to come to America, Americans tell themselves, even as the America the rest of the world is or is not dreaming about comes under threat from more draconian legislation, such as the USA Patriot Act, the second instalment of which you can't even read online. The site is never available. What will we do in a country where even things supposedly public are secret?

The war means less freedom for Americans, a state of alert set to last indefinitely. The 'Israelisation of America', some people in New York are calling it. Other people call it the 'hemispherisation of America', by which they mean to say that the US suffered a *coup d'état* in December 2000 and has become a banana republic, like the governments in Latin and South America that it has always preferred to deal with. But the voters could have repudiated the Republican Administration in the 2002 Congressional elections and they didn't. The successful prosecution of the war means not deferring to anybody else. It has reinforced a feeling that has been emanating from the mainstream for a while: Americans don't need Europe or European culture any more. After all, every other country wants to be like us and if they don't they're just jealous. The cocoon, fortress mood fits with the wilful dismissal of the rest of the world and may help to explain why popular culture in the US it at its lowest, meanest level in 50 years.

I'd been saying to British friends that an American could say anything on the margins, but the mainstream was very policed. I usually cited the *New York Post* attack on the actor Alex Baldwin a while ago when he suggested that our troubles began with the Supreme Court's decision about Florida in the 2000 presidential election. Websites sprang up, advocating in a humorous vein the deportation of liberal Hollywood types, who are written off as 'irrelevant' anyway. That is the new buzzword, the new triumphalist attitude: the nay-sayers are irrelevant, anachronistic, out of touch with the changed global reality. On some campuses, students have expressed their impatience with Leftist professors. Fear of being in the cold when the economy collapses and of not counting for much in the meantime may be why some young writers today sound like Irving Kristol when he switched from liberal to conservative. Yet the old liberal voices – Mailer, Schlesinger, Sontag – are among the clearest.

Some people say our troubles began with Bush Sr's appointment of Clarence Thomas to the Supreme Court in 1988. It's always been hard to explain to people from elsewhere, who could never see the difference between Republicans and Democrats, that it does matter which political party appoints our judges from top to bottom. Some people say that the nation state itself has become irrelevant in the age of global capitalism and supranational corporations. The bottom line and brand name mentality has wrecked the US. Big business bought up almost everything in the communications and cultural media market long ago. The prestige that used to belong to liberal culture is perversely withheld; seriousness is bestowed on the inanities of the right. It's hard to live here if you are not a success, which may be why the thousands of white-collar workers who got laid off during the Iraq crisis have stayed so quiet about their lost ways of life.

I blame Ayatollah Khomeini and the example he set for the Christian Right in the US in 1980 for the way things are now. Being an absolutist bastard gets results in politics; uncompromising fundamentalism works. The mission to bring democracy to the Middle East has accomplished the liberation of the Shiites. This worries people of a secular cast of mind, but not the religious Right. After all, among intellectuals respect and understanding for Islam implies the same protection from blasphemers for Christianity. A Middle East policymaker under Kennedy pointed out that even though the

US uses 30 per cent of the world's oil, most of the oil in the Middle East goes to the European and Far East markets. He argued that religion was the deeper motive behind the Bush policy in the Middle East. Maybe that's why there are so many black faces in front of the cameras: we're Christians and in the army, too. Some Christians believe that Christ won't come again, can't come again, if Christians are not in possession of the Holy Land. That is why we have the worrying situation of historically the most anti-Semitic people in the US now being the most pro-Zionist. Don't worry, Sharon, we'll take care of them. An acquaintance told me with much excitement that she was helping to prepare a big conference in New York on the rise of anti-Semitism. I didn't have the courage to ask if she planned on having non-Zionist Jewish people speak. They get accused of betrayal by other Jews. They are having a hard time here at the moment. Some of my non-Zionist Jewish friends tell me that they are reluctant to speak their minds in conversation with other Jews until they are sure they are in safe company.

Fear of speaking out, fear of surveillance, fear of what the Bush Administration will do next – though we are assured that the US is a nation in which 76 per cent of the population says that it is religious, I wonder. There are official answers and then the answers Americans don't give. We are becoming much like the Eastern bloc of old, a place where society has little to do with the state, a place where people try to live behind the backs of authority. That may explain why the percentage of registered voters in each US election in the past 20 years has steadily declined, no matter how crucial and critical the vote seems. Are people in the Department of Homeland Security thinking of the numbers of undocumented migrant workers who come regularly into California, where most of the produce consumed in the US is grown? Midge Dector, one of the original members of the neo-conservative movement of the 1980s, may be writing a biography of Donald Rumsfeld, but the internet is still alive with dissent, with emails that bring you Bush's Inaugural Address to a soundtrack of 'Burning Down the House' by Talking Heads. A consequence of the war may be greater, more upfront regulation of the world wide web.

I went to Times Square. On 42nd Street the voice of Dr Martin Luther King stopped me. I looked around. His voice was coming from a small speaker attached above the door of what looked like a disused club. Its doors were padlocked, though I could see a few people in what looked like an exhibition space. A sign in the window said that the broadcast of the historic speech against the Vietnam War that Dr King made at Riverside

Church on 4 April 1967, exactly one year before he was assassinated, was a project sponsored by a college in Queens. Dr King's voice exhorted the passers-by. His Christianity had led him to pacifism. Now and then a white kid would stop, smoke a cigarette, jot down a few lines on a notepad or a piece of paper. Meanwhile, the bustle of Times Square went on: traffic, the sirens, the sound of a band advertising some upcoming event, the crowds. 'I like my history where it belongs,' a sportscaster had said on television not long before, 'in the past.'

As we enter some sort of unimagined cultural and evolutionary regression, the prophetic voices of the past are drowned out. We have become a nation where many believe that the past is a problem and that we would be better off paying less attention to it. A black woman poet told me that when she heard Bush use the word 'crusade' after 11 September, she wanted to remind him that the Christians lost back then. ❏

Darryl Pinckney *is the author of* High Cotton

STRIP SEARCH by Martin Rowson

It is *typical* of cynical OLD EUROPEANS that they dismiss the **UNIDED STATES** of **AMERIKA** as a *benighted land* totally bereft of a **SENSE** of **IRONY**...
However, as with **EVERYTHING ELSE**, in Irony terms America *leads the world!*

For starters, we all know that Amerika is a *vibrant, classless, democratic* REPUBLIC, so is obviously run by **PLUTOCRATIC ARISTOCRATS** who know that it is their DESTINY to **REIGN LIKE KINGS!**

(Although they also know that, despite believing in DIVINE RIGHT, they also have to be elected, usually, so the aristos pretend to be ordinary *dumb* slobs like the electorate — see fig. 1)

ONE THINGY I LEARNIFIED AT **YALE** IS THAT I'M JUST AN **ORDINARY DUMB JOE JUS'** LIKE ALL THE OTHER LIDDLE GUYS OUT THERE, AN' VEESY VERSO!

Fig. 1.

A deeper Irony arises here. Although DESTINED to be KINGS, the aristos don't actually believe in Government, as it gets in the way of all that vibrant classless (but not necessarily *democratic*) stuff (fig. 2) ———

BUT! A KING needs a KINGDOM (Texas won't quite do) even if you don't intend to do anything apart from executing poor blacks when you come into your BIRTHRIGHT and become KING. This makes it all very confusing...

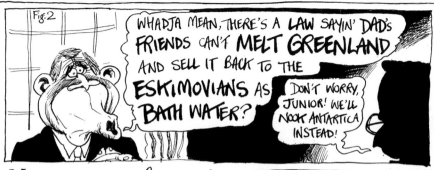

Fig.2

WHADJA MEAN, THERE'S A **LAW** SAYIN' **DAD'S FRIENDS** CAN'T **MELT GREENLAND** AND **SELL IT BACK** TO THE **ESKIMOVIANS** AS **BATH WATER?**

DON'T WORRY, JUNIOR! WE'LL NOOK ANTARTICA INSTEAD!

Worse, you can only *fuck* over the Economy & line the pockets of your Plutocratic Aristocrat buddies for SO LONG before your subjects start thinking you're a BAD KING! BUT, if you *do anything* to improve the lives of your subjects you will become, by your own lights, a TYRANT (fig. 3)

AN' WE MIGHT DO SOMETHIN' 'BAHT HEALTHCARE AN' SCHOOLS AN' ALL, BUT PROBABLY NOT...

GODDAM! THIS COUNTRY IS TURNIN' INTO NAZI GERMANY!

Fig.3

IRONIC? I THOUGHT THEY WERE NEXT! AIN'T WE STILL DEALIN' WITH THE IROQICS?

And thus the only option left to you, in order to uphold those FOUNDING (and clearly *ironic*) PRINCIPLES of democracy, liberty and all that old guff so that they shall not *perish from the Earth* is to become EMPEROR of a CONQUERED and RESENTFUL WORLD as a classic DISPLACEMENT ACTIVITY so that your impoverished and neglected subjects can democratically elect you (if absolutely necessary) to be KING BY DIVINE RIGHT. *Ironic, huh?*

@Martin Rowson '03

UNKINDEST CUTS

JACK G SHAHEEN

MOST AMERICAN MINORITIES CAN EXPECT
FAIR CINEMATIC REPRESENTATION FROM
HOLLYWOOD — BUT NOT ARAB-AMERICANS
AND MUSLIMS

Hollywood's role in preparing the way for the war in Iraq wasn't to churn out overt propaganda, but to condition audiences to perceive Arabs – and by extension all Muslims – as unrelenting enemies of Western values. To this day, Hollywood cinema continues to drive this other anti-Semitism in spite of the fact that Arabs, like Jews, are Semites sharing a common genetic make-up.

In cinematic terms we first went to war in Iraq in 1943, when Saddam Hussein was still wetting his diapers. The movie *Adventure in Iraq* featured the US Air Force staging a 'shock and awe' bombing of Iraq to free British and US hostages. The movie's Arabs were portrayed as pro-Nazi 'devil worshippers', fanatics or purring sheikhs. But *Adventure in Iraq* was nothing new. With increasing momentum from 1896 until 2003, film makers have collectively indicted all Arabs. Without let-up, movies displayed them as uncivilised religious fanatics or money-mad sheikhs bent on terrorising both Christians and Jews.

I use the word 'other' not because anti-Semitism against Jews is passé (it isn't), but because the most damaging films directed against Arabs were released in the last third of the twentieth century, at a time when Holly-wood was eliminating stereotypical portraits of other groups.

Regrettably, it remains acceptable to keep pushing anti-Semitism in movies provided the Semites are Arabs who, like yesteryear's stereotypical Jews, supposedly represent all that is evil and depraved. Hollywood's tiresome depiction of hook-nosed Arabs as money-grubbers out to take over the world, killing the innocent people in worship of a 'different' God, all the while scheming to seduce blonde virgins, parallels the image of Jews in Nazi-inspired movies such as *Jud Süss* (1940) and *Der Ewige Jude* (1940).

Who am I to be drawing such parallels with the 'other anti-Semitism'? I'm a Christian of Lebanese origin born in Pittsburgh, a veteran of the US armed forces and of our higher education establishment. I'm also, in a delicate phrase these days, an Arab-American. I've spent my adult life as a professional observer committed to analysing America's image factories and their reckless distortions, not just of Arabs, but of Native Americans, Asians, blacks, Italians, Latinos, Jews – you name it.

In my book *Reel Bad Arabs: How Hollywood Vilifies a People*, I appealed for the kind of fair play that would put an end to ethnic stereotyping across the board. I offer as proof nearly a thousand movies where Hollywood went out of its way to turn Arab Muslims – Egyptians, Palestinians and other dark-complexioned baddies from Lebanon to Libya, from Syria to the Sudan – into the most maligned group in cinematic history. In spite of the evidence, many people have a hard time accepting this fact. But think about it: how often do you see a movie featuring an Arab or Arab-American as a 'regular guy'?

How did it start? Film makers inherited and built on Europe's pre-existing Arab caricatures. During the eighteenth and nineteenth centuries, European writers wove tales and painted portraits of wild, obese merchants, of fleshy belly dancers in gauzy veils, gyrating to finger cymbals in corrupt desert milieus. Rejuvenated Arabs now stalk the screen in a hodgepodge of melodrama and mayhem. From the prowling creature from *The Mummy* (1932), the evil Palestinians in Arafat-style kaffiyehs in *True Lies* (1994), the terrorist shoot-'em-ups such as *Rules of Engagement* (2000) and even children's films such as Disney-Touchstone's *Kazaam* (1996) through to musical comedies such as *Road to Morocco* (1942) and Elvis Presley's *Harum Scarum* (1965), viewers stand and cheer when everyone – even, for heaven's sake, Vegas showgirls – trounce movie Arabs.

Films also dehumanise, demonise and exoticise Arab women. In movies such as *The Golden Blade* (1953), *Black Sunday* (1977), *Protocol* (1984) and *The Sheltering Sky* (1990), Arab women appear as subservient, mute and shapeless bundles of black; as beasts of burden carrying jugs on their heads; as bosomy belly dancers, scantily clad harem maidens or bombers.

Why perpetuate these images? The answer is The P Factor: Politics, Prejudice, Profit and Presence (lack of).

Take politics. Since the 1940s America's leaders have taken pro-Israeli positions, so it's no surprise that Hollywood should capitalise on US policy. These films have made it easier for Americans to embrace the occupation of Iraq and Palestine and minimise the deaths of innocent Arab civilians as collateral damage. And what's in it for Israel? More than half, 28, of Hollywood's 43 all-Palestinians-are-terrorists mythic movies were filmed in the

Jewish state. All through the 1980s, movies such as *The Ambassador* (1984), *Children of Rage* (1987) and *Wanted Dead or Alive* (1987) showed Palestinian aggressors killing Israeli civilians. How many movies during that decade showed Israeli settlers and/or soldiers gunning down Palestinian civilians? Not one.

So how does the other anti-Semitism fit that scenario? Turn the demonisation process around. Suppose Hollywood and Arab movie makers had worked together to project and export images of Israelis and Americans as terrorists? Who among us wouldn't properly condemn such films as blatantly anti-Semitic?

Accurate perspectives of the Arabs world are hard to come by. The information most people get comes from the nightly news reports and their selective presentations of the minority, Arab radicals who chant 'Death to America!' as they burn Uncle Sam in effigy. According to MSNBC TV journalist Ashleigh Banfield, one reason why the US is failing to 'win over the hearts of the Arab world' is the failure of the US media to consider the effect of the US government's partiality towards the Israeli position. 'As a journalist, I have been ostracised just from going on television and saying, "Here's what the leaders of Hezbollah, a radical Muslim group, are telling me about what is needed to bring peace to Israel,"' she said. 'And, "Here's what the Lebanese are saying." Like it or lump it, don't shoot the messenger, but that's what they do.'

Balanced images? It is not that audiences would or even should be expected to revel in a diet of Arab domestic life, let alone at the nostalgic level of the 1948 paean to the immigrant family, *I Remember Mama*. But, just to strike some needed balance, how about a feature film with an Arab-American in a heroic role, whether cleaning up in Wall Street or vindicating the innocent in a courtroom drama? Or simply laughing it up, as was seen in the rare example of de-stereotyped movie-making, the 1999 George Clooney film *Three Kings*?

Then there's greed. Youths flock to cineplexes and video outlets to watch their movie idols blowing Arabs to smithereens in films such as *Executive Decision* and *Rules of Engagement*.

What about presence? By now pretty much any Americans of whichever creed, colour or culture have had the opportunity to produce and project images of themselves and their heritage. With one remaining exception:

Opposite: Harum Scarum, *1965: Elvis gets the Arabian princess, and rescues good Arabs from evil ones. Credit: BFI Stills / Warner Bros*

ethnic bias continues to deny Arab-Americans a significant place in the creative process.

Exclusion of any people damages us all. That includes the industry itself. Yet nobody talks about this exclusion, or not openly. Other previously excluded groups have found their way to the Hollywood table; why haven't Arab-American and American Muslim organisations, who both take a share of the blame for allowing these caricatures to ride on, acted on behalf of their memberships? Every racial and ethnic group seems to have a lobby in Los Angeles, yet we Americans of Arab descent do not. Until Arab-Americans open the window and shout like the TV anchor in the classic satire *Network* – 'I'm mad as hell and I'm not gonna take it any more!' – the stereotypes will persist.

Silence, too, plays a role. The New York and Los Angeles trade papers – *Daily Variety*, *The Hollywood Reporter*, *Entertainment Weekly*, *Premiere* – have yet to mention *Reel Bad Arabs* in their book review sections.

Since 11 September America's Arabs and Muslims have been attacked, our freedoms have been threatened – by the government and the media – and we have been labelled as disloyal thugs and terrorist traitors. TV dramas are full of Arab-Americans ready to use mosques as hideouts, abuse the law, shoot dead our neighbours and lay waste the nation with dirty nukes. Speaking at a Writers' Guild symposium on perceptions of cultures in US TV and film, *West Wing* creator Aaron Sorkin warned: 'I am going to bring on to the show certain Arab Muslim characters and . . . you're not going to like them.' Sorkin's a man of his word. Since 11 September, his show and others have given prejudice a free pass.

Plato recognised the power of fictional narratives in *The Republic*, acknowledging that those who tell the stories also rule society. As the world's foremost industry for moulding public opinion, Hollywood also helps shape public policy. Feature films reach billions on video cassettes, DVDs, cable and TV systems – not just today but every day and everywhere in 150 world markets. TV networks worldwide recycle movies ranging from *Exodus* (1960) to *Freedom Strike* (1998), each one reaching back in time to dehumanise Arabs, then re-dehumanise them again on the rerun. Like books, films last for ever.

How to debunk this Arab mythology? PR experiments such as President George W Bush's US$15 million public diplomacy campaign won't do it. Muslims will not swallow the US government's words of loving propaganda as long as the basic problem of Hollywood's other anti-Semitism is ignored.

Producers are capable of making films that elevate the human spirit and deal with minorities in a considerate fashion – whether Native Americans in *Dances With Wolves* (1990) or Greek-Americans in *My Big Fat Greek Wedding* (2002). Even the Arabs can get a fair representation sometimes. *Three Kings* was an anti-war movie that helped erase damaging stereotypes, humanising a people who for too long have been projected as caricatures. *Robin Hood, Prince of Thieves* (1991) featured a Muslim character – on a visit to medieval Britain – as a dignified Saracen warrior with superior judgement and ready access to a host of technological innovations covering medicine to explosives.

Will image makers continue to denigrate Arabs as Nazi cinema once vilified their Jewish cousins? To advance diplomacy and to help ensure a durable peace path in post-war Iraq and throughout the Middle East, Hollywood must humanise the Arab Muslim. I have urged President Bush to host a White House conference to address the anti-Semitic images and violence-driving rhetoric that dominate silver screens and related media. High on his guest list could – most helpfully – appear such top officials and media moguls as Karl Rove, Ted Turner, Rupert Murdoch, Stephen Spielberg and Michael Eisner. I'd be happy to pass round the refreshments before I give my talk. ❑

Jack G Shaheen is professor emeritus of Mass Communication at Southern Illinois University, a former CBS news consultant and the author of Reel Bad Arabs: How Hollywood Vilifies a People

NOT-SO-SMART BOMBERS

SALIL TRIPATHI

THE ANTI-WAR MOVEMENT'S SELECTIVE
TARGETING LEAVES VICTIMS OF
INTELLECTUAL COLLATERAL DAMAGE
ABANDONED AND FORGOTTEN FROM THE
CONGO TO COLOMBIA

As I write this, thousands of men and women are fleeing Monrovia, trying to get away from the mayhem about to descend on their city. Rebel forces are advancing to the Liberian capital, ruled by a man, Charles Taylor, who has been indicted by a UN-sponsored tribunal in Sierra Leone for war crimes. Ghanaian officials allowed him safe passage back to the city instead of arresting him.

But strangely, my in-box has been silent, like a character in a Pinter play. This is unusual. The email lists that I subscribe to encompass a range of issues – literature, journalism, South Asian politics, post-colonial literature, globalisation, technology, East Asian politics, economics, trade and development – and during the lead-up to the war in Iraq the chatter was loud.

On these lists I had read eager academics and activists passing on impassioned articles by Jacques Derrida and Slavo Zizek and Tariq Ali and Robert Fisk and Arundhati Roy and Noam Chomsky and George Monbiot and John Pilger and Edward Said and Naomi Klein. I had also read fierce denunciations of Michael Ignatieff and Salman Rushdie and Vaclav Havel and Martin Amis and Christopher Hitchens, for having sold out.

I had seen polemical critiques of imperialism and globalisation and US hyperpower and the need for us to understand Islam and why the real problem is poverty, not terrorism. I had read conspiracy theories which only French thinkers with overactive imaginations could conceive. They must be giving a special degree at the Sorbonne for that sort of lateral thinking.

But in the last month, on all those lists, few have said anything about Liberia. Nor much about the Democratic Republic of Congo or Côte d'Ivoire. Occasionally, Sudan gets mentioned and, sometimes, Aceh. But not Colombia.

What could be wrong with my email lists? My many friends and acquaintances who were active in the hugely popular Stop the War Coalition campaign have not agitated much about these other wars. Has the failure to stop the war in Iraq dispirited them? Could they be tired? Do they have better plans for the summer? Why are no marches planned to protest against the massacre in Ituri, why are there no campaigns about the state of war in Lhokseumawe, no banners denouncing the greed driving the war in the Sudan?

When I raise this issue on one list, and hopefully post three articles and a report about the civil war in the Democratic Republic of Congo, and ask: do deaths in Congo matter less than deaths in Iraq? I'm told that's not a fair question. I shouldn't criticise their noble anti-war effort. There is a neat division of labour. Please keep doing your important work on Africa; but we are focused on this war. Let us not undermine each other, I'm instructed.

Africans, Asians and Latin Americans can fight each other all the time. They are consumed by 'ancient hatreds'. Economists like Paul Collier at the World Bank may tire of trying to convince us that the root cause of civil wars is greed, not ethnic grievance, but those ethnic explanations are so much easier to explain away pogroms. Hutu vs Tutsi, Sumatran vs Javanese, Muslim vs animist – best not to get involved.

This logic actually makes the selective pacifist a bedfellow of the isolationist conservative in America. Some, such as Edward Luttwak, argue that these countries should be allowed to play out their histories without intervention, which only interferes with historical progression. Tariq Ali is too decent a man to endorse such a conclusion, but he none the less argued at a *London Review of Books* debate that no intervention, 'humanitarian' or not, has ever been good. None? Really? What about Tanzanian forces overthrowing Idi Amin? Or Vietnamese troops aiding the toppling of Pol Pot? Closer still, the British in Sierra Leone? The interventions that ended the Balkan wars, ushering in the process that took Milosevic to The Hague?

The case of the DRC is particularly instructive. If one counts the toll since its independence, the number of dead in the DRC may be close to ten million. But those who marched in London on 15 February didn't carry placards denouncing that other, bigger war, which was more nakedly over access to natural resources than the war in Iraq.

In the DRC, unlike in Iraq, there has been indisputable evidence at the UN: its experts name elite networks exploiting the economic resources of that brutalised country. Diamonds, gold, copper, the secret mineral ingredient of your mobile phone, coltan – you name it, the DRC has it in abundance. Its neighbours, ranging from Uganda to Zimbabwe to Rwanda, want their cut.

But, on the DRC, the normally eloquent Corbins, Jacksons, Galloways, Cooks and Shorts have said little. Pinter too is silent. Perhaps there is a hidden meaning there. For when he wants to be, Pinter can be eloquent. He was exceptionally vocal during the Kosovo bombing, trying to outshout the avalanche of bombs, haranguing us about our complacency, complicity and responsibility.

Today, dead bodies mount in Kisangani and Lumumbashi: but where is Arundhati Roy, the poster girl of the anti-globalisation movement? Why, in New York, of course, where she is busy crafting elegant insults and criticising democracy and the Bush Administration, not necessarily in that order. (In her lexicon, democracy has become a euphemism for neo-liberal capitalism, whatever that means.)

My friends who marched against the war in Iraq will forever deny it, but I must conclude reluctantly that their pacifism has been selective. There are many honourable men and women among them and I will not accuse them for a moment of supporting Saddam and his tyranny – even if they'd extend that courtesy to those of us who welcomed Saddam's fall but are not George W Bush's cheerleaders. The anti-war movement's relative silence about the other wars can mean that they are not against all wars; they are against some wars. They are not against intervention per se – many would have agreed with the war if the Security Council had passed the 18th Resolution critical of Iraq – but they are against intervention by certain countries. They would like to see a tyrant removed, but they don't want certain countries to do it.

At heart, then, is this Swiftian logic. After the disintegration of the Soviet bloc, the US has grown so powerful that those who feel it is like Gulliver feel themselves to be Lilliputians. Best to tie him down. The US is disliked for its unilateralism, its perceived shallowness, its apparent anti-intellectualism, its brash celebration of wealth, its youthfulness which is confused with adolescence. Every country thinks it is older than America. And, in a sense, America is indeed a young country, but the US is an old democracy. Scandinavian countries apart, though flawed, the US has had one of the longest and most durable constitutional democracies in the world, one not interrupted by Napoleonic leaders redrawing a republic, or one travestied by a Hitler.

To that, add the confidence that a continent-sized country brings: Americans do believe they can reshape the world and tame nature, because

Phnom Penh, 1999: what price intervention? Marking the twentieth anniversary of liberation from Pol Pot. Credit: AFP / Rob Elliott

they've done some of that on their own territory. Its culture allows individuals to reinvent themselves, and it celebrates people breaking free and grasping the second chance.

That fluidity makes Americans feel they can reshape whatever they want. Problems are to be solved, and life has to move on; in Europe, problems are complex creatures that need to be studied. This combination of America's post-Cold War triumphalism, the relentless journey towards new markets, the sweep of multinational firms, and the perception that the so-called Washington Consensus is dictating the way the rest of the world should operate – that has generated this anger in Europe and elsewhere. It can get vicious, but it is often vacuous.

At a lunch discussion at the World Economic Forum in Davos earlier this year, a panellist was explaining why NGOs hated genetically modified foods. The litany was read out: these foods are unsafe, the precautionary principle prohibits them from experimenting, the technology is untried, but-we-are-not-Luddites. 'What if,' I asked him, 'the patents for GMOs were owned by a rural cooperative in Kerala, or a village enterprise in China, and not Monsanto? Would Europe and the non-government organisations still object to GM foods?' No; the panellist felt. The anger was greater because GM foods appeared as another example of US dominance.

Then in Florence last November I asked one of the anti-globalisers why their targets were inevitably McDonald's or Starbucks, not Costa Coffee; Nike, not Adidas? 'We are against big, large corporations,' I was told. But surely Costa Coffee and Adidas are large? I helpfully suggested: 'Could it be that McDonald's, Starbucks and Nike are American?' Well, there is something to that, but we are opposing their global power, I was told. And global power means American power.

That may explain the apparent apathy over the forgotten wars. There is no obvious American villainy, no America to blame. And that's why some wars, and their victims, remain less equal than others. ❑

Salil Tripathi *is a writer and freelance journalist*

THE TRIALS OF LIBERTY

MICHAEL MCCLINTOCK

THE UNITED STATES, A NATION THAT ONCE
LIKED TO THINK IT SET THE BENCHMARK FOR
CIVIL LIBERTIES, IS FAILING INTERNATIONAL
STANDARDS OF HUMAN RIGHTS ACROSS THE
BOARD, POST-11 SEPTEMBER

Returning to the United States in 1994 after almost 20 years in London in the international human rights movement, I found a surprising gap between the American civil liberties movement and the world of international standards and campaigning. American activists and lawyers fought hard for human rights – although that terminology was rarely used – but by and large within the framework of the United States Constitution and its Bill of Rights. They supported human rights campaigns abroad, but saw little use in applying international norms at home, believing that US law provided the highest standards and most effective protection.

This confidence persisted despite the failure to provide equal justice for all in practice, and as the nation fell below international standards on such issues as the death penalty and children's rights. Yet, despite setbacks, civil libertarians in the United States took particular pride in standards of freedom of expression, freedom of association, freedom of assembly, fair trial guarantees, and progress in extending the right to privacy. The right to be free from discrimination, the centrepiece of the twentieth-century civil rights struggle, had been advanced step by bloody step in the streets, the courts and the legislature.

Yet since 11 September virtually every aspect of human rights protection in the United States has been called into question – and the need to bring international standards into American courtrooms and to the American public has become more urgent than ever. The federal government's growing intrusion in public and private life was gradual and almost imperceptible to most Americans. It initially stirred little outrage outside the minority communities most immediately affected. The first steps to build in new powers generated most concerns when they threatened to impose permanent constraints on the fundamental freedoms central to most Americans' conception of their country.

These initiatives, particularly as they concerned privacy, free expression, due process and government secrecy, were gradually seen to threaten to transform both the dynamics of the American system of government and the very culture and values of the nation. On 14 September 2001, the United States Congress voted overwhelmingly to authorise the president 'to use all necessary and appropriate force against those nations, organizations, or persons he determines planned, authorised, committed, or aided the terrorist attacks that occurred on September 11 or harbored such organizations or persons, in order to prevent any future acts of international terrorism against the United States by such nations, organizations or persons'.

Sweeping emergency legislation – the USA Patriot Act – was rushed through Congress and signed into law on 26 October 2001. Despite its far-reaching consequences for civil liberties, there was virtually no public debate. The act removed constraints on police powers to conduct surveillance and collect information on citizens and non-citizens alike, while establishing new crimes and enhanced penalties. The rules changed almost overnight and almost without notice. Changes in law coincided with executive initiatives to alter government practices and an exponential growth of government intrusions into private life.

Freedom from discrimination and equal protection under the law was an early casualty. In the immediate aftermath of the September attacks, thousands of members of ethnic minorities were detained or called in for questioning on the basis of their race, religion or national origin. Many were deported after months in detention and secret hearings. In the second year after the attacks, tens of thousands more faced new registration procedures, often enduring abuse and detention when they applied voluntarily. Anthony Romero, executive director of the American Civil Liberties Union (ACLU), commenting on the Inspector General of the Department of Justice's June 2003 report on the post-11 September detentions noted how 'the war on terror quickly turned into a war on immigrants'.[1] Meanwhile, doors were closed to visitors and immigrants alike from many parts of the world, and the United States' traditional welcome to refugees fleeing persecution faltered.

Freedom of expression and of association suffered not least through new government powers to infiltrate community organisations, to tap into private records and even details of what citizens read. The security of one's own home and property and personal records became vulnerable to government intrusion without notice or explanation.

Due process of law was denied in the detention of citizens and non-citizens alike, within the United States and in offshore holding pens declared to be 'legal black holes' over which no court has jurisdiction. Some 650 people seized in the aftermath of the war in Afghanistan, including citizens of at least 43 countries, continue to be held in military detention at Guantánamo in Cuba, denied even the status determination hearings required by the Geneva Conventions. The United States continues to withhold even their names. Two American citizens are being held without charge or trial within the United States – designated 'enemy combatants' and denied the opportunity to contest this.

The executive's assumption of emergency powers in the immediate aftermath of 11 September has been buttressed with further broad powers, even while its actions remain largely insulated from oversight by the legislature and the judiciary.

In February 2003, a new legislative draft came to light. Nicknamed 'Patriot II', the Domestic Security Enhancement Act of 2003 would have expanded executive powers of surveillance and secret detention and made them a permanent part of the fabric of American law, while enhancing the government's capacity to exercise these powers in the shadows. Department of Justice officials had denied to members of Congress that a new draft was in the works, but the stealth legislative process was derailed when a leaked copy was posted on the internet by the Center for Public Integrity.

A mantle of secrecy enveloped the United States' executive branch after 11 September, largely with the acquiescence of Congress and the courts. This made effective oversight impossible, upsetting the constitutional system of checks and balances, while the executive branch accrued vast new powers. Government behind closed doors was a theme extending far beyond operations expressly directed at a terrorist threat. New regulations adopted administratively, without public debate and often without public disclosure, extended secrecy to many aspects of government formerly open to scrutiny.

The Freedom of Information Act (FOIA) itself, a cornerstone of accountability for government operations in all spheres, became a principal casualty. FOIA establishes a right of access to records in the possession of government agencies and departments. Before its enactment, in 1966, the burden was on individual citizens to establish a right to examine these

Opposite: Guantánamo Bay, Cuba, December 2002: Camp Delta librarian taking books to inmates (photograph released by US Army). Credit: AFP / Stephen Lewald-Ho

records. With the passage of the FOIA, the burden shifted to the government to make the case that particular records should not be released. On 12 October 2001, Attorney-General John Ashcroft turned this principle on its head, with a directive as the nation's chief legal officer to chiefs of executive agencies that the presumptive refusal of requests would henceforth be the norm. The FOIA policy covers not just information that might relate to terrorist activity, but *all* government information.

While denying citizens access to government information, the executive also denied basic information to Congress on its use of special powers. In particular, the administration was largely silent on the implementation of the USA Patriot Act until obliged by congressional action to report.

While citizens are increasingly in the dark about what the government is up to, their private lives are more and more in the government spotlight. The right to privacy is protected by the Fourth Amendment to the United States Constitution, which limits the government's search and seizure powers. The Constitution protects the 'right to be left alone', a right that US Supreme Court Justice Louis Brandeis termed 'the most comprehensive of rights, and the right most valued by civilized men'. In the wake of 11 September, this gold standard on privacy was tarnished, with many long-standing prohibitions on government search and seizure powers modified or revoked, with little public discussion or debate.

The post-11 September government's voracious appetite for data-gathering included new demands that retailers, libraries, schools, internet service providers and others turn over client information. Section 215 of the USA Patriot Act requires libraries, bookstores and other venues to turn over on demand business records, documents and other items the FBI requests for an ongoing investigation related to international terrorism or clandestine intelligence activities. Under the new rules, every book or video checked out of the local library or video store, every website called up for a school project, every essay written for a college course, and every online purchase can now become a part of an FBI profile – a ready index of citizens' ideological correctness.

Previously, US law allowed for special access to the personal records of suspected foreign agents. Now these norms can be applied to US citizens through broad police powers. This invasion of privacy is exacerbated by a new law that makes it a crime to reveal that the FBI has seized customer or reader records. This means, for example, that a librarian who reveals having been forced to disclose a patron's book selections can be subject to prosecution.

The American Library Association's Freedom to Read Foundation (FTRF) and the American Booksellers' Foundation for Free Expression (ABFFE), the ACLU and the Electronic Privacy Information Center challenged the threat on 24 October 2002 with a joint lawsuit brought to obtain information on subpoenas issued to bookstores and libraries under the USA Patriot Act. Public concern has generated some congressional action, including a draft 'Freedom to Read Protection Act' (in the House of Representatives) and a 'Library and Bookseller Protection Act' (in the Senate): both would exempt public libraries and bookstores from section 215 of the act.[2]

This notwithstanding, measures to extend further government access to personal information continued in 2003. In May 2003, a proposal to give extraordinary domestic police powers to the military and the Central Intelligence Agency was slipped into a broader intelligence authorisation bill, setting off fierce debate in a closed-door session of the Senate Intelligence Committee. The measure would have given the CIA and the military powers 'requiring internet providers, credit card companies, libraries and a range of other organizations to produce materials like phone records, bank transactions and e-mail logs'.[3] Unlike the powers now exercised by the FBI, the military and intelligence powers would have been executed through 'national security letters' – subpoenas issued by administrative order, sidestepping the courts.

Opposition to the proposal within the Senate committee resulted in its being withdrawn from the authorisation bill, 'at least temporarily'. An American Civil Liberties Union spokesman described the proposal as 'dangerous and un-American', adding that 'even in the most frigid periods of the Cold War, we never gave the CIA such sweeping and secret policing powers over American citizens'.[4]

In 2002 Ashcroft unilaterally lifted restrictions on domestic spying by the FBI that were put in place following revelations that the government had conducted oppressive surveillance on Martin Luther King and other civil rights leaders deemed 'subversive'. These measures pose new limits on freedom of expression and freedom of association and assembly – rights that, like the right to privacy, were also held in the past to enjoy higher standards of protection in US law than that accorded by international standards.

Proposals are now under consideration to lift court-supervised 'consent decrees' that prohibit illegal spying by state and local law enforcement agencies. The Justice Department argues that they inhibit 'effective cooper-

PATRIOTISM MEANS
NO QUESTIONS

A MESSAGE FROM THE MINISTRY OF HOMELAND SECURITY

ation' with the federal spying now permissible under the new guidelines. The draft 'Patriot II' Act would abolish virtually all these consent decrees and effectively prevent new ones. Ashcroft has said that the prohibitions are 'a relic'. Yet when asked at a recent Senate Judiciary hearing whether he could provide a single example of an instance where such a consent decree interfered with a terrorism investigation, he admitted he could not.

Some rights-restricting measures already in place before September 2001 were significantly expanded in scope. The Foreign Intelligence Surveillance Act (FISA) was enacted in 1978 to create a separate legal regime for the gathering of foreign intelligence information, as opposed to domestic law enforcement information. FISA grants the FBI exceptional authority to monitor foreign powers and their suspected agents in counter-intelligence operations within the United States. In using this authority, the FBI was exempt from the norms applicable to criminal investigations, but it was barred from spying on ordinary US citizens. The new norm, under the USA Patriot Act's Section 218, broadens the application of FISA warrants to US citizens, while requiring only that gathering foreign intelligence information be a 'significant purpose' of the warrant.

Operation TIPS (the Terrorism Information and Prevention System) was a Department of Justice programme intended to enlist public participation in homeland security – a system for reporting suspicious activity using millions of volunteer informants. Ultimately, TIPS was intended to recruit truckers, trash collectors, utility workers and others to spy on the daily activities of other ordinary Americans. Eventually, the goal was to enlist 11 million civilians (or about 4 per cent of the US population) to spy on their neighbours.

Operation TIPS first made the news in mid-2002, when journalists came across a description of the scheme on the website of the Department of Justice's Citizen Corps (with a 'Join Now!' button to click).[5] Operation TIPS set out to recruit people whose everyday activities put them in daily contact with people in their homes and businesses – phone repairmen, cable TV installers, postal workers, delivery drivers. The government website presented this as 'a formal way to report suspicious terrorist activity'. In July 2002, it was reported that the government hoped to have 1 million volunteers in the programme within months to test the system.[6]

Opposite: Remixed war propaganda, from You Back the Attack, We'll Bomb Who We Want *by Micah Ian Wright (Seven Stories Press, 2003). Credit: Seven Stories Press*

The ensuing uproar led to a rare assertion of congressional prerogatives to slow the executive's rush to transform the nation in the name of counter-terrorism. Ultimately, the bill establishing the Department of Homeland Security included a provision banning Operation TIPS.

The Bush Administration, however, is now pursuing an even more invasive initiative, initially termed the Total Information Awareness (TIA) Program. The programme, now the more palatable *Terrorism* Information Awareness Program, is a comprehensive data-mining project tapping into data from thousands of public and private databases – from private health-care records, to employment, educational and library records, even information on purchases, while monitoring domestic and international email traffic.

The programme aims to develop a comprehensive data profile of citizens and non-citizens alike. Press reports have said, for example, that the US government has purchased highly sensitive databases maintained by governments in Latin America, including Mexico's entire voter registration database, Colombia's national citizens' registry, and others.[7] Following a public outcry from many quarters, Congress passed a temporary ban on funding for the TIA until its impact on civil liberties could be assessed. However, the TIA is expected to continue in some form.[8]

Another 'Patriot II' bill proposal with far-reaching implications for privacy and due process rights is the creation of a 'Terrorist Identification Database'. This proposal would authorise the administration to collect the DNA of anyone considered a suspect and of any non-citizens deemed to have any form of association with a 'terrorist organisation'. Even those merely suspected of terrorist involvement would be required to submit DNA samples for inclusion in the database. Non-compliance would be a crime punishable by up to one year in prison and a US$100,000 fine.

The assertion and consolidation of executive power has not been without opposition. A drama is taking place in the United States' court-rooms and legislative corridors, where the separation of powers and the checks and balances underpinning human rights in the United States are at stake. In the legislature, the questioning of burgeoning executive power is slowly taking focus on new threats to privacy, the rights to receive and impart information freely, and the principles of open government. In the courts, the contest concerns both individual rights and the judiciary's responsibility to interpret the law and where necessary to judge and constrain the executive's assertions of power. And in what may be a turn of the tide, the media and the public are increasingly questioning the path taken since 11 September.

To date, the balance is in favour of an executive branch that has been largely successful in fencing out the courts, Congress and the public from a say in its actions. in the name of national security. But recent bipartisan action to challenge proposed domestic intelligence gathering, court challenges to detention without trial, secret hearings and public distrust of an increasingly secretive, intrusive and omnipresent government gives some hope that fundamental freedoms will not be permanently lost in the United States.

1   Cited in Adam Liptak, 'For Jailed Immigrants, A Presumption of Guilt', *New York Times*, 3 June 2003.
2   See Rep. Bernie Sanders, 'Pulling FBI's Nose Out of Your Books', *Los Angeles Times*, 8 May 2003, concerning HR 1157, the Freedom to Read Protection Act; and Travers Korch, 'Call Mounts to Weaken Patriot Act', *Santa Cruz Sentinel*, 1 June 2003.
3   Eric Lichtblau and James Risen, 'Broad Domestic Role Asked for CIA and the Pentagon', *New York Times*, 2 May 2003.
4   Ibid.
5   The Citizen Corps website is at www.citizencorps.gov/tips.html.
6   *Christian Science Monitor* commentary, 'Tipping off the Government', 25 July 2002. See also Gene Healy, 'Volunteer Voyeurs?', Cato Institute, at www.cato.org/dailys/07-29-02.html.
7   Oliver Burkeman and Jo Tuckman, 'How US paid for Secret Files on Foreign Citizens', *Guardian* (London), 5 May 2003.
8   The requested report was submitted by the Department of Defense to Congress on 19 May 2003; it is available on the website of the Freedom of Information Center at http://foi.missouri.edu/totalinfoaware/ reporttocongress.html. ❏

Michael McClintock is Director of Program, Lawyers Committee for Human Rights

This account draws upon the reports of the Lawyers Committee for Human Rights (LCHR), and in particular 'A Year of Loss, Re-examining Civil Liberties Since September 11' (September 2002), and 'Imbalance of Powers: How Changes to US Law and Policy Since 9/11 Erode Human Rights and Civil Liberties' (March 2003)

For these reports and other relevant documentation
⇨ www.lchr.org

IN GOD HE TRUSTS

MILTON VIORST

AMERICANS ARE BEGINNING TO SENSE
THAT GEORGE W BUSH IS LOWERING THEIR
NATION'S HISTORICAL BARRIERS BETWEEN
CHURCH AND STATE, BUT THE PROCESS IS
SO UNFAMILIAR TO THEM THEY HAVE YET
TO DEBATE IT SERIOUSLY

When President Bush called a conference with Arab rulers at Sharm el-Sheikh in early June to launch the now celebrated 'road map' to end the Israeli–Palestinian conflict, he enunciated what may be a new religious doctrine. 'Almighty God,' he declared in justifying his call for a Palestinian state, '. . . expects each person on the face of the earth to be treated with dignity.' It did not matter to which faith – Islam, Christianity, Judaism – one was pledged. 'This is a universal call. It's the call of all religions, that each person must be free and treated with respect . . . I feel passionate about the need . . . God bless our work.'

The statement seemed to transform Palestinian statehood, at least in Bush's mind, from a political to a divine cause. The Muslims in his audience, witness to his long indifference to the Palestinians, were in all likelihood puzzled by his innovation. But so too were the Americans, who are still trying to grasp the meaning, after two and a half years of his presidency, of George W Bush's religious faith.

Despite a growing piety in American society, American politics is a secular process, and few Americans have much sense of the religious background of their political traditions. By the time the country was established, the bloody wars within Christianity that racked Europe had passed. The Puritans were history. Our constitution was the product of the Enlightenment, which mandated the separation of church and state. Though we were never immunised against the West's religious prejudices, we never had a religious party, much less religious wars. Though our presidents have often engaged in public worship, and our Congress opens each day with a prayer, we have remained faithful to the Enlightenment notion that a citizen's relationship to God is a personal choice. Now, Americans are beginning to sense that Bush is lowering historical barriers between church and state, but the process is so unfamiliar that we have yet to debate it seriously.

Bush, from the time he entered elective politics in Texas in the 1980s, was actually quite open about his dedication to conservative Protestantism. He pushed, for example, a 'faith-based initiative', directing federal funds to religious institutions to run social programmes. He has offered federal money for a 'voucher' programme to the advantage of religious schools. His opposition to stem cell research and partial-birth abortion has admitted religious roots. Still, he began his presidency with a soft voice on matters of faith.

Like so much else in his administration, his restraint in invoking God changed only in the wake of the trauma of 11 September. The attacks imparted to all of American society a new sensitivity to the presence of religion in politics. The historian Bernard Lewis wrote: 'When modern man ceased to accord first place to religion in his own concerns, he also ceased to believe that other men . . . could ever truly do so.' Osama bin Laden made it clear that religion is a major source of political inspiration, most notably in the Middle East. What has been slower to dawn on Americans is that Bush has mirrored bin Laden by blurring the sharp line that has existed in our culture between the activities of church and state. The American press, no more sensitive to religion's role in politics, missed the clues that Bush provided to his thinking. In his 2000 autobiography, *A Charge to Keep*, Bush spoke frankly of the depth of his faith. Admitting to a drinking problem that dated back to his Yale days, at the age of 40 he experienced a life change, which he attributed to a meeting, initiated by his father, with the Reverend Billy Graham, America's most celebrated evangelist. Bush wrote: 'I knew I was in the presence of a great man. He was like a magnet; I felt drawn to seek something different. He didn't lecture or admonish; he shared warmth and concern. Billy Graham didn't make you feel guilty; he made you feel loved. Over the course of that weekend, Reverend Graham planted a mustard seed in my soul, a seed that grew over the next year . . . It was the beginning of a change in my life . . . It was the beginning of a new walk where I would recommit my heart to Jesus Christ.'

In his book, Bush writes emotionally of the impact made on him by the Bible study group he joined after his encounter with Graham. 'As I studied and learned, Scripture took on greater meaning, and I gained confidence and understanding in my faith.' Though he cited few details on the lessons, he named among his teachers, in addition to Graham, James Dobson and

Washington, DC, 2003: President Bush at the National Prayer Breakfast.
Credit: AFP / Luke Frazza

'my friend' Pat Robertson. All are Protestant evangelicals, dedicated to a fundamentalist vision of Jesus and the Bible. All are also known as Christian Zionists, whose theology embraces Israel as a virtuous force in the eternal struggle between good and evil.

While still governor of Texas, Bush once told a reporter he was convinced that only believers in Jesus go to heaven. It was probably a slip of the tongue, in that it risked alienating a swathe of his political constituency, and he never repeated it. But during the 2000 campaign, he declared that his favourite political philosopher was Jesus Christ. The assertion received little attention and few Americans interpreted the words as literally as Bush apparently meant them.

Bush deserves credit for declaring repeatedly, in the aftermath of 11 September, that America's dispute was not with Islam but with terrorism. Though government minions cast a dragnet that snared thousands of men with Islamic names, jailing many of them without charge, Bush publicly urged citizens to respect the rights of the nation's Muslims. He retracted the word 'crusade' which he had applied to his war on terrorism and he discreetly distanced himself from the anti-Islamic incitement of the

JESUS WANTS ME FOR A LASER BEAM

Even US Muslims have acknowledged that President George W Bush went out of his way – even if only out of strategic necessity – to make it clear that the United States was not waging war on Islam in the wake of 11 September. But three of his most prominent Christian ministers have not shied from the Crusades analogy. Some have revelled in it.

Speaking on his *700 Club* TV programme in February 2002, multimillion-aire Christian fundamentalist Pat Robertson disagreed with Bush: 'I have taken issue with our esteemed president in regard to his stand in saying Islam is a peaceful religion. It's just not. And the Qu'ran makes it very clear, if you see an infidel, you kill him.' Bush had earlier declared in an Oval Office meeting with UN Secretary-General Kofi Annan: 'Some of the comments that have been uttered about Islam do not reflect the sentiments of my government or the sentiments of most Americans.'

But Robertson's views echoed remarks by like-minded evangelist Revd Jerry Falwell in an appearance on CNN's *Crossfire* debate show. While declining to condemn Islam directly, he made it clear that he thought Islam was not a good thing. 'In the 30 or more nations in which Islam is in the majority and in control of the government,' Falwell asserted, 'there is zero religious liberty.'

Even Revd Franklin Graham, son of Billy Graham – the man credited by Bush himself for leading him 'back to the Christian Gospel' – called Islam 'a very evil and very wicked religion'. Graham later moderated his remarks, but Robertson actually turned up the heat. 'The Qu'ran teaches that the end of the world will not come until every Jew is killed by Muslims,' he was widely quoted as claiming. 'Now that is what it says in the Qu'ran, written by Mohammed.' And he added: 'In today's world, people say it is not possible for us to believe that a religious system could teach what the Qu'ran clearly teaches. It's the religion that's the problem, not necessarily the adherents to it.'

CNN *Crossfire* host Bill Press, considering Falwell's comments on his show, concluded that the evangelist 'didn't know what he was talking about' when he attacked Muslims. 'Nor did Robertson, when he attacked Islam for warlike passages of the Qu'ran,' he added. Indeed, he said, Robertson could find plenty of examples of similar viciousness in Christian history. 'Pope Urban promised Christian soldiers who lost their lives while slaying Muslims remission of all their sins and a direct ticket to paradise. Sound familiar?' ❑

RJ

evangelical movement. When Graham's son, the Reverend Franklin Graham – who had pronounced the invocation at Bush's inaugural – called Islam 'a very evil and wicked religion' and when Pat Robertson portrayed Mohammed as a 'wild-eyed fanatic . . . a robber and a brigand', Bush replied coolly that their words 'do not reflect the sentiments of my government'.

Bush, however, became more overtly religious as the Iraq war approached. In a nationally televised talk, he declared: 'My faith sustains me . . . I pray daily . . . for guidance and wisdom and strength . . .' He told a group of Christian religious leaders: 'Events aren't moved by blind change and chance. Behind all of life and all of history there's a dedication and purpose, set by the hand of a just and faithful God.'

Then, when the Iraq war ended, Bush faced the promise he had made to Britain's Prime Minister Tony Blair to resolve the Israeli–Palestinian conflict, and many wondered how he would behave. Throughout his first two years as president, Bush had ignored the conflict. In late 2002, international pressure forced him into negotiations with the European Union, the United Nations and Russia, which resulted in a 'road map' to peace, but he took no steps to implement it. Even though Blair, subjected to heavy antiwar pressure, insisted that an American commitment to the road map was necessary to legitimise the coalition against Iraq and the State Department agreed, Bush gave no ground. Finally, in a gesture to save Blair, he promised publicly to put the road map into effect after the coalition's victory. But such was his credibility that no one in the international diplomatic community believed him.

It was understood that, given the power of America's Jewish lobby, an ally of Israel's right wing, a peace policy in the Middle East offered few rewards. Bill Clinton's negotiations had brought him only aggravation. Bush, furthermore, scoffed at the high priority that Europe gave to Middle East peace, and he had only disdain for the Arabs. He was not even impressed by the argument that peace between Israel and the Palestinians – or, at least, the appearance of peacemaking – would serve him in the war against terrorism.

It took a while for analysts to contemplate – most Americans are still uncomfortable with the idea – that Bush's religious faith might be at the source of his outlook on the Middle East. Bush's beliefs are tightly linked to Christian Zionism, a theology born in England which influenced David Lloyd George and provided ideological underpinning for the Balfour Declaration that became the rationale for the Jewish state. This doctrine, radicalised in America in the twentieth century, teaches that the return of Jewish rule to the Holy Land will ignite a chain of prophetic events leading to Jesus' resurrection. At that time, it holds, Jews will cease to deny Christ and convert en masse to Christianity. If they continue in the path of rejection, however, the Jews will all be wiped out in a final battle at Armageddon. In 1948, many evangelicals saw Israel's establishment as nothing less than a fulfilment of biblical prophecy.

George W Bush, very early in his political career, perceived his fellow evangelicals as a rising political force and cultivated them aggressively. By 2000, the year he ran for president, they had become preponderant in the Republican Party and were a powerful electoral force. Evangelical ministers supported Bush's candidacy in huge numbers, and their congregations cast a significant block of ballots to elect him. As the new president, Bush was indebted in a major way to his evangelical constituency.

Since his election, evangelicals have lobbied Bush hard for conservative causes, including support for the right wing in Israel. Though he has not publicly taken a theological stand on Israel, he conveyed a strong hint of his preference in his book, describing an 'overwhelming feeling' during a 1998 visit to the Holy Land. Faithful to evangelical positions on domestic issues, he became equally unwavering in supporting Prime Minister Ariel Sharon's territorial designs. Even for those unaware of the evangelical connection, his backing of Sharon provided ample reason to doubt whether he planned to promote the road map seriously at all.

But at Aqaba in Jordan on 4 June he surprised even the sceptics. Photographed with one arm placed comfortably on the shoulder of Ariel Sharon, the other on the shoulder of Mahmoud Abbas, the Palestinian prime minister, Bush seemed to be saying something new. Both men went well beyond what their followers had expected in making public promises to carry out the road map's provisions. It hardly seemed to matter that the two were following scripts that had been heavily edited for them by Bush's officials.

As he left Aqaba, Bush suggested that he now recognised the relationship between the Israeli–Palestinian conflict and Islamic terrorism. 'The Holy Land must be shared between the state of Palestine and the state of Israel,' he said, and vowed to use his authority 'to keep the process moving'. But he went beyond the issue of terror to say: 'No leader of conscience can accept more months and years of humiliation, killing and mourning,' which seemed to amplify his new religious doctrine. It could have been said by a European diplomat, or a member of Israel's peace camp.

Bush gave no clue to the circumstances that lay behind his new line. Most observers, in fact, were sceptical that he would keep to it, especially with an election coming up next year. Yet, whatever the reason, Bush imparted a dynamic start to the journey that the road map charted. In doing so, he departed from conventional evangelical theology, but he did not abandon his dedication to the faith. His final words on the day in which he placed his hands on the shoulders of the two leaders, Jewish and Muslim, were: 'May God bless us in our work.' The evidence of George Bush suggests strongly that this was more than a politician's platitude; it suggests a man who sees himself on a divine mission. ❏

Milton Viorst, *who has written on Middle East politics for 30 years, is most recently author of* What Shall I Do With This People? Jews and the Fractious Politics of Judaism *(Simon & Schuster, 2002)*

UNCOMFORTABLY NUMB

THOMAS R ASHER

STUPEFIED BY MESSAGES OF FEAR,
PROPAGANDA AND OUTRIGHT FALSEHOOD,
THE CITIZENS OF THE UNITED STATES
FOLLOW A LEADERSHIP UNABLE OR
UNWILLING TO DISTINGUISH BETWEEN
TRUE STRENGTH AND RAW POWER

'Of course the people don't want war . . . That is understood. But after all, it is the leaders of the country who determine the policy, and it's always a simple matter to drag the people along whether it's a democracy, a fascist dictatorship, a parliament, or a communist dictatorship. Voice or no voice, the people can always be brought to the bidding of the leaders. All you have to do is tell them they are being attacked, and denounce the pacifists for lack of patriotism and exposing the country to danger. It works the same in any country.'

Hermann Goering, speaking at the Nuremberg trials in 1946
From GM Gilbert, Nuremberg Diary *(Da Capo Press, 1995)*

It is painful to explore how we Americans followed George Bush into Iraq; painful and embarrassing, akin to finding a strain of feeble-mindedness in one's family. Despite little evidence of an Iraqi threat, and much evidence that displacing Saddam Hussein was (and remains) fraught with costly dangers, 70 per cent of Americans supported the invasion. So far, closer to 80 per cent seem pleased with America's 'victory'.

The conventional wisdom among dissenters, who include many intellectuals and precious few legislators, is that Americans were frightened into endorsing the war by a drumbeat of falsehoods and propaganda, all magnified by a 'patriotic' mass media.

'The run-up to our invasion of Iraq featured the president and members of his cabinet invoking every frightening image they could conjure,' US senator Robert Byrd commented. 'The tactic was guaranteed to provoke a sure reaction from a nation still suffering from a combination of post-traumatic stress and justifiable anger after the attacks of 9/11. It was the exploitation of fear. It was a placebo for the anger.'

This widespread fear, coupled with predictions of a quick and easy victory, overrode international opinion and abundant historical and pragmatic evidence indicating that conquest and, especially, occupation of Iraq would be costly and messy; and that this escapade would heighten rather than quell global terrorism and disorder.

Egypt's President Hosni Mubarak, a US 'friend' and client, warns it will create 'a hundred bin Ladens'. Recent major terrorist attacks in Saudi Arabia and Morocco underscore this concern. Why then do most Americans believe or assume otherwise? There is no simple answer. However, a central factor is that Americans since 11 September have indeed suffered lingering shock, or what is called 'post-traumatic stress disorder', a numbness of mind and spirit.

People in such a fog apparently find it easy to follow leaders who speak in simple and confident antipodes: good and evil, power and weakness, action and vacillation, patriotism and betrayal – all within a subtext of American exceptionalism, extolling our uniquely great and God-blessed, if wounded/insulted, nation.

'You are either with us or against us,' Bush exhorts, and most Americans remain with him. Also, the absence of any credible opposition left us no constructive alternative except protest, which alas rarely is a substitute for leadership.

To be fair, Bush speaks one indisputable truth: 11 September did change everything, at least in America's perception of its vulnerability and role in the world. How, one might ask, can a single day of vicious and unprovoked attacks on two large cities, which killed under 3,000 people in a nation of 280 million, so traumatise a strong and rich people as to render them so politically disengaged? Consider the context: Americans were already upset by a sulking economy and 11 September was followed by several months of terrorism-by-anthrax. The cumulative impression was that our vaunted state-of-the-art systems – transportation, communication, the economy itself – were falling apart or turning on us.

Americans' anxiety has been magnified by our insularity. We are notoriously, often proudly, uninformed about the rest of the world. Our ignorance is geographic, cultural and historical; indeed, we regard the study of history, especially non-American history, as largely irrelevant. America is, after all, the paradigmatic land of the future, the 'New World' of liberty and abundance to which people came, and still come, to escape the ravages of the past.

In lieu of history we indulge the operatic myth of US exceptionalism, invulnerability and success – a strong (but apparently fragile) sense of security blessed by two protective oceans and God's manifest destiny.

America's is, and always has been, a rapid-fire story line. In Richard Goodwin's words, 'there is a heroic strain to American restlessness', an impatient desire to keep moving on and not looking back. Almost a year before invading Iraq, Bush spoke at West Point to America's future military officers: 'Our security requires all Americans to be forward-looking and resolute, to be ready for pre-emptive action where necessary to defend our liberty and to defend our lives.' There you have it. The future is ours, the threat is theirs, so our mission is wipe 'them' out before they cause further harm.

The American Dream of virtuous invulnerability has often, in troubled times, been interrupted by nasty bouts of hysteria and xenophobia. An economic recession in the wake of our bloody Civil War led to a 'Yellow Peril' scare that launched America's first anti-immigration law, the Chinese Exclusion Act of 1872. The decades preceding and following World War II were marred by paranoiac anti-communism: although the Soviet nuclear threat after 1953 was real, much of America's reaction was, in retrospect, unreal.

Many similar bouts of anxious defensiveness led historian Richard Hofstadter to write of 'the central preconception of the paranoid style [in US politics] – the existence of a vast, insidious, preternaturally effective international conspiratorial network designed to perpetrate acts of the most fiendish character'. On 11 September, just such a fiendish network struck the United States and, it seems, reignited residual paranoia with a vengeance.

Such overreaction is the product, in part, of ignorance of the ways of the wider world, its people and its endless, and invariably finite, hazards. A fretful insularity, then, is one taproot of America's many serious overseas misadventures. These include several with Cuba in the last two centuries, Vietnam and, now, Iraq. The Afghanistan of 2001–3 is a slightly different case. However, the United States' earlier anti-Soviet paranoia led us to arm the mujahidin in the 1980s, only to abandon the Afghans to local terror after the 1989 Soviet collapse – leaving Afghanistan to become the human rights horror and breeding ground of terrorism that struck us on 11 September.

A paradox, then: a strong nation filled with recent immigrants yet easily frightened, especially by foreigners. Of course, paradoxes abound in all cultures. However, America's are especially flamboyant and widely broad-

New York City, February 2003: high alert team at the Stock Exchange.
Credit: Paul Fusco / Magnum Photos

cast. Yet we have little patience for ambiguity, let alone enigma or paradox. For similar reasons, we possess a famously short attention span, preferring immediate gratification, and showing little tolerance for weakness and vulnerability. Therefore, in parlous times we lean towards easy, usually pseudo-optimistic, answers. It was and is much simpler to follow Bush than his thoughtful critics: if foreigners mistrust us, that's their problem; if the French, Arabs and others disagree with us, it's sheer envy, etc.

Furthermore, although most Americans appear to be a supremely self-confident folk, we are also riddled with stress, perpetually dissatisfied, often xenophobic and uncomfortable attempting to accommodate an activist self-image with the passive spectatorship that increasingly occupies our time at work and home: in a word, narcissistic.

The Culture of Narcissism: American Life in an Age of Diminishing Expectations was a seminal 1978 book by historian Christopher Lasch. It describes a *reductio ad absurdum* of individualism, a citizenry that increasingly behaves as consumers: anxious, historically oblivious, media-addicted, easily distracted, and caught up in a self-absorbed and insatiable, therefore self-defeating, pursuit of happiness.

A pertinent quotation from this work: '[The narcissist] does not accumulate goods and provisions against the future . . . but demands immediate gratification and lives in a state of restless, perpetually unsatisfied desire. The narcissist has no interest in the future because, in part, he has so little interest in the past.'

And a second: the 'propaganda of consumption turns alienation itself into a commodity. It addresses itself to the spiritual desolation of modern life and proposes consumption as the cure . . . Advertising institutionalises envy and its attendant anxieties.'

Advertising – brief manipulative images presented repetitively and in series – is the dominant mode of disseminating information to Americans now even more than when Lasch wrote 25 years ago. Television and computers use advertising to sell to spectator-consumers an array of products, political candidates, comedy, drama, sports and what passes for news, all packaged to entertain. The very same sound bite and quick-cutting visual images were used by Bush and his lieutenants to market the war: 'Axis of Evil', '9/11', endless video repetitions of the 'Twin Towers' collapsing in flames, 'War on Terror', 'Homeland Security', and so on.

Americans consume a daily diet of violent spectacle and Bush's circle-the-wagons advertisements for war in Iraq were, therefore, quite familiar: appealingly simple and clear. The only problem is that they led in a fundamentally wrong direction, factually, morally and geopolitically – a concern deflected by redundant moralistic labels: 'Freedom', 'Liberty', 'Democracy', 'God Bless America'.

Isolation, which Bush in 2000 proposed, is no longer an option for the United States. Al-Qaida, on 11 September, made clear that foreigners' views can be Americans' problem. Americans on one level realise this, but on another we deny it. Many Americans buy into the hawks' notion that US military might can dispel these invaders and restore our sense of security. However, with US troops still dying in Iraq, the myth of quickly and inexpensively pacifying and democratising that troubled land is already fading.

Moreover, the recent deaths from terrorism remain primarily abroad. However, even if new lethal terrorist acts hit our shores, the American public will likely remain confused, frightened and, in the absence of an equally clear but more astute alternative, willing to follow Bush, whose blithe aura of clarity and self-confidence is unruffled by external disorder.

Sooner or later, however, Americans will learn that: 1) the global economy, global environment and global responsibilities are more interconnected and more costly, as well as less prone to military domination, than we thought (or hoped), and 2) America's high-tech, high-altitude destructive capabilities are no more suitable to democratising poor nations or alleviating humiliation or terrorism than is a tank to fight Aids, Sars or loneliness.

Americans' self-absorption and narcissism are reinforced by a steady media stream of propagandistic euphemism: the Bush slogan 'Operation Iraqi Freedom' was used as a 24/7 'news' banner by at least two TV networks. We stand for 'liberty' yet tolerate the USA Patriot Act, a blunt expansion of arbitrary police powers; the 'Axis of Evil' obscures a world of nuance; we 'liberate' Iraq and will bring 'democracy' to the Middle East; a skimpy 'coalition of the willing' morphs into 'the allies', a false echo of World War II, accepted uncritically by most US media, including the authoritative *New York Times*.

In contrast to such broadcast propaganda, a close look at real history would invite greater humility. Beginning in 1961, in Vietnam, the US blundered into the 'rotten war' the French, after a decade of woe, had abandoned. Likewise, a review of Iraq's formation in 1916–19 and British efforts to control it for decades thereafter would have cautioned against the cakewalk-cum-welcome-party predicted by Vice-President Dick Cheney and his hairy-chested colleagues.

We could not afford to 'win' in Vietnam and now, seemingly, cannot afford to control and rebuild Afghanistan (or parts of Chicago and Los Angeles). Likewise, we lack the resources to intervene in more 'rogue states' with hostile brutal leaders who despise, taunt and blackmail the US – North Korea, Iran, Syria, etc – so we Americans will soon find the price of occupying Iraq beyond our thinning wallets and shrinking stomachs to watch our children die in the desert.

Also, sooner or later, we will be unable to ignore the costs of making a shambles of international order and American stature. The US needs the cooperation of many nations, even the 'despised' French and 'shaky'

Pakistanis, to pursue and interdict international terrorists and purchase our software. When this is clearer perhaps a majority of Americans will decide that we neither want nor can afford an empire.

Finally, Americans must learn that we are not immune or insulated from history. It has not ended, despite neo-conservative blather to the contrary, let alone in American triumph. Thoughtful steps to end hubristic notions of American exceptionalism, entitlement and empire, and lead towards the 'humility' that George Bush promised in his 2000 election campaign would bespeak a maturity that distinguishes true strength from raw power. Wouldn't that be nice, both for America and for a world that trembles before our missiles and marching feet?

In sum: combine a sheltered and gifted nation, marked by a rising tension between its heroic storyline and a frustratingly mundane reality, addicted to simplified media messages, with a false sense of physical security and a declining economy, and you have America of 10 September 2001. The 11 September attacks and the ensuing anthrax-by-mail terror produced profound agitation, anger and shock.

And Bush's people – who are, if nothing else, astute marketers of images and candidates – adroitly diverted attention from their economic and security failures by extenuating popular fears, while invoking lofty principles of Americans' freedom, worthiness and entitlement as the greatest people on God's earth. To date, most Americans remain in thrall to that storyline and the war it launched, and oblivious to the emerging costs and consequences. ❏

Thomas R Asher is a lawyer and president of the American Council, a public policy organisation in Washington, DC

IT'S OVER, OVER THERE

GARY YOUNGE

MUSLIMS AND ARABS WHO CAME
TO THE UNITED STATES TO REALISE
THE AMERICAN DREAM PAID A HEAVY
PRICE FOR ABIDING BY THE LAW IN
THE WAKE OF 11 SEPTEMBER

Ansar Mahmood had just delivered his last pizza of the day when he drove to Hudson's highest point to get a good view of the mountains, and asked one of two guards on duty to take his picture with the sunset as a backdrop. His family back home in Pakistan complained that all he ever talked about was work, so he wanted to give them an impression of where he lived. Also in the frame was Hudson's water supply. It was October 2001, at the height of the anthrax scare. While one guard took his picture, the other phoned the police.

By the time Mahmood got back to Domino's the police were waiting for him, asking him why he was taking pictures of the water treatment plant. A few days later, when tests of the water proved clear and investigations into his immigration status indicated that all his papers were in order, Mahmood thought he was in the clear.

But the police had also discovered that he had paid the first month's rent and car insurance for a Pakistani couple who were living in the country illegally. Mahmood had no idea that their immigration status was in question. Even more surprising, to him, the coveted green card he believed God helped him win in a US immigration lottery was about to be revoked. He pleaded guilty to harbouring illegal immigrants – a charge usually reserved for big-time people-smugglers – and was duly deported.

Mahmood's fate was no aberration. Since 11 September Arab immigrants have been the principal casualties of the erosion of civil rights in America. Some, like him, have been unlucky enough to be in the wrong place at the wrong time with a blemish that would previously either have gone undetected or been ignored. Others have been the victims of a systematic trawl. Men from countries regarded as potential sources of terrorism and who do not have a green card have been required to be registered, fingerprinted and photographed by the immigration service.

The round-up was severely criticised by the United States Justice Department's inspector general, who concluded that the FBI 'made little attempt to distinguish' between immigrants who had possible ties to terrorism and those who were swept up in the investigation. The report uncovered 'a pattern of physical and verbal abuse' at a detention centre in Brooklyn, where almost 100 inmates, guilty of no crime, were locked away 23 hours a day and placed in handcuffs, leg irons and heavy chains whenever they went outside their cells. Hundreds have fled either back home or to Europe or Canada – so many to the latter that some asylum hostels on the border can no longer cope. Of the 144,513 who registered, 11 have been accused of having links with terrorism and 13,434 have been issued with deportation orders.

'Families who came to the United States to realise the American dream who chose to abide by the law and to cooperate with the immigration authorities have been singled out on the basis of their ethnicity and religion,' said Emira Habiby Brown, executive director of the Arab-American family support centre in Brooklyn.

As Mahmood's experience shows, even those who do have a green card remain vulnerable. Almost 3,000 men, most of whom had little more than technical breaches of their immigration status and some of whom were simply victims of the inefficiency of the immigration service, were detained. 'Basically, what this has become is an immigration sweep,' said Juliette Kayam, a terrorism expert at Harvard. 'The idea that this has anything to do with security, or is something the government can do to stop terrorism, is absurd,' she told the *Washington Post*.

The episode has both traumatised and galvanised America's Arab communities, which have organised to protect their civil rights. 'These are the best of times and the worst of times,' Mary Rose Oskar, president of the Arab-American anti-discrimination committee, told the *New York Times*. 'People are energised when they see some of the difficult problems experienced by people who happen to be Middle Eastern.'

But it has also dealt a blow to the heart of America's self-image, not only as the home of successive generations of immigrants but the model for successful immigration itself. It is an image that goes back to *The Mayflower* carrying asylum seekers in search of a land where they could practise their religion, and stands high atop the nation's most coveted symbol, the Statue of Liberty, laying down its challenge to the rest of the world: 'Give me your tired, your poor, your huddled masses yearning to breathe free.'

Immigration in America concerns not just the continuous arrival of new people to its shores but the constant presence of dominant cultural myths within its borders. It is central to the notions of personal reinvention, economic meritocracy, ethnic diversity and class fluidity that lie at the core of the American dream. And while the treatment of Arab immigrants contradicts the myth, it is entirely consistent with the actual narrative of America's immigrant experience.

It is an entirely different narrative to the European experience. In American political discourse, the word 'immigrant' does not denote or serve as a code for non-white people, regardless of their place of birth, as it does in Continental Europe. Nor does 'immigration' represent a threat to a perceived and no less mythological ethnic cohesion as it does in Britain. In a nation where almost everybody lays claim to an identity from elsewhere – be they Mexican, Italian, Irish or Dominican – immigration per se is not the indelible, eternal blot on the political landscape that it is in Europe.

The swearing-in ceremonies, citizenship classes and language tests they have here are invoked not as a threat, as they were when British Home Secretary David Blunkett suggested them in the wake of the uprisings in the north of England two years ago, but a rite of passage. At a swearing-in ceremony I visited in Atlanta a few years ago, the official recalled the words of Roberto C Goizueta, a Cuban immigrant who became the head of Coca-Cola. In a rousing speech, he told the soon-to-be-citizens that there were three obligations that came with the opportunity they were now to be granted. 'First of all you have to seize it. Secondly you must live it and carry it with you. And thirdly you must defend it. Opportunity is ours to seize, live and defend. If you don't we will lose it.'

But while the rhetoric is far more upbeat (compare that with Norman Tebbit's 'cricket test'), the reality is none the less problematic. The debate here has for the most part rested not so much on whether immigration itself is good or bad, but whether certain immigrants at certain times are good or bad. The issue of which immigrants would be subject to scrutiny, and precisely what they would be under scrutiny for, varies according to the era.

During the 1850s, religion was the signifier. Following a huge increase in arrivals, primarily from Ireland and Germany, anti-immigration sentiment found political expression in a group called the Know Nothings. A group of native-born Protestants formed into select and secret orders; they were anti-booze and anti-Catholic. If anyone asked members for information about them they were told to say, 'I know nothing', hence their name. In 1882

Imad Bazzi, owner of a dry-cleaning shop in Dearborn, Michigan. He was interviewed by FBI agents in August 2002. Credit: AP Photo / Paul Sancya

there was the Chinese Exclusion Act which barred Chinese immigrants on the grounds that their presence 'endangers the good order of certain localities within the territory'.

Often it has been labour. In the early part of this century an Italian envoy was sent to Mississippi after pogroms against Italian migrant labour there left many dead. During World War II, Japanese immigrants as well as citizens became a target (while those of German descent were not), and were placed in internment camps for which they recently received reparations.

During the early 1990s in California, by far the most popular destination for immigrants, the issue was access to public services. California passed Proposition 187 in a referendum in 1994, which barred illegal immigrants from welfare services, non-emergency medical treatment and public schooling. In a 1998 referendum, language came to the fore with Proposition 227, which banned bilingual education in school.

Moreover, over the past 20 years, America, like most Western countries, has sought to insulate itself from the human fallout of globalisation in a more generalised way. The free movement of capital, which has intensified over the past two decades with the US leading the charge, has necessitated restrictions on the free movement of labour to prevent the poverty that accompanies it. Structural adjustment programmes, imposed on countries by the International Monetary Fund and the World Bank in return for loans, generally lead to swingeing cuts in health, education and welfare spending, and to mass privatisation. People in the South desperate for a better life will, not surprisingly, seek out better prospects in the West. With around half the world living on two dollars a day or less, there is a clamour to move to the wealthiest nation on earth and a clampdown to prevent that happening. Throughout, even as certain sections of immigrants were being scapegoated, the influx of immigrants into the country continued. Indeed, in the 1990s, during which the issue of Hispanic immigration dominated the political discourse, applications for citizenship increased more than sixfold.

Each episode was regarded not as a general trend in the narrative of American immigration, but as an isolated deviation from it which can be explained by the demands of the time. Americans see themselves not as a nation that has persecuted immigrants but as a nation of persecuted immigrants that has been forced, at certain moments, to marginalise the few in order to protect the many.

Since 11 September the issue has been terrorism, the focus has been on Arab-Americans and the logic has been the same. The 500,000 or so voters of the Arab-American community, relatively small and until recently relatively conservative, were more likely to have voted for George W Bush than for Al Gore.

Given that all the perpetrators of the terrorist attacks on 11 September were immigrants of Arab descent, it stands to reason that Arab immigrant communities would be one place the US authorities might look for leads as to whether terrorist cells remain intact. What makes no sense is the manner in which these investigations occurred, which were huge in scale, racist in their conception and heavy-handed in their execution. For it is a huge leap from Mohammad Atta to Ansar Mahmood – a move that you can only make if you start from the principle that all Arabs are potential terrorists and therefore to be treated as suspects.

This principle did not start on 11 September. The immediate suspicion following the Oklahoma bombing in April 1995 was that it was the work of Arab terrorists. It later transpired to be extreme right-wing Americans. The upshot was not a clampdown on white people with crew cuts but a sophisticated surveillance of extreme right-wing militia groups.

The Arab-American community, however, are not being targeted for what they have done or what they believe but simply for who they are. And while that discrimination existed before 11 September, it has intensified hugely since then. To force the registration of men from certain countries in the name of national security is about as crude a form of racial profiling as you can get. And, like all policing and security work that relies on racial profiling, it was incredibly inefficient. From the 182,000 men questioned, as of 1 June 2003 only 99 remain in custody.

'What the government is doing is very aggressively targeting particular nationalities for enforcement of immigration law,' says Lucas Guttentag, director of the immigrants' rights project at the American Civil Liberties Union. 'The identical violation committed by, say, a Mexican immigrant is not enforced in the same way.' There are many possible consequences to this action. The Arab community will become alienated; racism against the Arab community will grow – if the state discriminates against them then why shouldn't the mob? – and many miscarriages of justice will occur; and the state will increase its power over some of the most vulnerable people in the country, namely all immigrants.

The one thing it will have almost no impact on is terrorism. When it comes to 11 September, the few who were already suspected of terrorism were allowed into America because the US immigration service did not act on the information it already had or use the powers it already had. Now even more arbitrary powers have been given to agencies that have proved themselves to be incompetent or irresponsible with their existing powers.

We in Britain know this better than most because our own spectacularly unsuccessful war on terrorism was conducted in exactly the same way. According to Home Office statistics, 97 per cent of those arrested under the Prevention of Terrorism Act – a series of draconian measures supposed to thwart the IRA – between 1974 and 1988 were released without charge. Only 1 per cent were convicted and imprisoned. The act was used instead as an information-gathering exercise for the British security forces. 'It was a measure of social control,' says Penny Green, professor of law and criminology at Westminster University. 'It was used to repress political activity – a fishing expedition used for scanning information on a whole community.'

In this regard America is anything but exceptional. Powerful nations at war, whether it is Britain and Northern Ireland or France and Algeria, isolate certain communities they regard as sympathetic to the enemy and deprive all their citizens of their civil rights. The difference with America, compared not just with other countries but with other times in its history, is the nature of the enemy it has chosen to identify. The British and the French knew where Northern Ireland and Algeria were, and had some sense of what would constitute victory over them, even if they never achieved it. America's war on terror is endless against a foe that is stateless (terror has no nationality), invisible (it could be anyone) and ubiquitous (they could be anywhere).

As a result the Arab–American experience is not only consistent with America's immigration history, but with the overarching philosophy that guides the war on terror. They have been the victims of a pre-emptive strike on their civil rights. Just like the intelligence agencies with Iraq's weapons of mass destruction, the immigration services identify the guilty party first and then come up with evidence that is either inconclusive, unconvincing or unavailable for reasons of state security. It is a war, at home and abroad, based on assumption, presumption, prejudice, profiling, secrecy and political expediency. ❏

Gary Younge *is New York correspondent for the* Guardian *and the author of* No Place Like Home *(Picador, 2000), an account of his travels in the American South*

THE WAGES OF HATE

WALTER MOSLEY

**THE HATRED THAT SOME OF THE WORLD
FEELS FOR AMERICA IS PERHAPS EASIER
FOR ITS BLACK CITIZENS TO UNDERSTAND
THAN ITS WHITE**

When my father sat there in our darkened living room wishing that he
could go out and join the mêlée [of the 1965 Watts Riots], I saw something
that it took me many years to work out. He was far beyond simple outrage.
He wanted revenge for all of those years that he was mistreated and for all
the millions who had been murdered and robbed, raped and silenced. He
wanted to go out in the streets and yell and fire his gun into the void of his
oppression. Did he hate? Most definitely. Should the people he hated have
been afraid of him? Without a doubt.

LeRoy Mosley was the victim of a system of racism that had ruined his
people for six, eight, ten and more generations. He was the inheritor of that
bitter pill. He was the survivor who now found himself with the possibility
of finally getting revenge. 'Burn, baby, burn,' was the catchphrase of the
riotous sixties. Those words were screaming in my father's mind. He, and
millions of other black men and women, hated white America for the five
days of the Watts Riots; for those five days and for generations before and
after them. His smouldering wrath was justified in his experience. He never
once questioned his own culpability for the racist institutions and their
adherents. America was afraid of my father. More than ever, they wanted
the part of his mind that held this deep grudge to disappear. And if my
father, and the millions that felt like him, could not drop this hatred, they
wanted them to disappear.

This is only natural. No one wants someone who hates them to be
anywhere in the periphery. Their mere presence poses a threat. All the years
before the riots white people could ignore the history and the crimes. That
was a long time ago, we were taught in school. But then Lincoln freed the
slaves. But now the grandchildren and the great-grandchildren of those
slaves were cutting up, acting out hatred that went all the way back through
centuries of abuse.

Once again my father's seminal story rears its head. This time it's white America saying: they couldn't be at war with me. I never did anything to those people. But white America had to wake up, if just a little, and realise that dark America was writhing in an endless nightmare. Seeing my father so wretched over his decision to stay at home during the riots made me very insecure. After all, my mother was a white woman. The Luckfields next door and many of the people my father worked with were white. My father wasn't duplicitous, either consciously or unconsciously. His friends were his friends before and after the riots. He would have died to protect my mother from harm, and he would never have hurt her. He didn't bad-talk whites because of their race. He never excused himself because a white superior criticised him. If the criticism was wrong, then he'd say so. If the criticism came from racism, he boiled. But he was always rational and responsible.

My father would never become his enemy to make a point.

So why did he want to go out with his gun and a Molotov cocktail during the summer of '65? Why did his heart race with a dark pride when he saw his fellow black Americans wreaking havoc? Of course, I've already answered this question. The hatred lived inside my father; it lives in the hearts of so many black people in the United States today. It is part of the legacy of slavery, racism and Jim Crow. It is something that my father and most black Americans have learned to live with. He never fired his gun or burned a building. He never allowed himself to commit the crimes that were committed against him. Most of us haven't. We understand that the choice is between building and tearing down.

There is a long discussion issuing from that painful realisation, but that is not the topic of this book. The only purpose that my father's muted rage has here is to help us try and understand the rage that men and women around the world feel towards America today, especially the Muslim population of the Middle East. The similarities are undeniable: a group of people who feel intense political and economic pressures from an external culture; people who are pushed to adhere to standards that make them outcasts in their own culture, their own skins. We see them on CNN or on the cover of our magazines and newspapers: enraged dark-skinned people burning effigies and flags, marching and loudly denouncing the capitalist imperialists – us. From Pakistan to Saudi Arabia, they rage. For decades, they say, America has interfered with their religion, their money and their rulers. Sometimes, we run away. Often, we get involved with covert military actions. But lately, we've been preparing for all-out war.

This sort of international politics presents a deep quandary for black Americans. I realised that when I saw Colin Powell being burned in effigy on the streets of Pakistan. They didn't think of him as a black man, a Negro. They certainly didn't see him as a son of Africa. He was an American pressing American policies on a people who are sick of our policies and our representatives. They don't identify with him, but I see some of my father in their rage. I imagine ten thousand Pakistanis for every one that stands in protest. I imagine these men and women sitting in their houses feeling impotent and seeing America as their enemy. I see them wanting a world that is forever denied them. They are living in poverty in a nation surrounded by enemies. They are a people who want to realise their dreams in a world that vies to control their every thought.

They hate me. I wish that this hatred would disappear, in just the same way that white America felt about my father's hatred. I find myself, oddly, in the position that whites found themselves in regard to my father's generation. Here I am, feeling no enmity towards a people who hate me. They celebrate when I am attacked and damaged. They pray for my downfall.

White America recoiled at the images of black American hatred. They ran to the suburbs. They elected Richard Nixon. They complained of their innocence. And in ignorance of their own history, they believed in that innocence. White America has had centuries to hone the myth of American incorruptibility. It's hard to fault the full-faced happy Americans who believe in the Constitution and the right of every American to vote; who believe in democracy and freedom of religion and a free marketplace. Travelling in the limited circles of middle-class America, anyone would be hard pressed to deny the utopian majesty of our nation. We have clean water and automobiles, televisions in every home, and policemen who patrol the streets. We have firemen and elected representatives and free schools and vast quantities of food, clothing, medical aids, alcohol and tobacco.

The America that exists for the middle class is beautiful. But there are places that my father and I have both seen that deny this American Eden: poor America, working-class America and the grey area between those two suffering masses. The millions of men and women who travel the revolving door between the ghetto and prison, the children who go to bed hungry, the elderly who are shunted into systems of maintenance but not care, the mentally ill, the sick and the under-educated make up a large portion of this paradise. And these suffering masses are the lucky ones. At least they have

the chance of being associated with the American dream. There's the magic of wealth in America, but what about the rest of the world?

Afghanistan was the poorest nation in the world before the World Trade Centre attack. And while Aids decimates Africa, we only have to look at our recent history to see the carnage that we've created on a worldwide scale: the bombing of Cambodia and the senseless, endless war on the Vietnamese people; the slaughtering of thousands in Guatemala, and the invasion of Panama. We have embargos against the leaders of nations who never suffer want, leaving only the innocent populations to endure our punishments. Our freedom and comfort comes at a great cost for our own citizens and peoples around the world. Middle-class white America and its aspirants have been blissfully ignorant of this situation.

But black Americans are not so lucky. ❑

Walter Mosley *is a novelist. This text comes from his new book* What Next? *(Serpent's Tail, forthcoming September 2003). His latest Easy Rawlins mystery is* Six Easy Pieces *(Serpent's Tail, June 2003)*

Opposite: New Delhi, India, 2002: the new imperialist? Credit: ARP / Raveendran

CLEAR AND PRESENT DANGER

JIM D'ENTREMONT

A CORPORATE 'COALITION OF THE
WILLING' — ALLYING MEDIA NETWORKS
AND RECORD COMPANIES, AND
SPEARHEADED BY THE BROADCAST
BEHEMOTH CLEAR CHANNEL — IS
SILENCING DISSIDENT MUSICAL VOICES

'There has never been so much mixing of politics and music as there is now, not even during the Vietnam War,' said Pete Seeger in a 2 April interview broadcast in the US by National Public Radio. 'Of course,' he added, 'you don't find it in the media.'

The 84-year-old folk singer, whose career spans half a century of peace and civil rights activism, had just sung one of his Vietnam-era signature songs, 'Where Have All the Flowers Gone?' at an anti-war rally in New York City. Recently, Seeger was widely visible at demonstrations against US intervention in Iraq. His classic recordings are seldom heard on American broadcast outlets, however, and Stephan Smith's new single 'The Bell', an anti-militarist protest song with vocals by Seeger, has had minimal airplay.

Hundreds of independent radio and television stations, record companies and concert venues where, in the 1960s and 70s, solo musicians and bands could express dissent now belong to News Corporation, AOL Time Warner, Viacom, Vivendi Universal, Disney and a dwindling number of smaller but still formidable corporate entities. 'Music industry censorship,' notes free-speech advocate Nina Crowley, 'now starts in a place far away from the artists.'

In the boardrooms of communications conglomerates and retail chains, curtailment of expression arises out of fear that controversial language, imagery or themes might stain the corporate escutcheon – or lose money. Corporate censorship also serves premeditated attempts to influence American consciousness. Efforts to recast American culture in a right-wing corporate mould have been led by tributaries of AOL Time Warner, especially CNN; the Fox Entertainment subsidary of Australian-born Rupert Murdoch's News Corp, and a burgeoning broadcast empire called Clear Channel.

Before and during the invasion of Iraq, CNN and Murdoch's Fox News transformed the event into infotainment brimming with colourful iconography. Skewed glimpses of anti-war agitation were often juxtaposed with upbeat coverage of 'Rallies for America'. These jingoistic flag-fetish orgies were not the spontaneous outpourings of grass-roots patriotism they purported to be, nor did they outdraw peace demonstrations in major American cities. The events, instigated by Philadelphia radio personality Glenn Beck, were orchestrated and hyped by Clear Channel.

Clear Channel Communications was founded in the early 1970s by L Lowry Mays, now the patriarch of a San Antonio-based Republican business dynasty whose holdings and connections reach into the world of Texas oil and investment banking where the indefatigably presidential Bush family thrives. Clear Channel Worldwide Incorporated, active in 65 countries, now owns 1,225 radio stations and 39 television stations across the US. These serve as arbiters both of popular taste and, by promoting reactionary chat, popular thought.

According to its press material, the Clear Channel juggernaut also 'owns, operates, and/or exclusively books 135 live entertainment venues in North America and 30 in Europe'. Clear Channel runs scores of facilities like the New Jersey Performing Arts Center, whose management forbade anti-war leafleting at a recent Ani DiFranco concert, and controls the touring schedules of a host of artists, including Ozzy Osbourne and Madonna.

Following the 11 September 2001 terrorist attacks on New York's World Trade Centre and the Pentagon, Clear Channel issued a memo suggesting that its radio stations retire at least 150 songs whose content might seem anti-American, allusive to the attacks, or otherwise unpleasant. Apart from tracks by artist/activists such as Rage Against the Machine, the list included such standards as Don McLean's 'American Pie' and Martha and the Vandellas' 'Nowhere to Run'. While Clear Channel denies that it 'banned' these songs, the memo cast a chill over the US music industry.

In 2003, as war approached, the chill became polar and provoked self-censorship. When Sheryl Crow performed at the American Music Awards on 13 January, she wore a T-shirt reading 'NO WAR'; before appearing at the Grammy Awards on 24 February, she agreed to avoid such 'antics'. Madonna withdrew the promo video of 'American Life', her new album's title song, 'out of sensitivity and respect for the armed forces' – and perhaps out of awareness that Clear Channel controls 60 per cent of the American rock-music broadcast market and most venues where she performs, while

MTV and its parent company, Viacom, frown on provocation. The video's original imagery included a moment when she appeared to toss a hand grenade into the lap of US President George W Bush. In late April, a tamer version was released.

Less circumspect musicians paid a price. The best-known incident erupted at a 10 March concert in London, when Natalie Maines of the Texas-based Dixie Chicks told the audience, 'Just so you know, we're ashamed that the President of the United States is from Texas.' Maines's comment crossed the Atlantic via the *Guardian*'s online review, which noted that the remark 'set the audience cheering'. The news triggered hyperventilation among broadcast demagogues throughout the USA. Scores of US radio stations hastened to drop the award-winning bluegrass trio's music from their playlists or to reduce its airtime. In Kansas City, protestors hurled Dixie Chicks albums and concert tickets into trash containers; in Louisiana, country music fans pulverised Dixie Chicks merchandise under a steamroller.

More ominously, musicians involved in the anti-war movement drew the attention of the FBI. The mother of a member of the hip-hop/reggae band Spearhead, for example, was visited by government agents digging for information about her son, who helps perpetrate songs such as 'Bomb the World' ('You can bomb the world to pieces / But you can't bomb the world to peace'). Surveillance of anyone protesting against the war effort was facilitated by the Orwellian *Uniting and Strengthening America by Providing Appropriate Tools Required to Intercept and Obstruct Terrorism (USA PATRIOT) Act of 2001.*

In late March, as US and UK forces entered Iraq, pop stars such as Jennifer Lopez and a toned-down Eminem dominated the American music charts. Musicians with oppositional messages turned to the internet. On 22 March, Thurston Moore of Sonic Youth and Arab-American graphic designer Chris Habib unveiled Protest Records, a free online conduit using MP3 technology for samizdat recordings. Through her own website, Paula Cole released 'My Hero, Mr President' ('I love the way you take control and push the world around / United Nations, ha ha ha / No one can keep you down . . .'). John Mellencamp, Michael Stipe, Zack de la Rocha, the Beastie Boys and others made anti-war songs available for download. Rock the Vote offered visitors to its website a Lenny Kravitz composition called 'We Want Peace', whose mix includes contributions from Islamic musicians.

Paris, a rapper who first gained attention in the early 1990s with songs such as 'Bush Killa', his enraged appraisal of the first President Bush, used his

Paris's controversial cover, 2003.
Credit: courtesy Guerilla Funk

website, GuerillaFunk.com, to publish text condemning the Iraq war, the USA Patriot Act and the second President Bush. In May, he issued a new album, *Sonic Jihad*, whose cover-art image – a passenger jet bearing down on the White House – was in itself sufficient to ensure that no US distributor would touch the record, which is being sold primarily online.

Pro-war US citizens have also made use of the web. Visitors to ProBush. com are bluntly told, 'If you do not support our President's decisions, you are a traitor.' FamousIdiots.com incites boycotts of celebrities who have taken exception to US policy. (One measure of the boycott campaign's success is that during the April assault on Baghdad the Dixie Chicks' Grammy-winning *Home* slipped only briefly out of its top position in the Billboard country album chart, regaining first place the following week.) Chauvinistic music ranging from 'God Bless America' to Clint Black's 'I Raq and I Roll' can be downloaded at various sites.

While songs like Paris's angry, thoughtful 'What Would You Do?' have been kept out of earshot, *soi-disant* patriotic selections by Travis Tritt, Tobey Keith and others have been widely hyped. In March, Darryl Worley's single 'Have You Forgotten?' eclipsed the Dixie Chicks' 'Travelin' Soldier' in popularity. Written in support of the post-11 September US incursion into Afghanistan, the song appealed emotionally to partisans of war against Iraq. On 16 April, sharing a podium with Defense Secretary Donald Rumsfeld, Worley performed it at a pro-war concert in the courtyard of the Pentagon.

'Have you forgotten,' Worley sings, 'how it felt that day / To see your homeland under fire / And her people blown away?' The lyrics fuel a new-found heartland affection for New York City, a place Middle America once regarded with the populist contempt it now reserves for pacifist France. The song also aids government efforts to influence public perceptions of why 'regime change' in Iraq had to happen. Failing to trace a link between Iraq and al-Qaida, the Bush Administration has been seeking to foster faith in such a connection regardless of the facts. In the opening days of the war, polls revealed that more than half the population of the US believed that Iraq had played a role in the 11 September attacks. Relentlessly aired by Clear Channel affiliates, 'Have You Forgotten?' feeds that belief.

In his book *The Media Monopoly*, journalist Ben Bagdikian observes, 'The impact [of media consolidation] on the national political agenda has been devastating.' Overlapping corporate and governmental forces now shape what America believes by telling its people what to hear, watch, read, imagine and think. Corporate power began to circumscribe American reality when the Reagan Administration initiated deregulation in the 1980s. In 1996, the Telecommunications Act increased the number of broadcast outlets a single company could own – a boon to operations like Clear Channel. In 2003, Federal Communications Commission chairman Michael Powell, son of the US Secretary of State, is pressing to relax the few remaining curbs on oligopoly.

Immersion in a corporate propaganda bath may ease America's justifiably distressed response to 11 September, but it also enhances Main Street USA's predisposition to view the world in insular and Manichaean terms. Songs like Tobey Keith's revenge diatribe 'Courtesy of the Red, White and Blue' provide a thought-free education, redefining the American way in terms of global vigilantism and authoritarian might.

Many citizens are now so ill-informed about the actual contents of the US Constitution that they neither know what rights they have to lose nor why the loss would be of any consequence. Conditioning tells them, however, that America is always right; that international law does not apply to the United States; that individuals from other cultures are Americans manqués; and that anyone who challenges prevailing wisdom flirts with treason. As its sociopolitical vacuity grows, American pop culture is emerging as an endless, gaudy merchandising circus where celebrities gyrate to a top-40 beat provided by Rupert Murdoch, L Lowry Mays and their handful of peers. ❏

Jim D'Entremont, an arts journalist and playwright, is head of the Boston Coalition for Freedom of Expression

'They that can give up essential liberty to obtain a little temporary safety deserve neither liberty nor safety' Benjamin Franklin

NOAM CHOMSKY ON
ROGUE STATES

EDWARD SAID ON
IRAQI SANCTIONS

LYNNE SEGAL ON
PORNOGRAPHY

... all in INDEX

SUBSCRIBE & SAVE

SUBSCRIBE & SAVE

ON BECOMING AN AMERICAN

PATRICK MCGRATH

> BECOMING AN AMERICAN AT THIS
> PRECISE MOMENT IN HISTORY FEELS
> NOT EXACTLY LIKE A POISONED
> CHALICE, BUT IT CERTAINLY LEAVES
> A BITTERSWEET TASTE IN THE MOUTH

There's a wonderfully grisly story by WW Jacobs called *The Monkey's Paw* in which an old couple are granted three wishes. What they want most of all is to see their long-lost son again. The son, however, has just been killed by a piece of heavy machinery in a ghastly factory accident. The climactic moment comes when they hear his mangled corpse sloshing horribly towards their front door, and the old man uses the last of the three wishes to send him back to the grave.

I detect a curious parallel here to my own recent experience. Having devoutly hoped for many years to acquire American citizenship, now that I have it there's a sense that something monstrous attaches to the fulfilment of the wish. That monstrous thing is of course the Bush Administration, and becoming an American at this precise moment in history feels not exactly like a poisoned chalice, but it certainly leaves a bittersweet taste in the mouth.

My sentiments towards this country, where I have lived for more than 20 years, have been like those of many immigrants: fascinated, affectionate, grateful, though somehow never easy to articulate without resort to large vague abstractions. Extensive reading in the history of the revolutionary period, undertaken for the writing of a historical novel, gave me a largely romantic picture of the colonists' struggle: this plucky band of farmers and fishermen challenging the greatest army in the world, with the wilderness landscapes of early America as a backdrop, and the idea of Liberty shimmering at the heart of it all. I felt in addition a strong sympathy with their robust hatred of kings, but above all an admiration, verging on awe, in fact, at their intellectual audacity. The act of political imagination it took to write first the Declaration of Independence and then the Constitution, the vaunting idealism of those documents, and the eminent efficacy of the republican model they created so as to establish at least the possibility of social equality and exclude a future in which tyranny could take hold – this is truly heroic stuff.

But it is hard to detect in our current leaders the spirit of Sam Adams and Tom Paine, Jefferson and Franklin and all the rest who risked the king's rope for the sake of a republican ideal. Senator Robert Byrd of West Virginia is a keeper of the flame. In a speech on the Senate floor in late March he said he wept for his country. America is mistrusted round the world, he said, its intentions are questioned, it ignores its friends and risks undermining international order by adopting a radical doctrinaire approach to using its awesome military might. He said America's true power lay not in its ability to intimidate, but to inspire.

I am one of those who have been inspired by America, but the way forward now is dark and uncertain in the extreme. The behaviour of this administration, not least its squandering of the immense goodwill and sympathy the world felt towards us in the wake of 11 September, provokes intense anxiety. Many of us continue to reject the legitimacy of the Bush election victory, and indeed this is one of the dilemmas facing the large field of contenders for the Democratic nomination currently jockeying for position. Do you speak to the many millions of Americans who regard the Bush presidency as illegitimate, distrust his motives in foreign policy, and tremble at what another four years of his neo-conservative cabal will do to civil rights, the environment, the domestic economy, the courts, the labour unions and, not least, tolerance of dissent? Or do you emphasise your hawkishness, on the assumption that nobody who isn't strong on defence can be elected president in 2004?

Most of all, I think, at least at this moment, as the dust settles in Baghdad and hostile eyes are turned towards Syria and Iran and North Korea, we tremble at the implications of the Bush foreign policy. It has its theoretical foundations in the work of Leo Strauss, an obscure professor at the University of Chicago who died in 1973, and whom James Atlas in the *New York Times* one recent Sunday described as the political guru of many of the senior Bush people. Rejecting the moral relativism of the 1960s, in a book called *On Tyranny,* Strauss wrote that 'to make the world safe for the Western democracies, one must make the whole world democratic, each country in itself as well as the society of nations'. He asserted 'the natural right of the stronger' to prevail, although he did warn of the dangers of foreign occupation: 'Even the lowliest men prefer being subjects to men of their own people rather than to any aliens.' Whether or not the administration heeds this last caveat, their commitment to Strauss's programme of domination is borne out in the clumsy arrogance of American 'diplomacy' in the run-up to the invasion of Iraq.

Reading Melville's *Billy Budd, Sailor* last week, I came across this description of the Napoleonic Wars: '. . . like a flight of harpies [they] rose shrieking from the din and dust of the fallen Bastille.' Substitute 'Twin Towers' for the last word in that sentence, and you have what many of us fear is the foreign policy agenda of this administration.

Melville is on other minds too, at this fraught time. Jason Epstein, in an essay entitled 'Leviathan' in the *New York Review of Books*, suggested that *Moby Dick* is prophetic, even if Bush is no Ahab, and Iraq will not sink the United States as the white whale did the *Pequod*. It is, rather, a thirst for vengeance Epstein recognises in both Ahab and the Bush people, Ahab's zeal resembling the administration's twisted passion to 'Americanize the world, as previous empires had once hoped with no less zeal to Romanize, Christianize, Islamicize, Anglicize, Napoleonize, Germanize, and Communize it'.

Melville saw the America of his era – and symbolised it in the whale-ship *Pequod* – as a nation bent on self-destruction, as in fact it was, in that it would shortly tear itself apart over the question of slavery. But the *Pequod* stands for America in a better, higher sense too – an inspirational sense – in that men of disparate races ship out aboard her, not only Ishmael and Quee-queg but Daggoo and Tashtego and Fedallah the Parsee – men of all colours and religions, 'federated along one keel'. The ship has been at sea for some time before Ahab actually appears from below decks, and it is only then that Ishmael glimpses the man who will lead the entire crew, himself excepted, to their deaths, having diverted the ship, as Jason Epstein notes, from her proper purpose, the hunting of whales, to his own private purpose, the seeking of vengeance on the whale which 'dismasted' him.

In similar fashion did I – and the hundreds of others who became citizens with me – board the good ship America, with no idea what sort of a captain would eventually emerge from below, and it's this that gives my citizenship its distinctively bittersweet flavour. In vain do I assert that I have joined the America of Adams and Jefferson and Franklin and Paine, for I live in an America whose leaders espouse a Manichean vision of a world starkly divided into good folks and bad. And if it is true that the real national treasures of the United States are her documents – the Bill of Rights, the Constitution, the Declaration of Independence – then the Bush people are

no less vandals of our heritage than the Iraqis who, after the fall of Baghdad, looted and destroyed the ancient artefacts of Mesopotamia.

I suspect that much of my ambivalence was shared by my fellow citizens-to-be at the immigration centre in Garden City, NY, that warm clear day in late April. During the oath ceremony – which was resolutely American, in that all those presiding were jovial and informal, and seemed genuinely happy at what they were about – the official at the podium gave a short speech in which he reminded us that henceforth we must be loyal to our new country 'through thick and thin'. Was it my imagination, or was he suggesting that this, now, is an extremely thin bit, but if we just hold on, and vote with our consciences, we will have thicker times in future? I certainly plan to cast my vote for regime change in Washington, and look forward enthusiastically to exercising this most valuable right of the American citizen. Will my single, solitary vote matter? It might, if Florida 2000 is anything to go by – as long, that is, as a right-wing Supreme Court does not step in and award the election to its own favoured candidate. ❏

Patrick McGrath *is the author of a story collection and six novels, including* Spider, Asylum *and* Port Mungo *(forthcoming, spring 2004)*

Opposite: New York, 2001: pledge of allegiance. Credit: Camera Press / Brian Snyder

IN MEMORIAM: KAVEH GOLESTAN

Photo journalist Kaveh Golestan, 52, a long-time champion of free expression and a friend of *Index on Censorship,* was killed by a landmine on 2 April in Northern Iraq. The Pulitzer Prize-winning photographer was working as a cameraman for the BBC; he died instantly when he stepped on a mine as he climbed out of his car.

Kaveh Golestan, a veteran cameraman and photographer, had worked for the BBC for about three years. He lived in London and travelled extensively. During his career, he also worked for Associated Press Television News and *Time* magazine. He covered the Shah's departure from Iran and the 1979 takeover of the US Embassy in Tehran by student militants.

His work took him to the very sharpest ends of the battle for free expression. As a photojournalist he risked his life to help break the story of the gas attack on the Iraqi Kurdish town of Halabja in 1998; in his home country he received a suspended sentence from Iran's Revolutionary Court, which banned him from working in Iran after his film about the conditions inside the Hazrat Ali Children's Asylum in Tehran was shown on CNN. The film showed horrific scenes of naked children manacled by their hands and feet.

It took years, and a change of government in Iran, to see his press accreditation and his right to work restored, in what he told his supporters was a 'victory for freedom of expression in Iran'. Tellingly, he marked the occasion by filing a report for CNN on popular demands for Iran's new president, Khatami, to allow new social and intellectual freedoms.

Kaveh said that it was the knowledge that he was not alone in campaigning for greater freedom of speech in Iran that sustained him: 'Everyone has become aware of the struggle for more press freedom. I have been able to reflect on what was happening in my society – there were other people calling out for change.'

'Kaveh Golestan's commitment to freedom of expression showed in his work, his care for the people he represented and in the personal courage he showed at all times,' said *Index on Censorship*'s editor-in-chief, Ursula Owen. 'That he was also a fine photographer and a great artist simply deepens the loss.'

His father, Ibrahim Golestan, is a well-known Iranian film maker. Kaveh is survived by his wife, Hengameh, and their 19-year-old son. ❏

RJ

Opposite: the women's prison, Evin, Iran, one of a series of photographs taken by Nahid Ranjibar, a pupil of Kaveh Golestan who oversaw the project. Golestan's commitment to teaching is well known. Credit: Nahid Ranjibar

PUTTING THE 'DEAD' INTO 'DEADLINE'

DAVID JARDINE

The major offensive by the Indonesian National Armed Forces (TNI) against the Free Aceh Movement (GAM) which is fighting for secession from Jakarta has had direct consequences for the local media. Martial law was put into effect on 19 May with a decree signed by President Megawati Soekarnoputri, which gave TNI the green light to 'crush' the separatists in the province popularly known as Serambi Mekah, 'Mecca's Front Verandah'.

Martial law is to run for six months, after which it can be prolonged by a further presidential decree. Borrowing openly from the US 'management' of the media during the recent Anglo–American aggression against Iraq and saying so, TNI has insisted that Indonesian media personnel in the resource-rich province are 'embedded'. At the same time it has invoked the right to use Law 23/59 which enables it to impose a news blackout and to confiscate and destroy personal letters, if it so wishes.

However, fresh from seeing its high-ranking officers Brigadier General Tono Suratman and Major General Adam Damiri walk free after a Jakarta court cleared them of human rights abuse charges relating to East Timor, the military has gone further. It has obliged media personnel to undergo military training. Journalists and camera crew assigned to Aceh were obliged to attend a tough three-day training course at the HQ of the Army Strategic Reserve Command (KOSTRAD) in Sanggabuana, West Java. 'Sanggabuana was chosen,' according to Deputy Chief of the TNI Information Centre Brigadier General Tono Suratman, 'because the environment is not much different from Aceh.'

Military discipline was applied to the 'new recruits'. Forced to live in barracks and wear army combat fatigues, they were also liable to punishment. According to Abdul Manan of the leading bilingual current affairs weekly *Tempo*, the training was indeed rigorous. Those failing to sing the song 'Hallo, Hallo Bandung' in chorus were made to do the squat-walk. Manan quoted Lieutenant Colonel Nachrowi, head of TNI's General Information Section, as saying, 'From this second on you must obey military law and follow military discipline. This is why every violation must be punished.' The media workers were made to take part in nocturnal war games and other exhausting exercises.

This remarkable attack on the independence of the Indonesian media reflects the renewed TNI emphasis on its 'national security' role as well as the self-composure it feels now that the East Timor-related human rights cases have been cleared from the national agenda. The TNI leadership is demanding that local media deliver what it prefers to call 'patriotic journalism'.

Martial law administrator Major General Endang Suwarya stated the case bluntly: 'I want all news published to uphold the spirit of nationalism. Put the interests of the unitary state of Indonesia first and don't give statements by GAM any credence as they are made without factual evidence.' TNI seeks to forbid the use of any quotes from GAM, whose combat leadership can be easily reached by mobile phone. Major General Sjafrie Sjamsoedin, a suspect in the 1999 attack on the Dili residence of East Timor's Bishop Belo, said: 'We require all media personnel to work within the unitary Republic of Indonesia . . . news reports from the field may disturb the ongoing restoration of security [in Aceh].' He then added the threat that the president herself would take legal action against those 'issuing unfavourable reports' from or about Aceh.

Coordinating Minister for Security and Political Affairs, Lieutenant General (retired) Susilo Bambang Yudhoyono, now seeks to ban all foreigners from Aceh. 'This ban is urgent to avoid any foreign victims in the province and to help make the military operation a success,' he says. In early June TNI troops shot dead Lothar Engel, a world-touring German cyclist, and injured his wife as they camped on a beach. A US freelance journalist with an Achenese wife surrendered to the military on 24 June and may yet face espionage charges. The military is also seeking to expel all the personnel of the Henri Dunant Centre, which brokered the failed Cessation of Hostilties Agreement between TNI and GAM.

TNI's 'security' approach to the media has not gone without protest. Agus Sudibyo of the independent Institute for the Study of the Free Flow of Information (ISAI) has protested against the ban on quoting GAM. 'This is not about taking sides. The issue is that the media must give the same coverage to each of the sides,' he told the daily *Jakarta Post*.

Meanwhile, TNI enjoys considerable support both for its overall Aceh strategy and its strong-arm approach to the media from members of Indonesia's House of Representatives, notably members of Megawati's Indonesian Democratic Party of Struggle (PDI-P). TNI, for its part, is relishing the chance to return to centre stage and muzzle the media. ❏

David Jardine *is a freelance writer and editor based in Jakarta*

A censorship chronicle incorporating information from Agence France-Press (AFP), Alliance of Independent Journalists (AJI), Amnesty International (AI), Article 19 (A19), Association of Independent Electronic Media (ANEM), the BBC Monitoring Service Summary of World Broadcasts (SWB), Centre for Human Rights and Democratic Studies (CEHURDES), Centre for Journalism in Extreme Situations (CJES), the Committee to Protect Journalists (CPJ), Canadian Journalists for Free Expression (CJFE), Democratic Journalists' League (JuHI), Digital Freedom Network (DFN), Glasnost Defence Foundation (GDF), Human Rights Watch (HRW), Indymedia, Information Centre of Human Rights & Democracy Movements in China (ICHR DMC), Institute for War & Peace Reporting (IWPR), Instituto de Prensa y Sociedad (IPYS), the United Nations Integrated Regional Information Network (IRIN), the Inter-American Press Association (IAPA), the International Federation of Journalists (IFJ/FIP), International Press Institute (IPI), the Media Institute of Southern Africa (MISA), Network for the Defence of Independent Media in Africa (NDIMA), International PEN (PEN), Open Media Research Institute (OMRI), Pacific Islands News Association (PINA), Radio Free Europe/Radio Liberty (RFE/RL), Reporters Sans Frontières (RSF), The Southeast Asian Press Alliance (SEAPA), Statewatch, Transitions Online (TOL), the World Association of Community Broadcasters (AMARC), World Association of Newspapers (WAN), World Organisation Against Torture (OMCT), Writers in Prison Committee (WiPC) and other sources including members of the International Freedom of Expression eXchange (IFEX)

AFGHANISTAN

The Afghan Transitional Administration approved a new law on 2 April restoring to Afghans the right to hold public assemblies – granted them in 1964 and denied them in 1973. Deputy Chief Justice Fazel Ahmad Manawi said the law was essential 'to give people the courage to express their lawful and legitimate demands' but warned against the misuse of the law. (DPA, RFE/RL)

On 23 April, **Zohur Afghan**, editor-in-chief of the *Erada* newspaper in Kabul, received eight phone calls threatening him with death if he did not repudiate his criticisms of the Education Ministry's performance. Afghan was briefly detained when the article was published on 17 April by order of the deputy education minister. (RFE/RL)

On 2 May, the Committee to Protect Journalists (CPJ) placed Afghanistan fourth in its list of the world's top ten worst places to be a journalist, citing the unchecked threat of physical intimidation and assaults carried out on the order of politicians and military commanders. (CJP, RFE/RL)

ALGERIA

On 24 March, 40 parliamentary deputies were prevented from protesting against the war in Iraq outside the US embassy in Algiers. The deputies came from two Islamic movements, the Movement for National Rebirth (MRN) and the Social Peace Movement (MSP), and the Trotskyite Workers' Party. Public demonstrations have been banned in Algiers since the 2001 Berber community protests (*Index* 3/01). (AFP)

On 20 May, cartoonist **Ali Dilem** (*Index* 2/02, 2/03) of the daily *Liberté* received a suspended six-month sentence for his cartoon of the army's chief of staff, General Mohamed Lamari, published in January 2002. He was fined US$285, the paper's editor **Abrous Outoudert** US$570 and the paper itself US$4,270. (RSF)

ARMENIA

Two men attacked **Mger Galechian**, a journalist with the opposition newspaper *Chorrord Ishkhanutyun*, on 29 April. They had earlier complained about an article critical of the country's National Security Service chief, Karlos Petrosian. (CPJ)

Armenia's Telecommunications Centre suspended broadcasts by local Ankyun+3 TV in the city of Alarverdi on 20 May, on the grounds of its failure to broadcast state programmes. Staff linked the ban to the station's decision not to support Hovhannes Qochinyan, brother of the leader of the regional government, who was due to stand in legislative elections five days later. (RSF)

AZERBAIJAN

On 20 May, a Baku court found editor-in-chief **Rovshan Kabirli** and journalist **Yashar Agazade** of the opposition weekly *Mukhalifet*, guilty of libelling MP Jalal Aliyev, brother of the president, in an article headlined 'Azerbaijan's Grand Mafia'.

BE ALERT, BUT NOT ALARMED

THE AUSTRALIAN FEDERAL GOVERNMENT

24-hour National Security Hotline 1800 123 400 www.nationalsecurity.gov.au

POSSIBLE SIGNS OF TERRORISM

• **Unusual videotaping or photography of official buildings or other critical infrastructure** Videotaping is one of the ways terrorists gather information about a target. In 2001, a major terrorist plot in Singapore was averted when videotapes of buildings to be attacked, including the Australian High Commission, were discovered.

• **Suspicious vehicles near significant buildings or in busy public places** Terrorists use vehicles for many different purposes, from surveillance to planting bombs, as in Bali. Vehicles may be parked for an unusually long time, sometimes in no-parking areas. Explosives can be heavy, so cars and vans may sit abnormally low on their suspension. They may be out of registration, or have false or missing number plates. Overseas, a terrorist attack was foiled after police became suspicious of a car with front and rear number plates that didn't match.

• **Suspicious accommodation needs** The way terrorists use, rent and buy accommodation is often suspicious. In the UK, a rented garage was turned into a bomb factory. A member of the public reported strange comings and goings of men wearing gloves, which led to the arrest of terrorists who had already attacked Heathrow airport three times.

• **Unusual purchases of large quantities of fertiliser, chemicals or explosives** Fertiliser is a widely available product that has been used in many terrorist bombs. In 1995, a bomb in Oklahoma City killed 168 people. One of the people involved was arrested following the discovery of a receipt for nearly a tonne of fertiliser that was used to make the bomb.

• **A lifestyle that doesn't add up** While planning an attack, terrorists may lead lives that appear unusual or suspicious. Before the 11 September 2001 attacks, terrorists in the US undertook flight training but weren't interested in learning how to take off or land. The leader of that group also paid cash for many large purchases such as the flight training, accommodation, vehicles and air tickets.

• **False or multiple identities** Terrorists frequently use stolen or fake documents, including passports and driver's licences. They can also have several identities and may give conflicting details to those they come into contact with. Overseas, alert bank employees noticed a series of unusual transactions and identified an account that had been opened in a false name. They reported it to authorities, who uncovered links to a terrorist group. ❏

Editor's note: taken from the so-called Terrorist – *what the* Sydney Morning Herald *called a 'comforting' Federal Government booklet detailing how to spot a terrorist and survive an attack. Every household in Australia was mailed a copy in the run-up to the war in Iraq. It included a letter from Australian Prime Minister John Howard and a handy fridge magnet with crisis contact numbers on it.*

The two were promptly amnestied, but they retain criminal records. (CPJ)

On 21 April, **Rauf Arifoglu**, editor of the independent daily *Yeni Musavat*, was detained at Baku Airport on his return from Turkey, and accused of smuggling religious literature into Azerbaijan. Arifoglu said the journals were published by the Azerbaijani Cultural Centre in Ankara and were not religious. (*Turan*)

On 26 April, the newspaper *Yeni Azerbaycan* reported that embattled human rights activist **Eldar Zeynalov** has changed his first name to Eduard – inferring from this that Zeylanov was not of 'pure' Azeri extraction – and thus 'incapable of doing anything good for the country'. (RFE/RL)

On 13 May, the head of the Baku subway system Tagi Akhmedov lifted a week-long ban on the sale of opposition newspapers at metro stations. According to the country's Council of Editors, the ban was ordered by the head of the presidential administration, Ramiz Mekhtiev. (*Turan*, RFE/RL)

BANGLADESH

In April, a court in the town of Feni issued arrest warrants for 13 suspects in the attack on **Tipu Sultan** (*Index* 2/01, 3/01, 4/02), who was nearly killed in January 2001 by supporters of Awami League politician Joynal Hazari. (CPJ)

On 21 May, **Atahar Siddiq Khosru**, correspondent for the national daily *Ittefaq* and

president of the Sitakunda Press Club, was found beaten but alive, his hands and legs chained, on a road near Sitakunda. Khosru's problems began after BNP cadres accompanied Sitakunda police in a unsuccessful 29 April raid on the home of **Mahmudul Haq**, the editor and publisher of local magazine *Upanagar*. The raid took place because Nural Islam, general secretary of the local BNP branch, had accused Haq of extortion. Haq, who was not home, had angered Islam with his critical articles about corrupt politicians and police in the town. On 30 April, Khosru was allegedly phoned and threatened by Islam while visiting Haq's home and, subsequently, kidnapped. On 6 May, police in Dhaka arrested Haq, who had gone there to obtain pre-arrest bail and meet officials about Khosru's abduction. The next day, **Osman Ghani Mansur**, the Chittagong bureau chief for *Ittefaq* and a relative of Khosru's, was threatened on his mobile phone. Fifteen journalists were beaten in Sitakunda on 6 May for delivering a petition to the town's chief administrative officer protesting about Khosru's disappearance. (RSF, CPJ, *Daily Star*)

Recent Publication: *Bangladesh: Urgent need for legal and other reforms to protect human rights* by Amnesty International, 16 May 2003

BELARUS

Nikolai Markevich, editor-in-chief, and journalist **Paval Mazheika** of the opposition newspaper *Pagonya* were released from jail on 4 and 21

March respectively. They had been jailed for 18 months in September 2002 for their reports linking President Aleksander Lukashenka to the disappearances of government opponents and TV journalist **Dmitri Zavadski**. (RSF)

In a joint communiqué on 26 March, RSF and the Belarusan Association of Journalists (BAJ) demanded the reopening of police investigations into Zavadski's assumed murder. He disappeared nearly three years ago, and his body has never been found. (RSF, BAJ)

On 28 May, Information Minister Michail Padhajny banned the independent daily *Belorusskaya Delovaya Gazeta* and its monthly supplement *Dla Sluzhebnoho Polzovaniya* for three months for its reports romantically linking Lukashenka and Russian beauty queen Svetlana Koroleva and its coverage of the trial of businessman Mikhail Leonov for alleged theft of public funds. (RSF)

The Belarusan Information Ministry has issued a second warning to newspaper *Predprinimatelskaya Gazeta*, for an article entitled 'Legalised Lawlessness' on the dismissal of **Uladzimir Tselesh**, director of the state-owned *Chyrvonaya Zorka* printing house. (RFE\RL)

BENIN

On 1 April, three journalists from *Le Télégramme* were arrested, beaten and detained, accused of publishing 'misleading information' about National Police Director-General Raymond Fadonougbo and police chief

Francis Awagbe Behanzin. When publisher **Etienne Houessou** went to investigate, he was detained and beaten as well. On 7 April, the country's media went on strike in protest. (RSF)

BULGARIA

The Bulgarian Helsinki Committee and Article 19 reported in June that the number of criminal lawsuits brought against people in the country's media industry had risen in comparison to 2001. They also warned against the current rise in damages demanded by plaintiffs. The record is being held by an Italian businessman who is seeking more than a million dollars in damages in a criminal case against journalist **Ekaterina Dzhuguburia** from *Duma* daily. However, the monitors discovered that lawsuits against journalists rarely succeeded and if fined the defendants had to pay reasonable sums. (Article 19)

BURMA

U Win Tin, one of the country's leading journalists and a member of the opposition National League for Democracy celebrated his 73rd birthday in detention in Rangoon general hospital on 12 March. He had been transferred there from prison in November 2002 for treatment for a heart condition. (RSF)

Opposition leader **Aung San Suu Kyi** was placed in what the military junta described as 'protective custody' on 30 May, after an attack on her and her supporters in northern Burma apparently orchestrated by what the US has termed 'government-affiliated

thugs'. Senior UN official Razali Ismail finally gained access to Aung on 10 June after mounting international concern over her health and well-being. The detention brought an end to the junta's slow process of rapprochement with Aung's National League of Democracy (NLD) and infuriated Asian nations. Japan, Burma's biggest single aid donor, suspended funds on 25 June and sanctions against the junta have already been stepped up by the European Union and the United States. British Foreign Office Minister Mike O'Brien said on 25 May that he would shortly meet the main British investor in Burma, the British American Tobacco Company (BAT), to urge it to withdraw from the country. If the EU, US and ASEAN member state sanctions under consideration – including discouraging investment and tourism and imposing restrictions on contacts with the leadership – did not work, then the issue might be taken to the UN at the end of the year, he said. (BBC)

CAMBODIA

On 12 May, **Nou Sath**, an activist for the opposition Sam Rainsy Party (SRP) was charged with disinformation and defamation. He had distributed leaflets entitled 'The people will not choose a bad guy to be prime minister,' which accused Prime Minister Hun Sen of, among other things, acquiescing to Vietnamese territorial demands, pillaging Cambodia's natural resources, instigating the July 1997 coup and permitting his wife to assassinate his alleged former mistress. (HRW)

CAMEROON

On 23 May, Communications Minister Jacques Fame Ndogo banned the Freedom FM radio station the day before it was due to open. Ndogo alleged the station had not applied for a licence. Station manager **Pius Njawe** denied the charge. (RSF)

The state printing press in Yaoundé refused to print the 13 April issue of *Mutation* newspaper, to block a planned article about the country's president entitled 'After Biya: The uncertainties of the end of his rule'. Publisher **Haman Mana** was briefly detained, as was editor-in-chief **Alain Blaise Batongué** and editor **Emmanuel Gustave Samnick** in the days that followed but the paper finally appeared on 16 April, complete with the disputed article. (CPJ)

On 14 March, Communications Minister Jacques Fame Ndongo received a plea from RSF not to close Magic FM, a privately owned radio station based in Yaoundé. The station was accused of broadcasting false and defaming news against the government and the president. It was closed two months after the closure of two other privately owned TV stations, RTA and Canal 2, on 19 February. (RSF)

CHAD

Weekly *Notre Temps* publications director **Nadjikimo Bénoudjita** and deputy-in-chief **Mbainaye Bétoubam**, who had been imprisoned on 6 February (*Index* 2/03), were released on 1 April. Their release was reported to be

ASEAN'S RAY OF LIGHT ON RANGOON
PRISCILLA CLAPP

Those who have been dismayed by recent events in Burma can take heart at the 16–17 June Association of Southeast Asian Nations (ASEAN) ministerial meeting in Cambodia. In an historic departure from past practice, the ASEAN ministers took Burma's military regime to task for its brutal attack on the National League for Democracy, called for the release of NLD leader Aung San Suu Kyi, and urged the government to negotiate with the democracy forces for a political transition.

ASEAN has firmly resisted past entreaties from the United States and Europe to take a stand against Burma's military regime, arguing that this would constitute interference in the internal affairs of a member state. Instead, ASEAN has favoured 'constructive engagement' with Burma, largely in the form of trade and investment, hoping that the military leadership would, on its own, develop the self-confidence and maturity to restore civilian government.

Thus ASEAN's turnaround was nothing less than a collective recognition by Burma's closest neighbours and traditional support base that its military regime, the State Peace and Development Council (SPDC), is no longer simply an internal matter for Burma, but has become a blight on ASEAN itself. The turnaround also signifies that ASEAN governments are disillusioned with the results of their attempts at 'constructive engagement'.

In fact, the SPDC has misused and abused ASEAN and other Asian investors for years, causing most of them to leave and reducing new investment to almost zero. The SPDC's brutal attack on the NLD on the eve of a key regional meeting demonstrated once again the regime's blatant disregard for the outside world, finally testing ASEAN's patience to breaking point.

The United States and Europe have, quite understandably, reacted with outrage to the SPDC's flagrant violation of its own promise to engage with the NLD in a negotiated transition to parliamentary democracy. But even the authors of new sanctions against Burma by the US Congress admit that US measures alone can have only limited impact, because Burma does not look to the US and Europe for its economic and political survival. If anyone can have an impact it will be Burma's neighbours. ❏

Priscilla Clapp *was the former US chargé d'affaires, the top US diplomatic position in Burma, from 1999 to 2002. This comment was first published by the* Bangkok Post provisional on a review of the case scheduled for 22 April. (RSF)

CHILE

Several journalists from *La Nación Domingo*, the Sunday supplement of *La Nación* newspaper, resigned on 24 May in protest at the management's demanded cuts to an article written by journalist **Alejandra Matus** on state funding to small farms which the staff claimed had been amended under politcial pressure. (PFC)

Governments across the Americas have reaffirmed the importance of free expression and access to information as essential components of democracy by issuing a declaration calling for a 'new commitment of governance' for the continent, at the annual meeting of the Organisation of American States (OAS) in Santiago, Chile. The OAS general assembly also adopted a resolution on Access to Public Information and Strengthening of Democracy. (IFEX)

CHINA

On 11 March, prosecutor Han Zubin reported that 3,402 people had been arrested in China for 'endangering state security' in 2002 as part of the fight to wipe out separatism, terrorism and religious extremism. No breakdowns were provided, and he did not say how many people were arrested for subversion, but Chinese political dissidents, including activists clamouring for democracy and internet essayists opposing the Chinese government on the web, are often charged

with 'attempting to subvert state political power'. (AFP)

On 18 March, journalist **Jiang Weiping**, had his prison sentence reduced by two years and he could now be eligible for parole in January 2004. Jiang, a reporter for the Hong Kong-based newspaper *Wen Hui Bao*, was arrested in December 2000 after writing articles on local corruption. He was sentenced to eight years in jail in January 2002 for revealing state secrets and incitement to subvert state power. (CPJ)

On 27 March, a 17-year-old girl was arrested for posting 'harmful information' in a central Chinese internet chatroom at an internet café in Xinmi city, Henan Province. The girl, identified only as **Zheng**, was arrested by a special internet police force after a nationwide search. (AFP)

A court in Yantai, Shandong Province, handed down a two-year jail sentence to South Korean freelance photojournalist **Jae Hyun Seok** on charges of human trafficking on 22 May. Seok, who has worked for the *New York Times* and South Korea's *Geo* magazine, was arrested on 18 January while photographing North Korean refugees attempting to board fishing boats in Yantai bound for South Korea and Japan. He had been investigating the plight of North Korean refugees in China. (CPJ)

On 28 May, the Beijing Intermediate Court sentenced internet journalists **Xu Wei, Jin Haike, Yang Zili** and **Zhang Honghai** on subversion charges. Wei and Haike

were sentenced to ten years' imprisonment and Zili and Honghai to eight years. Xu, a reporter for the *Consumer Daily*; Jin, a geologist and writer; Yang, a writer and website publisher; and Zhang, a freelance writer, were imprisoned on 13 March 2001. Prosecutors focused predominately on the group's writings, including two essays circulated online titled 'What's to be Done?' and 'Be a new citizen, reform China'. These articles were cited as evidence of the group's intention 'to overthrow the Chinese Communist Party's leadership and the socialist system and subvert the regime of the people's democratic dictatorship'. (CPJ)

On 9 May, the Chengdu Intermediate Court in Sichuan Province sentenced **Huang Qi** to five years' imprisonment and one subsequent year without 'political rights' for the crimes of 'splitting the country' and subversion. In 1998, Huang, 40, and his wife, **Zeng Li**, launched the Tianwang website (http://www.6-4tianwang. com) from Chengdu as a missing persons search service. Gradually, people began posting articles about a variety of topics on public forums hosted by the site. (CPJ)

Freelance journalist **Jiang Qisheng** was released from prison after completing his four-year prison term on 17 May. Jiang was arrested in May 1999 after writing a series of essays and petitions marking the tenth anniversary of the June 1989 Tiananmen Square massacre. He was charged with 'incitement to subvert state power'. (CPJ)

MEANWHILE, BACK AT THE RANCH
GEORGE W BUSH

Letter from the President to the Speaker of the House of Representatives

June 20, 2003

Dear Mr Speaker

Consistent with section 3204(f), title III, chapter 2 of the Emergency Supplemental Act, 2000 (the 'Act'), as enacted in the Military Construction Appropriations Act, 2001, Public Law 106-246, I am submitting a report prepared by my Administration that provides 'the aggregate number, locations, activities, and lengths of assignment for all temporary and permanent US military personnel and US individual civilians retained as contractors involved in the antinarcotics campaign in Colombia.'

This report is classified because of force protection considerations and the high level of terrorist threat in Colombia. However, the aggregate numbers given below are unclassified.

The report indicates that as of May 13, 2003, the end of this reporting period, there were 358 temporary and permanent US military personnel and 308 US civilians retained as individual contractors in Colombia involved in supporting *Plan Colombia*. This report further indicates that during March, April, and May 2003, these figures never exceeded the ceilings established in section 3204(b) of the Act, as amended. ❏

Sincerely,

Editor's note: Human Rights Watch, the Washington Office on Latin America and Amnesty International maintain that the Colombian government is failing to satisfy human rights conditions on US military assistance to Colombia. There continue to be numerous and credible reports of joint operations between the military and right-wing paramilitary terror groups, including the sharing of intelligence and propaganda. The paramilitaries are the leading violators of human rights in Colombia and have been indicted for massacres, selective killings, enforced disappearances, torture, death threats and forced displacement. Paramilitary forces continue to operate with the tolerance and often support of units within Colombia's military. In areas such as the Middle Magdalena, southern Colombia, and Urabá, paramilitaries reportedly move uniformed and armed troops unhindered past military installations or operate in mixed units with them.

On 30 April, the Communist Party newspaper *Renmin Ribao* reported a crackdown by Beijing, Chongqing and Guangdong police on rumourmongers and people who have exploited the severe acute respiratory syndrome (Sars) outbreak for commercial gain. One mobile phone service provider in Guangdong fell foul of the authorities when text messages about new Sars outbreaks caused panic. One message called on users to send the message to others in order to qualify for free talk time. (BBC)

On 8 May, police reported 107 cases nationwide of people arrested for using the internet or mobile phone texts to pass on unfounded Sars rumours. One man was arrested for posting an article on the internet saying that 400 people had died from Sars in one single city alone. (AFP)

CÔTE D'IVOIRE

The body of 51-year-old **Kloueu Gonzreu**, who had been missing since 11 January, was found on 19 March, in the western region of Toulépleu. Gonzreu had been a correspondent for the state-owned Agence Ivoirienne de Presse (AIP) since July 2000. He had been accused of being in favour of the rebels of the Côte d'Ivoire conflict by the pro-government newspaper *Notre Pays* on 30 January. (RSF)

CUBA

In a harsh crackdown on the political opposition and independent media, Cuban authorities arrested at least 20 independent journalists and 90 political activists throughout the country. The arrests, which began on 18 March, were announced in an evening news programme broadcast on state-owned television. (IFJ, CPJ)

The police also raided the home of **González Alfonso**, director of the Cuban journalists' association. They confiscated a fax machine, printer and laptop computer used to publish the association's bimonthly magazine, *De Cuba*.

On 4 May, eight videotapes belonging to French freelance journalist **Bernard Briançon** were confiscated as he left the country after interviewing families of the dissidents and journalists arrested in the March crackdown. A tape of an interview with the wife of one of the 26 jailed journalists was among the items seized. (RSF)

CYPRUS

Turkish-Cypriot journalist **Sener Levent** has been confined to the Turkish region of Cyprus after being prevented from crossing into the Nicosia area to attend a scheduled meeting on 4 May. (SEEMO)

DEMOCRATIC REPUBLIC OF CONGO

Joseph Nkinzo, director of the Sauti ya Rehema (Voice of Mercy) Anglican community radio station based in South Kivu province, was briefly detained in May after the station broadcast a report that the RCD-Goma rebel movement had decided to withdraw from negotiations for new transitional institutions. (IRIN, JED)

Journalists were harassed during a recent rally held along Kinshasa's Triomphale Boulevard on 17 May, despite the fact that many had been officially accredited by the presidential office to cover the commemoration event marking President Joseph Kabila's sixth year in power. (IFEX)

DJIBOUTI

Daher Ahmed Farah, deputy editor of the newspaper *Le Renoveau*, was detained on 20 April and held pending trial, accused of libelling deputy army chief general Zakaria Cheik Ibrahim. Farah is the head of the opposition Movement for Democratic Renewal and Development (MRD). On 17 March, Farah was given a suspended sentence of six months' imprisonment and a 200,000 FD (US$1,200) fine. (IFEX)

DOMINICAN REPUBLIC

The government has seized a media network of three newspapers, four television stations and 70 local radio stations belonging to a prominent banker accused of fraud. Media rights groups believe that irrespective of the eventual outcome of the charges made, the seizure by the government may have a negative impact on press freedom in the Dominican Republic. (WAN)

EGYPT

On 19 February, journalists **Mohammed Abdallah** and **Ahmad Haridi** were sentenced to one year in prison and fined US$1,270 plus US$340 to be paid in damages, having been found guilty of slandering Ibrahim Nafie, editor-in-chief of the state-owned *al–Ahram* press group. The former had accused Nafie of plagiarising a book he had written, while Haridi had published a series of articles criticising Nafie and President Hosni Mubarak on his website. (*Cairo Times*)

It was reported on 13 March that Lebanese documentary maker and film director **Jocelyn Saab** had been refused permission to make a film in Egypt by government censors who alleged that it would 'harm Egypt and Islam and incite depravity'. The censors alleged the film was to have covered subjects including female sexual pleasure and female circumcision. (*Cairo Times*)

On 15 March, 21 men were jailed for three years each for practising homosexuality. The other 29 of the 50 defendants jailed in the Queen Boat nightclub case (*Index* 1/2002) were acquitted in the retrial, ordered after their original sentences were quashed on presidential orders. Those convicted face equal or in some cases longer sentences than after the original trial at a state security court, although they will now have the right to appeal. (BBC)

On 18 March, Professor **Saad Eddin Ibrahim** (*Index* 3/01, 4/02) was acquitted of tarnishing Egypt's image abroad and misappropriating funds. Three co-defendants from the Ibn Khaldun Centre for Development Studies also walked free from the retrial. Originally jailed for seven years, Ibrahim had been released from prison on

3 December after an appeals court overturned the sentence and ordered a retrial. The director of the Ibn Khaldun Centre was accused of defaming Egypt's reputation after making a documentary about electoral fraud and reports on discrimination and massacres against the Coptic Christian minority. (AI, BBC, EOHR)

EL SALVADOR

Businessman **Jorge Zedán**, part owner the country's TV Doce network, claimed that President Francisco Flores had forced the cancellation of the station's commentary programme *Sin Censura* on 24 March, despite – or because of – its reputation for sharp political comment. (*Probidad*)

ESTONIA

The Russian government is pressing Estonian authorities to shut down the pro-independence Chechen website *KavkazCenter*, hosted on a server in the country. The campaign was triggered by the posting of a video clip on 20 April that purported to show rebels ambushing a bus full of Russian paramilitary police in Chechnya. Estonian Prime Minister Juhan Parts said the government will not interfere because the site is run from a privately owned web server. (CPJ)

ETHIOPIA

Wosenseged Gebrekidan, deputy editor-in-chief of *It 'op* newspaper, was imprisoned on 14 May after failing to pay a 2,000 birr (US$236) bail order applied after he was charged with libelling Ambassador Habte Mariam Seyoum

in the paper. His editor, **Melese Shine**, was already in detention, having been charged with defaming the administrator of a hospital, and then refused bail. (EFPJ)

On 14 April, **Ato Melese Gessit**, former editor-in-chief of *Gemoraw* newspaper, was fined 11,000 birr (US$1,300) for violating Articles 10(1) and 20(1) of Press Proclamation No. 34/85 and Article 480(b) of the Penal Code. He was accused of fabricating reports. (EFJA)

EUROPE

A new report on media ownership, *Eastern Empires: Foreign Ownership in Central and Eastern European Media*, released on 25 June by the European Federation of Journalists (EFJ), warned that foreign takeovers of the national media have devastating consequences for local independent groups. The report also shows that in the years since the fall of the communist regimes in Central and Eastern Europe, the encroachment of Western media conglomerates into these countries has prevented the growth of independent nationally based media groups. (*EurActiv*)

FRANCE

On 9 April, justice minister Dominique Perben proposed a law requiring anyone who has information that may be of value to a legal investigation to hand it over, even if held in personal files. The proposed law is regarded as a serious threat to journalists' right to protect their sources, enshrined as one of the corner stones of press freedom by the

European Court of Human Rights. (RSF)

Far-right leader **Jean-Marie Le Pen** has been suspended from the European Parliament for a year for assaulting an opponent. (*Guardian*)

The editor of *Le Figaro* newspaper **Jean de Belot** is under investigation for alleged insider trading. The case goes back to 1999, when he ran the paper's business section. Judicial officials allege de Belot bought up shares of a supermarket chain after learning confidential information about a coming merger. (IHT)

FRENCH GUYANA

Journalist **Frédéric Farine** of RFO Guyane TV was reportedly attacked by gold prospector Jean Béna on 14 May. Farine had frequently been threatened by interested groups as a result of his investigative reporting on the gold-mining industry in French Guyana for French and Caribbean broadcasters and newspapers. (RSF)

GABON

The National Communications Council ordered the closure of the bimonthly *Misamu* on 12 May after a legal dispute over the newspaper's ownership. On 15 May, the weekly *Le Temps* was suspended for three months after publishing an article about state mismanagement of funds. Two more magazines, *Jeunesse Action* and *L' Espoir*, were threatened with suspension; the first for publishing overly violent photographs and the latter for failing to register itself properly. (RSF)

GEORGIA

The Supreme Court published a statement in the 10 March edition of the state-owned Tbilisi daily *Sakartvelos Respublika* calling on the state prosecutor to investigate *60 Minutes*, a news programme on the independent, Tbilisi-based television station Rustavi 2. In its 16 February edition, the programme had revealed that government officials who had been fired for corruption had been later rehired. (CPJ)

On 8 May, **Malkhaz Gulashvili**, the president of the Georgian Times Media Holding company, said that a high-ranking official had warned him that his life was in danger. It was the second death threat Gulashvili had received that month. The company's newspapers had been sued three times in the past two months, including one writ from the head of the Ajara Autonomous Republic's Supreme Council. (JuHi)

On 28 March, four men broke into the office of Radio Dzveli Kalaki and chopped down its antenna with axes, putting it off air for two weeks. Station staff have faced harassment from Georgian Orthodox extremists who oppose the station's weekly 20-minute programme for the country's Catholic minority. (CPJ)

On 6 March, President Eduard Shevardnadze approved a new three-year programme to counter religious intolerance and racism. (*Caucasus Press*, RFE/RL)

GREECE

Gazmend Kapllani, an Albanian journalist and PhD student who has lived in Greece since 1991, has had his application for visa renewal refused because of 'reasons related to the country's public order and security'. These are widely believed to be related to the views he expresses in publications such as national daily *Ta Nea*. (Greek Helsinki Monitor)

GUATEMALA

On 25 May, the body of radio journalist and student **Milton Oswaldo Martínez** was found in a ravine. He had gone missing on 21 May. He had been working at the Ke Buena radio station and had been studying at Mariano Gálvez University. (CLPA)

GUINEA-BISSAU

Secretary of State of Information João Manuel Gomes ordered the dismissal of the national radio station's editor-in chief, **Ensa Seidi**, on 8 March. Seidi was accused of broadcasting a report regarding the former prime minister's possible return to the country. (RSF)

HAITI

On 30 April, Haitian journalist **Lilianne Pierre-Paul** received a letter containing a bullet and a written demand that she read a statement calling on France to pay Haiti an indemnity of US$21.7 billion as compensation for the 90 million francs indemnity it demanded from Haiti in 1838 to recognise the country's independence from French colonial rule. (RSF)

INDIA

On 4 March, the offices of the Nepalese-language newspaper *Sunchari Samachar*, in Siliguri, West Bengal, were damaged by a bomb. No one was hurt. The attack is linked to the paper's coverage of the situation in the Darjeeling Gorkha Autonomous Hill Council region. (RSF)

In March, Gujarat state passed a 'Freedom of Religion' bill that would make it illegal for anyone to convert to another religion without prior permission from the state authorities – on pain of up to a year in jail and a fine of 1,000 rupees (US$20) – even if conversion is voluntary. The new legislation also allows for three years' imprisonment for people using 'allurement' or 'force' to carry out conversions, as well as a fine of 50,000 rupees (US$1,000). (BBC)

RR Gopal, editor of the biweekly magazine *Nakkheeran*, was arrested by police in Chennai on 11 April, in connection with an investigation into a 1998 bandit murder. He was also charged with sedition for allegedly possessing a pamphlet that supported the separatist Tamil National Liberation Army (TNLA), and for being in possession of an unlicensed revolver. Police said Gopal subsequently confessed to links with banned separatist groups and allegedly led the police to a cache of weapons and communication equipment. But Gopal's supporters say his arrest and detention is driven by Tamil Nadu's Chief Minister J Jayalalitha's desire to punish *Nakkheeran* for exposing corruption in one of her previous administrations. (*Frontline*, RSF, BBC, IANS, *The Hindu*)

On 26 April, five people were killed in a suicide car attack on the offices of state-run television and radio in Srinigar, the summer capital of Indian-administered Kashmir. An Islamic group called the al-Madina Regiment claimed responsibility. Three days later, the militant group Tehrik-ul-Mujahideen issued a death threat against all journalists working in the area, accusing them of working for Indian intelligence. (BBC, CPJ)

The Hindu reported on 12 May that **Ghulam Mohideen Bhat**, editor of the newspaper *Kashmiri*, had been detained under the Prevention of Terrorism Act (POTA) after Delhi police recovered documents that linked him with the pro-Pakistan group Hizbul Mujahideen. A large sum of money, a wristwatch camera and a pistol were also said to have been found in Bhat's possession. (*The Hindu*)

INDONESIA

Journalists from the broadcaster TV7 were ambushed by snipers in Teupin Raya Subdistrict on 21 May while the crew was travelling from Banda Aceh to Lhokseumawe and on 24 May on their return to Banda Aceh from Lhokseumawe. TV7 reporter **Rizal Wahyu** was in the vehicle at the time, along with his cameraman, **Yusrizal**. The two said there were several blasts of automatic gunfire. (CPJ)

On 20 May, Major General Endang Suwarya warned journalists that they should neither report on statements issued by the separatist Free Aceh Movement (GAM) nor carry news supporting the separatist cause. He also ordered journalists to adjust their coverage and that all journalists will have to be accredited by the military command in Aceh. Military officials issued warnings to the regional daily *Serambi Indonesia* and the broadcaster Metro TV for carrying reports considered to favour GAM. Meanwhile, the radio station Nikoya FM, based in the provincial capital, Banda Aceh, received a telephone call from someone claiming to be a GAM commander threatening that the rebels would kill a reporter if the station did not start carrying more balanced news. (CPJ)

US freelance journalist **William Nessen**, who spent several weeks with separatist rebels in the Indonesian province of Aceh, has given himself up to Indonesian troops. Indonesian officials have questioned whether Nessen should be regarded as a journalist or a spy. On 26 June, Indonesian soldiers detained a Japanese photographer in Aceh for allegedly working in the war-torn province without permission from authorities. **Tadatomo Takagi**, 25, was arrested in the north of the province. (BBC)

IRAN

Alireza Eshraghi, a journalist at *Hayat-e-no*, was released on 9 March after 53 days' detention on bail of 250 million rials (US$33,078).

Eshraghi had been detained on 12 January (*Index* 2/03) following the closure of the newspaper for publishing an old US cartoon that was suspected to be a caricature of the late Ayatollah Khomeini. (RSF)

Narghues Mohamadi, a journalist at newspaper *Peyam Ajar*, was given a one-year sentence on 9 March for interviews she gave while her husband, journalist **Taghi Rahmani**, was imprisoned. (RSF)

On 10 March, **Ahmad Zeid-Abadi**, a journalist for the reformist newspaper *Hamchahri* and *Iran-é-Farda*, was given a 13-month sentence and a ban on 'public and social activity' a term including journalism, for five years for 'publishing false news' and 'propaganda against the regime'. (RSF)

Journalist **Ali-Reza Jabari** was rearrested on 17 March following his release on 6 February after commenting on the conditions of his detention. Jabari had originally been arrested in December 2002 for an article that appeared in the Canadian Persian-language paper *Charvand* (*Index* 2/03). On 19 April, Jabari was sentenced to four years in prison, 253 lashes and a fine of 6 million rials (US$794). The official charge was 'consuming and distributing alcohol', although this is a charge often laid at non-religious people. (RSF)

Siamak Pourzand, contributor to several US-based opposition Persian-language radio stations, was arrested on 30 March and taken to Evin

prison in Tehran. He had originally been granted a conditional release, an unofficial procedure allowing arbitrary reimprisonment. (RSF)

Seven journalists, all members of the banned National Religious Movement, were sentenced to a total of 52 years' imprisonment by the country's conservative courts on 10 May. **Ezatollah Sahabi, Taghi Rahmani, Hoda Saber, Reza Alijani, Saide Madani, Ali-Reza Redjaï** and **Morteza Khazemian** were given sentences ranging from four to seven years. (RSF)

IRAQ

Observer journalist **Farzad Bazoft**, hanged on the orders of Saddam Hussein 13 years ago, was innocent and was not a spy, according to Kadem Askar, a former colonel in the Iraqi intelligence service. The reporter was executed on 15 March 1990. (*Observer*)

Al-Jazeera TV claimed that British forces in Basra detained its reporter, **Mohammad al-Sayed Muhsen**, confiscated his equipment and banned him from reporting in Basra 'until further notice'. A British spokeswoman said British forces had told Muhsen to stop filming a burning tank for security reasons, but said he had neither been forced out or detained. (*Guardian*)

The war in Iraq took a heavy toll on the media. On 22 March, Australian ABC TV cameraman **Paul Moran** was killed by a suicide bomber in Northern Iraq. On 30 March, British Channel 4

reporter **Gaby Rado** was found dead after he apparently fell from the roof of his hotel in northern Iraq. Freelance Iranian cameraman **Kaveh Golestan** — a long-time supporter of *Index on Censorship* — was killed by a landmine as he got out of his car in northern Iraq on 2 April (see p134). The former editor-in-chief of *Atlantic Monthly*, **Michael Kelly**, died on 3 April in an accident involving the US jeep he was travelling in. BBC translator **Kamaran Abdurazaq Muhamed** was killed on 6 April when the convoy he was travelling in was attacked by a US warplane. On 7 April, a Spanish reporter with *El Mundo,* **Julio Anguita Parrado**, and **Christian Leibig** of *Focus* magazine were killed in an attack on a US communications centre in southern Baghdad. Three journalists were killed on 8 April. Two were killed when the hotel they were in came under US tank fire. Reuters cameraman **Taras Protsyuk** was killed immediately, and Spanish journalist **José Couso** died later of injuries sustained in the attack. The hotel acted as the main media centre in Baghdad and was known by the Americans to house the majority of journalists reporting from inside the regime. In a separate attack, al-Jazeera journalist **Tarek Ayoub** was killed in a US air raid on the building from which he was filming. Three more journalists died in car accidents: **Mario Podestá** and **Victoria Cabrera** of Argentina's America TV and **Elizabeth Neuffer** of the *Boston Globe* along with media worker **Waleed Khalifa al-Dulami**. Cameraman **Fred Nerac** and

LETTER FROM THE SUNNI TRIANGLE

BORZOU DARAGAHI

I sit down for a glass of sweetened tea. The story of the five men trickles out: during the attack that night, one of the Americans' flares landed on the family's farm and set a field afire. The old man ran out of the house to douse the flames. He was 70. His three sons couldn't let him go out alone, and ran out behind them. A young cousin followed. The Americans, just under attack, fired at everything that moved. Through night-vision goggles, the five men might have looked like people trying to attack them or flee. In any case, all five were killed.

Back beneath the tents, the women weep and wail. The men work their prayer beads and shake their downturned heads. The Americans, one relative says, were supposed to come here and offer an apology. They have yet to show up.

An army colonel up in northern Iraq once explained to me the triple pressures under which US soldiers strain. In the mornings, they might work at a ministry handing out meagre salaries to mobs of angry desperate Iraqis. In the afternoons, they patrol neighbourhoods, playing with the local children and acting like jolly ol' Officer Friendly with an M-16 and flak jacket as well as a sidearm. In the evenings, they go out on night patrol, shooting down Fedayeen. You can imagine the confusion: am I here to help, make friends with or kill the Iraqis?

The intense conditions have bred a sense of camaraderie among all the foreigners here. In Oja we asked a bunch of Marines if we could tag along as they conducted house-to-house raids. 'Sure,' said the squad commander, 'just stay out of the line of fire.'

'Ah, man, it's just so good to talk to an American,' one soldier told me after a 20-minute chat – a Chicago-area native whose high school played mine in football and basketball. A good guy.

This is why I don't understand the appeal of the embed programme [the attachment of journalists to military units]. You get so little for all that you give up, which includes the freedom to publish what you want when you want. I mean, sure, during the war being embedded was about the only way to get safely to the action. But these days, soldiers offer to give me rides and join in patrols and without my having to sign away my freedom as a journalist.

Besides, I've ridden in a Humvee. The windows are narrow slits on the world. I prefer my wacky young translator's little red Audi. ❑

Borzou Daragahi, a Tehran-based journalist, writes his occasional 'Letters from . . .' for family and friends. You can subscribe by sending a blank email to borzou-subscribe@topica.com media worker **Hussein Osman** are still missing after the vehicle they were travelling in on 22 March came under fire in the same attack in which ITN reporter **Terry Lloyd** was killed (*Index* 2/02). **Fabienne Nerac**, the wife of the missing journalist, later confronted Colin Powell at a press conference, where she asked for information about her husband's fate. (RSF, *Guardian*)

ISRAEL

On 17 April, reporter **Arnaud Müller** and cameraman **Harold Bellanger** of the French TV channel Canal+ were prevented from entering Israel and held in detention at an Interior Ministry detention centre. The journalists were travelling to Beersheva in southern Israel to report on the international pacifist and civilian peace movement in the country. (RSF)

ITALY

The MP and former defence minister Cesare Previti, Silvio Berlusconi's lawyer and close friend, was sentenced to 11 years' imprisonment on 29 April for bribing judges in cases including that which approved Berlusconi's takeover of the press-publishing giant Mondadori. (*Il Manifesto*)

Italian legislators voted in June to pass an immunity law that would save the media tycoon Silvio Berlusconi from prosecution for as long as he is prime minister. Deputies in the lower house of parliament approved a legal amendment, proposed by Berlusconi himself, which would protect

Italy's five highest-ranking officials from trial while in office. The law brings to an abrupt halt Berlusconi's trial in Milan where he is accused of bribing judges in a 1980s corporate takeover battle. The prime minister said the change in the law was necessary to protect the country from the 'communist threat' posed by prosecuting judges. (*Guardian*)

JORDAN

Three journalists from Argentina's Channel 13 TV – director **Juan Castro**, producer **Rubén Vivero** and camera operator **Cristian Sedam** – were detained on 1 March by the Jordanian authorities as they attempted to enter Jordan from Iraq. The three were arrested for allegedly filming Jordanian troops and held for six hours, during which their equipment and film footage was destroyed. (IFJ)

A Japanese photojournalist jailed in Jordan for causing the death of an airport security official was released through a pardon from Jordan's King Abdullah II. **Hiroki Gomi**, 36, a former photojournalist for the *Mainichi Shimbun* just back from covering the war in Iraq, was sentenced to one to 18 months' imprisonment after a souvenir cluster bomblet in his luggage killed an airport security officer and injured five other people at Amman airport on 1 May. (*Japan Times*)

KAZAKHSTAN

On 11 March, the Almaty Oblast court rejected opposition journalist **Sergei Du-**

vanov's appeal against a lower court's rape sentence. The court acceded to the prosecution's request and altered the sentence to the more serious charge, knowingly raping a minor. The prison term of three and a half years set by a lower court remains unchanged. Duvanov's lawyer said that his client was spared a harsher sentence because of his 'positive references', and plans to take the case to the Kazakh Supreme Court. On 12 March, Almaty Oblast prosecutor Dzhaksylyk Baytukbaev said there were no political motives behind the rape charge on which the journalist was sentenced. On the same day, Duvanov's daughter, **Dinisa Duvanov**, was granted political asylum in the United States. (RFE/RL, *Interfax-Kazakhstan*, CJES)

The state-owned Kazakhtelekom telecoms firm is blocking access to internet sites run by the opposition, which carry unofficial reports or criticise corruption in the administration of President Nursultan Nazarbayev and officials suspected of corruption. The list of affected sites includes *Navigator* (www.navigator.kz), www.eurasia.org, newspapers *Vesti Pavlodara* (www.vestipavl.kz) and *Assandi Times* (www.respublika.kz), and those run by opposition leaders **Mukhtar Abkyazov** (www.ablyazov.info), **Galymzhan Zhakiyanov** (www.zhakiyanov.info) and **Akezhan Kazhegeldin** (www.khazegeldin.addr.com). (RSF, CJES, IRIN)

On 28 April, Ermuhamet Ertysbaev, President Nazar-

OCCUPATIONAL HAZARD
DANI FILC

After 12 years of service in the brigade, including several times in the occupied territories, I have reached the conclusion that I can no longer serve in the territories. Although I have always been against the occupation, and for many years I have been aware of the human rights violations in the territories, I debated with myself because of my feelings of fellowship with the soldiers in the unit, because of the problematic issue of matters that are decided by governments elected by a majority, and because of the fact that my position there was that of a physician who treats everyone and might even be able to relieve some distress.

None the less, the past two years have brought me to the decision that I can no longer collaborate with what is being done in the territories. The killing of [Raed] Karmi by the IDF a day or two prior to the end of the 'quiet period' set by Sharon brought me to the conclusion that there is no real interest in negotiations.

Moreover, I reached the conclusion that in regards to my beliefs in democratic values, the affront to them caused by the occupation is inestimably more severe than any affront caused by the act of refusal. I also understand that the attempt to convince myself that I could be different there, or that by my being a physician I am not directly involved in human rights violations, is not true. From the moment we are in the territories, we are part of a mechanism of oppression.

I made *aliya* [Jewish immigration to Israel] as a Zionist who believed in the right of the Jewish people to self-determination. However, I also immigrated as a person who believes in equality between human beings and equality between nations. One cannot argue in favour of the right to Jewish self-determination while denying the same right to the Palestinian people. The occupation negates this right and therefore it is wrong, and it is wrong to attempt forcefully to preserve it.

The same principles which brought me to the decision to move to Israel bring me to the decision to refuse to serve in the territories. ❏

Dr Dani Filc, faculty member in the Department of Politics and Government at Ben-Gurion University and a board member of Physicians for Human Rights, was sentenced to 14 days' imprisonment in early June for his refusal to serve in the occupied territories. Dr Filc serves as a brigade physician with the rank of Major in the armoured corps. For further information please contact Miri Weingarten or Shabtai Gold of PHR-Israel, 03-687-3718.

bayev's adviser on political affairs, said that the ability of the country's information media to freely express its views will soon be reduced, because 'they violate certain articles of the constitution, legislation and the press law'. Speaking at the Second Eurasian Media Forum, Ertysbaev pointed out that the Kazakh constitution protects freedom of speech, but said that freedom is not absolute. (RFE/RL, *Interfax, Deutsche Welle*)

KENYA

Contempt of court charges were brought against the *East African Standard* and the *Kenya Times* in April when they reported a pending court case involving President Emilio Mwai Kibaki and unpaid petrol bills run up by Kibaki and his party staff from the National Rainbow Coalition before his election in December 2002. (CPJ)

KUWAIT

On 8 March, Information Minister Sheik Ahmed al-Fahd al-Sabah threatened journalists with legal action if they passed on any information to Israeli media organisations. Kuwait hosted over 1,000 foreign journalists reporting on the war in Iraq. Israeli journalists were not allowed visas. (RSF)

KYRGYSTAN

On 4 April, *Agym* newspaper published an article criticising the business activities of Khikmatullo Abdullayev, a member of the Osh city legislature. The legislature immediately responded with a letter to the newspaper's editor-in-

chief, **Melis Eshimkanov**, saying that the publication would face a US$200,000 fine if he did not repudiate the article. (CJES)

On 30 April, a Bishek court rejected an appeal by the newspaper *Kyrgyz Ordo* against its US$6,000 fine for libelling State Customs Service deputy head Aydarbek Duyshaliev. He had originally demanded US$8,500 in compensation and the closure of the newspaper. *Kyrgyz Ordo*'s equipment was seized and it has not appeared since the lower court's mid-January ruling. (RFE/RL)

On 23 May, all copies of the *Moya Stolitsa Novosti* newspaper were seized on a court's orders, which also covered the paper's property. However the bailiffs were told that the paper's equipment was on loan from the US embassy and could not be impounded. The paper has been sued 37 times by officials, including Prime Minister Nikolai Tanaev, who wants it closed. Court awards to plaintiffs of US$2.3 million are outstanding against the newspaper. (*Deutsche Welle*, RFE/RL, CJES)

Officials in Kyrgyzstan are systematically threatening media outlets with legal action, effectively shutting down the independent press in the country. 'The recent pattern of lawsuits targeted at independent newspapers in Kyrgyzstan is particularly troubling,' said *Freedom House* Executive Director **Jennifer Windsor**. President Askar Akayev's administration, increasingly impatient with critics of the regime, has recently taken a number of

steps to curb or control opposition media outlets. (IFEX)

LEBANON

Lebanon's chief prosecutor, Adnan Addoum, launched an investigation on 13 March against the *an-Nahar* newspaper, after it ran an article entitled 'Letter to God' written by Christian poet **Alk Awit**. The chief prosecutor was responding to anger at the article expressed by some Muslim leaders. (RSF)

LIBERIA

On 9 April, **Grody Dorbor**, editor of *The Inquirer* newspaper, and **Oscar Dolo, Nyahn Flomo** and **William Quiwea**, local correspondents for the radio station Talking Drum Studio–Liberia, were reported missing by RSF. By 6 May, all had reappeared except Quiwea, who was still missing. (RSF)

MALDIVES

President Maumoon Abdul Gayoom kicked off his 2003 presidential re-election campaign by banning 22 publications on 4 March. An amendment to the law tripped up almost all the country's print media, though the real targets of the act were the magazine *Dhanfulhi* and the *Monday Times*. *Dhanfulhi* was planning to publish an article by **Mohamed Nashid** (*Index* 2/02, 3/02,4/02), a prominent political activist and former MP. (maldivesculture.com)

MAURITANIA

Eleven members of the Ba'athist Party Nouhoud were arrested between

30 April and 3 May and were then detained incommunicado, including Secretary-General **Mohammed Abdallah Ould Eya**, without official warrants or charge. (OMCT)

MEXICO

On 25 April, **Conrado de la Cruz Morales**, son of the general manager of *Cuarto Poder* newspaper, was arrested in Cancún by officers of the Chiapas State Prosecutor. The government has previously harassed the paper and arbitrarily detained *Cuarto Poder* journalists who were accused of defamation. (*Periodistas*)

On 4 April, **Humberto López Lena**, director of *Expresión* newspaper and the radio news agency Corporación de Medios Informativos (CMI), was arrested. López Lena is accused of defamation by local Representative Juan Díaz Pimentel and Anauar Karim Said Murat, the state governor's brother. *Expresión* has featured critical articles accusing Pimentel and Governor José Murat Casab of abusing their authority and numerous procedural irregularities. (*Periodistas*)

MOLDOVA

Police raided the premises of Flux Publications on 13 May, seizing computers, files and emails in connection with a report by the news group suggesting links between Mahmoud Hamoud, a Moldova-based Lebanese businessman, and an alleged terrorist group. Police want to know the sources for the reports. (RSF)

MOROCCO

Maria Mokrim, a journalist with the independent weekly *al-Ayyam*, received a series of threatening phone calls in March linked to her reports on the Moroccan secret services. On 13 March, she was called on her mobile by 'one of the people you dared insult', and as she hung up was then struck by a man with a stick. She was then called again and asked if she 'had learned her lesson'. (CPJ)

On 4 April, al-Jazeera TV was barred from using state TV facilities to feed material to its headquarters in Qatar. The communications ministry said the station had been barred because of its 'erroneous reports' including one about the alleged closure of the US embassy in Rabat. (CPJ/*El Mundo*)

On 8 May, the publishers and three editorial staff of the daily *Aujourd'hui Le Maroc* were ordered to pay US$1,000 each in damages to Spanish journalist **Ignacio Cembrero**. The *El País* reporter had been accused of spying and plotting against Morocco. Cembrero said he would donate the money to Moroccan NGOs. (*El País*)

On 21 May, **Ali Lmrabet**, editor of the weekly *Demain* (*Index* 2/03), was sentenced to four years in prison and fined US$2,300 for 'insulting the person of the king' and 'offences against territorial integrity' relating to the publication of an interview with a former political prisoner who declared himself a 'republican' in monarchist Morocco and satirical images deemed to be insulting to the king. The

weekly and its Arabic edition were banned. Lmrabet went on a hunger strike which ended on 25 June. The cousin of King Mohammed VI, Prince Moulay Hicham al-Alaoui – a supporter of liberal reform in Morocco – visited Lmrabet in a Rabat hospital and advised him that the cause of freedom of expression 'needs him alive, not dead'. (RSF, BBC, *El Mundo*)

MOZAMBIQUE

On 22 April, Supreme Court president Mario Mangaze sued the weekly newspaper *Zambeze* for libel after it alleged that he had tried to intervene in the decision of a lower court in return for gifts of land in Maputo province. Mangaze's lawyer accused the paper of failing to check its sources; newspaper director **Salomão Moyana** said officials had told his reporters that 'affairs of a state institution are not discussed in the press'. (MISA)

NEPAL

On 25 March, the BBC reported that the pro-Maoist rebel *Janadesh* newspaper had resumed publishing after a ban of nearly 16 months. The move came two months after a ceasefire agreement was signed between the government and the rebels, and in the run-up to proposed direct peace talks between the two sides. (BBC)

On 27 March, Reporters sans Frontières and the local Centre for Human Rights and Democratic Studies called on both the government and Maoist rebels to release journalists still held in the country. The government is holding

10 journalists: **Komal Nath Baral, Muma Ram Khanal, Janardhan Biyog, Arjun Thapaliya, Bharat Sigdel, Dinesh Shrestha, Anjan Kumar Himali, Niva Shah, Sanga Tamrakar** and **Kumar Pandit**. Although never acknowledged by the authorities, **Krishna Sen**, the former editor of *Janadesh*, died in government detention last year. Rebels hold **Dhana Bahadur Rokka Magar** of Radio Nepal. (RSF)

Recent Publications: 'Role of International Community for Peace Initiation in Nepal' by Padma Khatiwada in *Informal*, Vol 15 No 2, April 2003; *'We Don't Want to Be Refugees Again'*, A Human Rights Watch Briefing Paper for the Fourteenth Ministerial Joint Committee of Bhutan and Nepal, 19 May 2003

NICARAGUA

After reporting on how drug traffickers operate along Nicaragua's Atlantic coast, journalist **Sergio León** has received a number of threats from drug dealers. León said: 'Ever since this whole affair began, my wife and I have not been able to sleep from fear that something will happen to us in the house.' (PFC)

NIGERIA

On 16 April, the Committee to Protect Journalists urged the country's new lawmakers to pass the Freedom of Information Bill. The lawmakers of the Ruling People's Democratic Party of President Olusegun Obasanjo had promised to pass this bill at the commencement of their term, in May 1999, but did not do so. Modelled according to the US Freedom of Information Act, the Nigerian Freedom of Information Bill would allow journalists and citizens free access to government information and consequently contribute to the media's ability to report more freely. (CPJ)

PAKISTAN

On 10 March, Ejaz Shah, the home secretary of Punjab province, allegedly threatened **Ilyas Mehraj**, the publisher of the *Weekly Independent*, over the phone. Shah apparently told Mehraj that the provincial government thought that the paper was working against the national interest because of articles it had published critical of the army, and that its' operations should be rolled back if he wanted to remain in business and stay safe. Shah, a retired army brigadier and former head of the Punjab division of the powerful Inter-Services Intelligence, is a close associate of General Pervez Musharraf's military government. (CPJ)

On 4 April, a bomb attack took place outside the home of **Awardeen Mehsood**, Laddah correspondent for the Urdu-language national daily *Khabrian* and the NNI news agency. Although no one has claimed responsibility for the incident, it is believed that the explosion has something to do with Mehsood's reports about the calls for change of status for the tribal areas. (RSF)

In mid-April, it was revealed that Fazal Karim, a suspect in the murder of *Wall Street Journal* reporter **Daniel Pearl** (*Index* 2/02, 3/02, 4/02), had been in police detention since July 2002. The BBC reported on 17 April that **Khawaja Naveed**, Karim's lawyer, claimed his client had been held incommunicado for eight months because the police feared that he might give evidence that would compromise the conviction last year of British-born Islamic militant Ahmed Omar Saeed Sheikh for the murder. According to a report by the *Gulf News* on 20 April, the four men sentenced to death in the Pearl case 'were believed never to have been in the small shed where Pearl was killed'. Karim, along with **Naeem Bukhari** and **Zubair Chisti** (who are also thought to be in police custody), led Karachi police to Pearl's body in May last year. Karim used to work as a driver for Saud Memon, an industrialist believed to be a key financial backer of the Harkatul Mujahideen al-Almi, an Islamist group that was named in connection with Pearl's murder. Memon, who owns the land where Pearl's body was found, was able to leave the country last year at a time when all airports were on the alert for suspects in the case. (BBC, *Gulf News Online*)

On 27 May, the BBC reported that the government in North West Frontier Province was about to introduce legislation that would make sharia law superior to secular law. Provincial deputies are also considering a bill to establish a new Taliban-style Department of Vice and Virtue. While many women's groups have expressed fears about the moves, it is also expected that the legislation will outlaw 'honour killings', in which women are killed for adultery. Both bills are expected to be passed since Islamist hardliners have a majority of the seats in the assembly. (BBC)

PALESTINE

On 6 March, two Palestinian journalists, cameraman **Shams Odeh** and photographer **Ahmad Jadallah**, received shrapnel wounds from an explosion caused when they were fired on by an Israeli tank in the Jabalaya refugee camp during a raid by Israeli troops. Both journalists required surgery, Jadalah for two broken legs and a severed artery, and Odeh for foot injuries. (RSF)

Rachel Corrie, 23, an American peace activist, was killed on 16 March after she was run over by an Israeli Defence Force bulldozer she was attempting to stop from demolishing a Palestinian house in Rafah. On 11 April, British activist **Tom Hundall**, 21, was shot by Israeli troops as he attempted to take children to cover as the street they were on in Rafah came under fire; he later died. The Israeli government has declared a 'zero tolerance' policy on peace activists after a British suicide bomber, Asif Hanif, detonated a bomb in Tel Aviv. Hanif had previously joined peace group the International Solidarity Movement (ISM) in laying flowers at the site in Rafah where Rachel Corrie had been killed. On 9 May, members of the Israeli Defence Forces and police arriving in over 20 vehicles raided the ISM offices, confiscating equipment and taking three

women into custody. Those arrested were **Christine Razowsky**, from Human Rights Watch, an Australian woman who did not want her name released, and Palestinian **Fida Gharib**, a secretary for the organisation. (Labournet)

On 19 April, **Nazih Darwazeh**, a cameraman for Associated Press Television News (APTN) and the Palestinian Broadcasting Corporation (PBC), was killed while filming clashes between Israeli soldiers and Palestinians in the West Bank city of Nablus. Witnesses said an Israeli soldier shot Darwazeh, who was wearing a yellow vest marked 'Press' and died on the way to hospital. On 3 May, British cameraman and film producer **James Miller** was shot dead in Rafah in the Gaza Strip by Israeli tank fire. Miller was filming a documentary for the American cable network HBO and was filming in the dark at the time. (IFJ, *Index on Censorship*)

On 20 May, two journalists, **Shaban Kendil**, a photographer for Arab News Network (ANN), and **Joseph Handal**, a photographer with France 2, were beaten by Israeli soldiers and sustained serious injuries when their car was stopped in Beit Sahur. The journalists reported that at the time there were no clashes in the town. (RSF)

PANAMA

Dutch journalist **Okke Ornstein** and Panamanian journalist **Carmen Boyd** of *El Siglo* newspaper claim to have been threatened following an investigation into the San Cristóbal land development company, which is suspected

of having swindled foreign investors. Ornstein says he received an email from San Cristóbal company president Tom McMurrain telling him that he knew where the journalist lived. Ornstein's lawyer was later found shot dead in May. (*Panama News*)

On 11 April, Gaspar Arosemena, a radio show host and the husband of the mayor of La Chorrera, assaulted a journalist at a town council meeting where problems with the garbage collection service were under discussion. (*Periodistas*)

PAPUA NEW GUINEA

A proposed law to prosecute anyone who publicly criticises the country or its government was announced on 3 April by a parliamentary committee. An Australian and a naturalised Papua New Guinean have already been summoned by a parliamentary committee for criticising the country in remarks that appeared in the Australian press. The government's position is still unclear but a spokeswoman for Prime Minister Sir Michael Somare said on 6 April that the government did not necessarily agree with it but she warned that the media had to show responsibility by not publishing negative news about the country. (RSF)

PARAGUAY

Gustavo García, journalist at the *Ultima Hora*, received a telephone death threat on 28 April. He had been reporting on the illegal diversion of Banco Oriental funds to offshore accounts in an operation that subsequently led to the charging of Chinese national Wai Fu Chan and members of his family along with a former director of Paraguay's Central Bank. (PFC)

PHILIPPINES

Two men were arrested on 22 May in connection with the 17 May killing of DWTI-AM radio announcer **Apolinario 'Polly' Pobeda**, in Lucena City, Quezon. The two men, Eulogio Patulay and his brother Eric, who are bodyguards of Lucena city politicians Ramon Talaga Jr and Romano Franco Talaga, were positively identified by an eyewitness. (CPJ)

On 14 March, three armed men broke into dxRM Radyo Natin (Our Radio) station in Surigao del Sur. They tied up three station employees, including an anchorman and a reporter. Afterwards, they destroyed the station's equipment. It is believed the attacks took place because the station might have angered certain government officials because of its critical programmes. (CMFR)

Philippine Daily Inquirer Central Luzon correspondent **Tonette Orejas** began to receive death threats by telephone and SMS messages on 15 March. She claims the death threats started just after she submitted a 13 March story about the filing of sexual abuse charges against Augusto Sanchez, the chief of staff for Pampanga province Vice-Governor Miguel Arroyo, who is President Gloria Macapagal-Arroyo's son. (CMFR)

John Villanueva, an announcer for the station DZGB in Legaspi City, south of Manila, was shot dead on 29 April after being ambushed while riding his motorcycle. The motive for his killing is unknown. The day after, radio announcer **Jun Pala** was attacked and wounded in the southern city of Davao by five men who opened fire on his taxi. (AFP/CPJ)

QATAR

The Arabic- and English-language websites of al-Jazeera were subjected to attack from hackers on 27 March. Visitors to the Arabic-language site were sent to a porn site, while visitors to the English site were sent to a page displaying the US flag and the message 'let freedom ring' or 'God bless our troops'. Al-Jazeera won the award for the best circumvention of censorship at *Index on Censorship*'s third annual Freedom of Expression awards on 26 March. (*Guardian*)

On 29 April, Qataris voted overwhelmingly in a referendum in favour of plans to give the monarchy a written constitution and increase democratic representation within the kingdom. The new constitution would create a separation of executive, legislative and judicial powers, although political parties would not replace representation through traditional tribal associations and one-third of the members of the legislature would be chosen directly by the Emir. In the vote, 96.6 per cent (68,987 people) voted for the proposal, while 2,145 voted against. (arabic-news.com)

On 6 May, the government announced the appointment of the state's first female government minister, **Sheikha al-Mahmoud**, as minister of education. The appointment of a female into government follows a series of reforms including the formation of a government human rights committee on 5 May with the ministries of foreign affairs, interior, justice, health, education and the civil service represented on it. (arabic-news.com)

The Jordanian journalist **Firas al-Majali**, who was sentenced to death for allegedly spying for Jordan in April (*Index 2/2003*), was pardoned on 18 March as a mark of the visit of Jordan's King Abdullah II to Qatar. (IFJ)

ROMANIA

The body of the investigative journalist **Iosif Costinas** was found on 21 March in a forest near the western city of Timisoara, eight months after he was last seen alive. The police have reported the cause of death as unknown. Costinas, who was 62 years old and worked for the daily newspaper *Timisoara*, disappeared at a time when he was working on a book on the city's mafia. During the course of his investigation he touched the issues of unsolved murders during the 1989 anti-communist revolt and the presence of former members of the communist-era secret police in positions of responsibility. (RSF)

RUSSIA

On 28 May, the Military Collegium of Russia's Supreme

Court overturned the acquittals of six men accused of involvement in the murder of **Dmitriy Kholodov**, military correspondent of the newspaper *Moskovskiy Komsomolets*, killed on 17 November 1994 by a booby-trapped briefcase. Kholodov had published a number of articles exposing high-level corruption in Russia's Defence Ministry, involving the then minister of defence, Pavel Grachev. Six men, including Colonel Pavel Popovskikh, formerly head of intelligence for Russia's airborne forces, were charged with the murder, but in June 2002 were acquitted by the Moscow District Military Court. On 27 May, the Supreme Court ordered a retrial, stating that the lower court had wrongly rejected as 'unreliable' statements by Popovskikh, who had allegedly told investigators that Grachev had repeatedly ordered him to 'settle accounts' with Kholodov, threatening Popovskikh's unit with disbandment otherwise. (RFE/RL)]

On 18 March, **Olga Kobzeva** of Don-TR television station, was attacked by a man who slashed her face with a broken bottle. It is believed that the attack might be connected to Kobzeva's most recent television report, about the illegal privatisation of buildings in the city. (CPJ)

Directors of several leading national broadcast media outlets, among them **Konstantin Ernst**, director of the pro-government Channel One television network; **Anton Zlatopolsky**, director of the state-run Rossiya television network, and

Aleksandr Lyubimov, president of the pro-government Mediasoyuz journalists' union, accepted voluntary restrictions on their coverage of terrorism and anti-terrorist government operations by signing an agreement during the Anti-Terrorist Convention on 8 April. They pledged to obtain official authorisation before interviewing terrorists live on air, ban journalists from acting as independent mediators during a crisis situation, be mindful of the tone of their coverage and follow a series of other restrictions. (CPJ)

On 18 April, Murmansk television station owner **Dmitri Shvets** was shot dead in front of the station's office. Shvets was co-owner and deputy managing director of the TV-21 station that had recently broadcast criticism of the municipal government and of candidates in the 2004 municipal elections. TV-21 journalists were previously verbally threatened by mayoral candidate Andrei Gorshkov, who warned he would sue if they broadcast an interview that he found unflattering. (CPJ)

The opposition radio station Krasnaya Armiya in the city of Noyabrsk was raided by police on 6 May, after the City Election Committee annulled the results of 4 May mayoral elections. The station was a supporter of **Anatoly Kudryashov**, the main challenger of incumbent mayor Yuri Link, and had received various threats before the raid. (CPJ)

Aleksandr Stetsun, a journalist with Ural Television Agency (TAU), an independ-

ent station in the city of Ekaterinburg, was attacked on 19 May by an unknown man. It is believed that the attack might be connected to the journalist's work and his critical reports on local politicians. (CPJ)

Russia's upper house of parliament approved a bill that will give authorities the right to shut down any news outlet during an election campaign if it violates election laws. The bill was passed by the lower house in June and must be signed by President Vladimir Putin to become law. In the past, media that violated a similar law risked only a fine. (*ABC News*)

After the Russian Media Ministry halted independent TVS's television broadcasts in June, *Ekho Moskvy* editor-in-chief **Aleksei Venediktov** concluded that 'the frequency the TV station used has been nationalised and that 'all federal channels are now under the state's control'. **Igor Yakovenko**, general secretary of the Union of Journalists, said: 'It is not an accident that all this occurred on the eve of elections. It is necessary to cement up fully the information field.' (RFE/RL)

RWANDA

On 22 April, the police seized all the copies of the first issue of *Indorerwamo*, as they were arriving from Uganda, and detained its representative without giving any reason for the confiscation. The paper's publisher, **Ismael Mbonigaba** (*Index* 2/03), had been arrested and imprisoned on 22 January. (RSF)

SENEGAL

On 20 March, two journalists from Radio Manore FM, **Fanta Badji** and **Mame Cira Konate**, were attacked by GMI riot police as they covered a police operation to remove the inhabitants of Terrain Foyer, an illegal shanty in Dakar. (WAJA)

SERBIA & MONTENEGRO

Milovan Brkic, Belgrade correspondent for the Podgorica daily paper *Dan*, and **Dragisa Petrovic**, the paper's correspondent in Kragujevac, were arrested on 7 April on suspicion of involvement in the assassination of Serbian Prime Minister Zoran Djindjic. The two journalists had written articles accusing Djindjic's government of having ties with gangsters. (RSF)

On 11 April, the Independent Association of Serbian Journalists, the Association of Independent Electronic Media (ANEM) and the Spectar association of Serbian broadcasters media associations demanded the dismissal of two members of the Serbian Broadcast Agency Council, whom they said had been appointed illegally. (ANEM/SEEMO)

The Belgrade weekly *Nin*, curently being sued by Serbian government communications chief Vladimir 'Beba' Popovic, has accused Popovic of using lawsuits as a whip to wave over the heads of the media. 'We hope the Serbian government does not wish to promote this model of relations, despite the fact that he is a senior employee of the government,' it said in the statement. (B-92)

Vukasin Obradovic, editor-in-chief of *Novine Vranjske* in the southern town of Vranje, received threatening phone calls related to articles linking Serbian Orthodox Bishop Pahomije to paedophilia. His car was damaged on 19 April – the day public prosecutors announced that they would charge the bishop. (SEEMO)

SIERRA LEONE

On 11 March, journalist **Paul Kamara** was released from Pa Demba Road Prison, Freetown. He had been convicted by the Sierra Leone High Court on 18 counts of criminal libel, under sections 26 and 27 of the country's Public Order Act. He had been jailed on 12 November 2002 for six months. Kamara was offered the option of either serving his full sentence or paying a fine and serving half of it. He was released after serving four months of his sentence and having paid the fine. (CPJ)

SOUTH AFRICA

According to a report released in May by the Free Expression Institute, the deepening of the gap between rich and poor has contributed to the rise of censorship in South Africa. Accordingly, there seem to be very few cases of traditional censorship such as jailing of reporters or closing down of media companies. Instead, censorship increasingly involves the hindrance of public assemblies and demonstrations as well as restrictions on public graffiti and leafleting. These are brought forward both by the state and private corporations. (IFEX)

On 17 March, Dennis Neer, Eastern Cape Member of the Executive Council (MEC) for Provincial Safety, Liaison and Transport, accused the press of being biased in favour of 'those who had benefited from apartheid' and who resisted the reconstruction of the South African Police Service (SAPS). The charge came after the *Herald* newspaper reported that a junior policewoman was being investigated by a national task force on suspicion of talking to the media. (MISA)

SPAIN

Pello Zubiria, **Joan Mari Torreldai**, **Txema Auzmendi**, three of the six journalists from Basque newspaper *Egunkaria* who were jailed in February, have been released on bail. However, three journalists remained in prison, and Spanish authorities announced on 10 March that they would be suing four of them for accusing Civil Guards of torture. (Guardian)

SRI LANKA

On 7 May, **Ponniah Manikavasagam**, the Vavuniya-based correspondent for the Tamil-language daily *Virakesari* and a regular contributor to the BBC World Service Radio's Tamil service, received a telephone death threat. Although there have not been any arrests, police traced the call to a Mannar office run by the Varatharajah Perumal faction of the Eelam People's Revolutionary Front, a group that is strongly opposed to the Liberation Tigers of Tamil Eelam.(CPJ, AP)

Recent Publications: *Child Conscription and Peace: A Tragedy of Contradictions – Special Report No 16,* by University Teachers for Human Rights (Jaffna), 18 March; *The North-East: Democracy on Death Row – Information Bulletin No 32* by University Teachers for Human Rights (Jaffna), 2 May.

SUDAN

Sudanese journalist **Edward Terso Lado**, a reporter for the English-language daily *Khartoum Monitor* was reported to have been detained by the General Security Service in Khartoum on 17 March. Some have claimed that his work on a history of Islam in Sudan may be connected to the detention. (CPJ)

Noureddin Madani, editor of the daily *al-Sahafa*, told CPJ that **Yousef al-Bashir Moussa**, the newspaper's correspondent in the city of Nyala, had been arrested on 4 May, a few days after he reported that the Sudanese president was considering firing the governors of the three states of Darfur, a region in western Sudan. (CPJ)

SWAZILAND

The Southern African Development Community (SADC) and the media rights group IPI have urged the Swazi government to repeal its new censorship policy in a 15 April letter to Minister of Information Abednego Ntshangase, who says national TV and radio would not be allowed to cover anything with a negative impact on the government; any media

opposing the government would be prevented from airing their views. (IPI)

SYRIA

On 18 April, Syrian opposition member **Jamal Mahmud al-Wafa'ei** was arrested on his return to the country after nearly 20 years' exile. It is alleged that al-Wafa'ei's family were forced into asking him to return to the country by the Syrian authorities.

TAJIKISTAN

On 22 April, access to two internet sites was closed, one registered in the UK and one in Russia but both operated by an opposition party banned by the country's Supreme Court. (CJES, IRIN, RSF)

THAILAND

On 3 May, in a joint statement marking UNESCO-designated World Press Freedom Day, the Thai Journalists Association (TJA) and the Thai Broadcast Journalists Association (TBJA) urged all of society to recognise the importance of press freedom by staging a public vigil on the government's existing legal and policy obstacles to their rights to search for truth, free expression and access to information. The outlined indicators of these obstacles include the government's intimidation of some journalists, its lack of sensitivity to the media and public calls for the abolition of the 1941 Printing Act, and its insincere position in pushing for an amendment to the 1997 Official Information Act. (TJA, SEAPA)

TOGO

On 7 May, **Sylvestre Djahlin Nicoue**, managing editor of *Le Courrier du Citoyen*, was set free. Nicoue had been arrested on 26 December 2002 (*Index* 2/03) and had been detained for four months, at the Lomé Civil Prison, without trial. (RSF)

After foreign correspondents neglected to cover a forum on African elections that opened in Lomé on 24 March, the Ministry of Communications press attaché informed them that they were being barred from practising their jobs 'until further notice'. With the exception of the correspondent for *Africa No 1*, this order affected all foreign correspondents including those with Radio France Internationale, Agence France Presse, Reuters and the BBC. (RSF)

The alarm was first raised following the closure of Tropik FM radio in Lomé in March on order of the High Authority for Audio-visual Communications (HAAC). The government had earlier accused the station director **Albert Biki Tchekin** of allowing the opposition to insult the ruling regime on air. (CPJ)

TONGA

On 2 April, **Lopeti Senituli**, director of the Tongan Human Rights and Democracy Movement, **Reverend Simote Vea, Ofa Simiki, Tavake Fusimalohi**, the retired general manager of the Tonga Broadcasting Commission, and **Sangster Saulala**, editor of the newspaper *Tonga Star* and president of the

Tonga Media Association, who were involved in a television debate on their government's ban on the New Zealand-published newspaper *Times of Tonga*, were charged with contempt of court. The Supreme Court claimed the issue was sub judice, because it was hearing an application by the Auckland-based bi-weekly newspaper for a judicial review of the government action at the same time. (PINA)

On 4 April, the authorities introduced a tough new media law which, the government says, cannot be subject to judicial review by the courts. The decision came immediately after the kingdom's Supreme Court ruled that the ban on the import of the biweekly newspaper *Times of Tonga* and the declaration that it was a prohibited document were invalid. The kingdom's Privy Council issued an ordinance making it unlawful for any person to publish, sell or offer for sale, distribute, copy or reproduce, possess or import any publication to which it applies, including the *Times of Tonga* newspaper and other Lali Media publications. (PINA)

TUNISIA

On 11 December, Amnesty International reported a violent assault on **Mokhtar Yahyaoui**, President of the Centre de Tunis pour l'Indépendance de la Justice (CIJ), and founding member of the Association Internationale de Soutien aux Prisonniers Politiques (AISPP). While on his way to visit fellow human rights lawyers, Yahyaoui was dragged to an alley and beaten up. The

attack took place the day after International Human Rights Day, when the AISPP published an appeal signed by Yahyaoui calling for the lifting of the prolonged solitary confinement of political prisoners in Tunisian prisons, and for the guarantee of their basic rights. Yahyaoui was dismissed as a judge in December 2001 after calling for the constitutional principle of the independence of the judiciary to be respected. (AI)

Jailed internet journalist **Zouhair Yahyaoui** (*Index* 4/02) was said by members of his family on 3 April to have begun another hunger strike after having been placed in solitary confinement for two days, accused of inciting other prisoners to fast. He was physically weakened and claimed to have been deprived of reading materials, letters and daily exercise periods. (RSF)

It was reported on 18 February that 20 young men from Zarsis had been arrested as a result of viewing banned websites, such as that of the proscribed Islamist al-Nahda Party. Their lawyer told the press that they were suspected of committing subversive acts and were being interrogated in Tunis with no right to receive family visits. (BBC online)

TURKEY

The national security council complained about the showing of a film called *Ararat*, claiming the film would have a worse effect on the public than the 1970s film *Midnight Express*. The NSC claimed the film was hostile to Turks

and 'propagates a genocide against the Armenians'. The film portrays the Turkish military as torturers, rapists and destroyers and as being corrupt. A decision has not yet been reached on whether or not the film is to be shown. (IMK, *Milliyet*)

On 12 March, the case against the owner of the daily *Yeniden Özgür Gündem*, **Ali Çelik Kasûmogullarû**, and editor-in-chief **Mehmet Çolak**, concluded at Istanbul SSC. The journalists were being tried in connection with an article by **Abdullah Öcalan**, published in the daily on 15 September 2002. The Court fined Kasûmogullarû and Çolak and ordered the closure of the daily for seven days. The same day, the court found against **Ümit Gök**, editor-in-chief of the journal *Sanat ve Hayat* (Art and Life), judging that the articles written by professor of economics **Haluk Gerger** and the Kurdish writer and critic **Muhsin Kûzûlkaya** contained 'separatist propaganda'. Gök was given a prison sentence of one year, one month and ten days and the journal was closed for ten days. (*Özgür Gündem*, *TIHV*)

Leyla Zana and three other imprisoned Democracy Party (DEP) parliamentarians were retried on 28 March. The court denied requests that they be released pending the conclusion of the retrial; and that a member of the judiciary be removed due to concerns about his impartiality. The State Security Court also rejected requests to acquit the parliamentarians in the light of the nine years they have already served in prison. The court maintained that an acquittal could not be granted on the basis of the 'case dossier and evidence'. The DEP parliamentarians, Zana, **Hatip Dicle, Selim Sadak** and **Orhan Dogan**, have been imprisoned since 1994. (KHRP)

On 17 April, an Istanbul court started to hear a case against **Handan Ipekçi**, director of the film *Big Man, Little Love,* who is charged with insulting the armed forces. In March 2002, the Ministry of Culture had banned the film, which shows a retired Turkish judge speaking Kurdish, on grounds that it violated the principle of the indivisible integrity of the State. The ban on the movie had been lifted in June 2002. (*Cildekt, TIHV*)

On 9 May, the European Court of Human Rights found that Turkey had violated the European Convention for its failure to investigate the killing of **Ferhat Tepe**. Isak Tepe of the DEP (Democracy Party) in Bitlis, south-east Turkey, alleged that in July 1993, his son, Ferhat Tepe, reporter for the pro-Kurdish *Özgür Gündem* newspaper, was tortured and killed by undercover agents of the state, and that the authorities had failed to carry out an adequate investigation into his death. The court confirmed that the circumstances in which Ferhat Tepe had died supported his father's allegations, and noted that there had been striking omissions in the conduct of the investigation into Tepe's disappearance and death. The judgement of *Tepe v. Turkey* (27244/95) can be found at http://www.echr.coe.int/ Eng/Judgments.htm (Kurdish Human Rights Project)

On 13 March, the pro-Kurdish People's Democracy Party (HADEP) was permanently banned for allegedly aiding the outlawed Kurdistan Workers' Party (PKK) and carrying out activities challenging the state. The court also pushed to ban its successor DEHAP, the Democratic People's Party. Over 40 HADEP members, including its founders, have been banned from becoming members, founders, administrators or inspectors of any political party for five years. Turkey has a long-standing record of banning a succession of pro-Kurdish political parties. In May last year a European Parliament delegation warned, 'If HADEP is closed down, this would be a serious setback in relations between the European Union and Turkey.' Forty-one HADEP offices were raided and 393 formal arrests of HADEP members were made in 2002. DEHAP was the leading party in 12 provinces in the Kurdish regions in the 2002 general election, scoring an average of 47 per cent of votes in Diyarbakir, Batman, Sirnak, Hakkari and Van. However, the Turkish electoral system denies parties with under 10 per cent of the vote nationwide from securing parliamentary seats. (Kurdish Human Rights Project)

Prisoner of conscience **Fikret Baskaya** faces two new cases. His book *Paradigmanin Iflasi* (Bankrupt Paradigms) was published in April 1991 and Baskaya was sentenced to 20 months' imprisonment. The book has been reprinted eight times. The European Human Rights Court found Turkey guilty in the first case against Baskaya, judging that the sentence was an open violation of freedom of expression and sentencing Turkey to pay compensation. The second case is for an article on secularism that he wrote after the aSivas massacre – in which 38 artists were burned in a hotel by a crowd provoked by fascist militants – in July 1993. (*FoeX*)

TURKMENISTAN

On 29 March, the Open Society Institute's Turkmenistan Project reported that a Baptist church had been closed by the authorities in the town of Balkanabat. The local authorities said that the church was unregistered and that its members were engaged in religious extremism. Under current Turkmen legislation small religious confessions are unable to register, and Baptist congregations have often had their services disrupted in the past by the police and security services. Individual Baptists were harassed, fined and arrested. (RFE/RL)

UGANDA

Monitor photographer **Wandera Ojumbo** was beaten by prison wardens in May for allegedly attempting to take pictures of them. The photographer was in the process of photographing one of the inmates being escorted to prison by one of the wardens. The journalist was, however, rescued by police who arrived at the scene of the crime. (*The Monitor*)

The Red Pepper – a tabloid notorious for its sex and scandal coverage – came under criticism from Christians in the Nkoyooyo area in Kampala, Uganda. Protestors called on the government to ban the paper. The demonstration was organised by the Uganda Joint Christian Council (UJCC) and the Family Life Network (FLN), a local NGO which is 'fighting against pornography'. (*New Vision*)

UKRAINE

The Presidential Administration has advised TV networks on news topics to cover – and how they should be presented – in a report distributed to top managers and editors. Noncompliance invites a wide range of informal sanctions, including tax audits, licence cancellation, arbitrary libel suits, demotions and pay cuts. Many journalists have been demoted, dismissed, had their wages cut and faced other negative consequences. Others have quit their jobs to protest against censorship, while others continue to practise their profession resorting to self-censorship or reporting impartial news despite constant risks. (HRW)

On 3 April, the International Federation of Journalists (IFJ) issued a report on the media crisis in Ukraine calling for unity among journalists to combat governmental interference in journalism. The report condemns forms of political censorship and the Ukraine's failure to meet European standards of press freedom. The report also says that within journalism political pressure on reporters and editors is compounded by corrupt labour practices and alarming working conditions. (IFJ)

On 6 May, a court in Kiev convicted and then amnestied Serhy Obozov, the former prosecutor of Tarashcha District, for obstructing the criminal inquiry into the September 2000 disappearance and murder of journalist **Georgy Gongadze**. Obozov, who was arrested in August 2002, was sentenced to a two-and-a-half-year prison term. He was released after the hearing under an amnesty law allowing convicted criminals with young children to be freed. (CPJ)

UNITED ARAB EMIRATES

The former Iraqi Information Minister **Mohammed Saeed al-Sahaf** has been offered a position at the Dubai-based satellite television station al-Arabiya, which currently runs a series of live programmes on Iraq featuring the former Iraqi ambassador to the United Nations, Mohammed al-Douri.

UNITED KINGDOM

Conservative MP Christopher Chope told the House of Commons on 3 April that the BBC's reporting of Iraqi statements meant British taxpayers were being 'forced to subsidise Saddam Hussein's propaganda campaign'. He called on the BBC to withdraw its journalists from Baghdad. Defence Minister Geoff Hoon attacked the *Independent* and its correspondent, **Robert Fisk**, implying he had allowed himself to be fooled by the regime and had dubious sources. Home Secretary David Blunkett complained on 2 April that journalists reporting behind 'enemy lines' were treating

the US and British forces and the Iraqi regime as moral equivalents. Foreign Secretary Jack Straw said on 1 April that the kind of media pressure surrounding the Iraq war would have made World War II more difficult to win. (*Guardian*)

The deputy director of BBC news, Mark Damazer, has warned that the BBC's credibility is on the line with overseas audiences, because it shies away from showing shocking war images on its international news channel. He said this had led to BBC World showing one version of the recent war in Iraq, while other news channels such as al-Jazeera were broadcasting something completely different. Damazer said that for too long the BBC and other UK news broadcasters had sanitised their coverage from war zones. (*Guardian*)

The owner of Britain's 14th largest regional press group, Sir Ray Tindle, was criticised for ordering his papers to ban articles and letters to the editor that were 'anti-war'. The Tindle Newspapers chief said he would allow withheld letters to be published after the end of hostilities. (*Guardian*)

Channel 4 was forced to withdraw street billposters advertising the TV series *Six Feet Under* after complaints. The adverts featured spoof ads for undertakers' products and models made up to look like corpses. The ad campaign was also taken up by a number of glossy and newspaper listings magazines. (*Guardian*)

Director **Ken Fero** screened his documentary *Injustice* on the wall of Channel 4's building on 1 May, to protest at the channel's decision not to broadcast the film, about the deaths of black people in police custody. (*www.injustice-films.co.uk*)

Lord **Puttnam**, the former film director now leading a House of Lords rebellion over the government's communications bill, published a compromise amendment to reflect their fears that media moguls such as Rupert Murdoch could 'lock up' whole sections of the media without safeguards. It aims to allay concerns over cross-media ownership provisions by subjecting such deals to a 'plurality public interest' test to be conducted by Ofcom, the media regulator created by the bill. (*Financial Times*)

UNITED STATES

The popular Texan band **The Dixie Chicks** came under fire after one of the group criticised president George W Bush while performing in London. Their records were publicly destroyed and scores of radio stations banned them. But as one of the station bosses put it: 'It's been a difficult decision, because how can you ignore the hottest group in country music?' Two DJs, **Dave Moore** and **Jeff Singer**, were suspended from country station KKCS on 6 May for defying their employers' ban and playing the group's records. (Media-Channel.org)

The Rock and Rap Confidential website reported that some phone calls from supporters of *The Dixie Chicks* ban were traced by caller ID back to Republican Party

offices in South Carolina GOP headquarters. (Media-Channel.org)

MSNBC disciplined star reporter **Ashleigh Banfield** after she criticised US TV's presentation of the Iraq war at a university lecture. Banfield was made to apologise for 'demeaning the work of her colleagues'. One of her colleagues at MSNBC, Michael Savage, had called her a 'slut' on air, but was not reprimanded. (www.newsworld.org)

Former vice-president **Al Gore** has been reported to be working to foster the creation of a liberal media network, to counter what he has called the malign influence of conservative talk-show hosts and news organisations. Gore, who began his working life as a newspaper reporter, has held talks with wealthy liberals, Hollywood stars and television executives, *Time* magazine said. (*Time*)

Harry Potter books that had been banned from one Arkansas school district at the request of Christian groups last June are back on the shelves there. (IHT)

Congress has approved a total of US$62m for a US Arabic-language television station to be broadcasting to the Middle East by the end of this year. Voice of America Middle East director Norman J Pattiz accused existing Arab broadcast media in the region of 'a sensationalist approach that includes incitement to violence and disinformation'. (*The Hill*)

Monster.com, the largest US-based internet job board,

blocked the posting of résumés or job openings originating from Cuba, Iran, Iraq, Libya, Myanmar, North Korea, Sudan or Syria, all countries under US sanction. Résumés that mentioned the countries would have the references deleted. (Media-Channel.org)

UZBEKISTAN

On 3 March, acting deputy education minister Rustam Qosimov announced the closure of the new *Natzionalnoye Obrazovaniye Milli talim* newspaper due to its 'grammatical mistakes'. The paper's editor-in-chief **Istam Kushev** said the authorities feared independent editors would cast too much light on the problems of culture and the press in Uzbekistan. (RFE/RL, CJES)

The director of political programmes at Uzbek public television, **Akhmatzhon Ibragimov**, was fired on 15 May, after a live broadcast from the annual general meeting of the European Bank for Reconstruction and Development showed President Islam Karimov sleeping just as EBRD chief Jean Lemierre was criticising Uzbek human rights violations. On 23 May, two cameramen were reprimanded and network chairman **Farkhad Ruziyev** was blamed for having allowed Ibragimov to report the conference live. (CJES)

On 26 May, **Ruslan Sharipov**, a journalist and head of an independent media freedoms group and two colleagues, **Oleg Sarapulov** and **Azamat Mamankulov**, were detained in Tashkent.

Sharipov was charged with sexual abuse and homosexuality, a criminal offence in Uzbekistan. (IRIN, RSF, HRW)

VENEZUELA

The country's controversial TV and radio 'contents law' passed its first reading in the National Assembly on 13 February. The legislation proposes to regulate the contents of radio and television under the guise of protecting children from crude language, sexual situations and violence. (IAPA, HRW, IPYS)

On 2 May, journalist **Roberto Giusti** was assaulted by a group of individuals when he arrived at the Radio Caracas studios. He has received unidentified death threats which he has linked to his reports on the presence of Colombian guerrillas in Venezuela and the so-called Bolivarian Liberation Forces on the Colombia–Venezuela border. (IPYS)

VIETNAM

Tuong Lai magazine editor **Nguyen Dan Que**, 61, previously jailed for more than 20 years, was arrested again at his home in Ho Chi Minh City on 17 March. His arrest is thought to be linked to a statement he issued criticising the lack of press freedom in the country. (CPJ)

On 21 April, assailants set fire to the car of journalist **Hoang Thien Nga** of the daily *Tien Phong*, in apparent retaliation for her reports on Dai Hung, a fugitive lawyer with alleged ties to the criminal underworld and senior government officials. In an unrelated case,

the day before **Bui Tan Son Dinh**, a reporter for the newspaper *Nong Nghiep Vietnam*, was attacked by a group of unidentified assailants while reporting on prostitution in Ho Chi Minh City. (CPJ)

YEMEN

Yemeni journalists not working for state-owned newspapers were barred from attending the trial of alleged terrorist Ali Jarallah on 7 May. He is accused of murdering three US doctors in December 2002 but has refused to answer to the court unless independent media are present. The prosecution has called for a death penalty to be imposed on the 32-year-old Islamist.

ZIMBABWE

On 16 May, **Andrew Meldrum**, the *Guardian*'s correspondent in Zimbabwe, was deported, despite three court orders prohibiting his expulsion. One of the last foreign correspondents remaining in the country, he had been fighting against deportation for a year. (MISA, *Guardian*)

Section 80 of the Access to Information and Protection of Privacy Act (AIPPA) was struck down as unconstitutional by the country's Supreme Court on 7 May, the result of a challenge by journalists **Lloyd Mudiwa** and **Geoff Nyarota** of the *Daily News*. Section 80 made it 'abuse of journalistic privilege' to publish false information, whether it was intentional or not. Journalists convicted of violating this provision faced up to two years' imprisonment. It was

used almost exclusively to target the independent media. (MISA)

On 18 March, *Daily News* legal adviser **Gugulethu Moyo** and photographer **Philemon Bulawayo** were released on the evening of their detention after the High Court ruled it was illegal and no charges were laid. They were both badly injured by beatings and taken to the Avenues Clinic for treatment. (MISA)

Compiled by: James Badcock (North Africa); Ben Carrdus (East Asia); Gulliver Cragg (Western Europe, North America); Ioli Delivani (Southern and Western Africa); Veronique Dupont (South America); Hanna Gezelius (Britain and Ireland); Monica González Correa (Central Asia and Caucusus); Javier González-Rubio (Russia, Poland, Ukraine, and Baltic States, South East Asia and Australasia); Andrew Kendle (India and subcontinent); Gill Newsham (Turkey and Kurdish areas); Jason Pollard (Gulf States and Middle East); Shifa Rahman (East Africa); Jugoslav Stojanov (Eastern Europe); Mike Yeoman (Central America and Caribbean)

Edited by Rohan Jayasekera and co-ordinated by Natasha Schmidt

EDGES OF THE MAP

EVERYONE KNOWS WHAT'S NEEDED FOR ISRAELIS AND PALESTINIANS TO LIVE IN PEACE. BUT DO THEIR LEADERS HAVE THE COURAGE TO MAKE IT HAPPEN?

Gaza Strip, 2003: Palestinian refugees lean against the wall of Gush Katif Jewish Settlement. Credit: Larry Towell / Magnum Photos

ELUSIVE PEACE

ISRAEL'S DAILY 'HA'ARETZ' BROUGHT TOGETHER
TWO WRITERS, AMOS OZ AND DAVID GROSSMAN,
WHO HAVE BEEN WORKING FOR PEACE. THEIR
LUCID DISCUSSION RANGES OVER THE
DISASTROUS POSITION OF THE LEFT IN ISRAEL,
TERRORISM AND THE FUTURE OF THE COUNTRY

AMOS OZ was born in Jerusalem in 1939. More than 20 of his books have
appeared in translation. He now lives in the Arad new town in the Negev
desert. His works include *In the Land of Israel*.

DAVID GROSSMAN was born in Jerusalem in 1954 and still lives there. His
books include *Sleeping on a Wire: Conversations with Palestinians in Israel*, *The
Smile of the Lamb*, *See under: Love*, *The Yellow Wind*.

What scares you the most, and is there hope?

OZ The good news is that for the first time in 90 years of conflict, everyone
knows what the solution will be. Today the Jews know that the Palestinians
are not going to disappear and the Palestinians know that the Jews are not
going to disappear. And everyone knows exactly what the solution will be.
We even know where the lines of partition will be.

If things are so good, why are they so bad?

OZ Because the patient is more or less ready for the operation but the
surgeons are cowards. I can't remember a time when there was such a nadir
of leadership in both nations. If there were a leadership today capable of
saying, 'Let's do what everyone knows has to be done,' the whole thing
would come to pass within a few months. Everyone knows that most of the
settlements will have to go, that a few blocs will remain in return for an
exchange of lots, that there will be no sweeping right of return. So what are
they waiting for?

The calamity resides in the personal cowardice of the two leader figures.
Sharafat, I call them. And of them it can definitely be said that like has
found like. Because I have a deep suspicion that both of them prefer this

reality to the post-solution reality. What for us seems to be a new dawn is for them dusk.

David Grossman, do you agree? What we just heard sounds fairly optimistic. The whole problem boils down to Sharon and Arafat.

DG I agree that what we have here is the personal cowardice of two individuals whose reputation rests on bravery, on the ability to face up to danger. I also agree that it's possible that the solution is close. Both because it is known and because the Americans are fed up and the world is fed up and they might impose a solution on us. But I am more pessimistic than Amos. I am afraid that even if we arrive at peace it won't be a rosy, eternal peace. It will be a series of spasms of periods of peace followed by violations and then more peace. But not in the lifetime of those present in this room.

You asked what the most frightening thing is. What most frightens me is that I am no longer confident of Israel's existence. That doubt was always there. I think that everyone who lives here also lives the alternative that maybe Israel will cease to be. That's our nightmare. But over the years we stabilised the nightmare and patched it up and whitewashed it. What has happened here in the past two years is that suddenly the possibility that Israel will no longer exist has become concrete. It's no longer a mere nightmare. The possibility exists that the great, heroic experiment that took place here will cease to be.

When in the past two years did that existential fear seize you?

DG Consider what happened in the Central Elections Committee or in the Likud primary. Suddenly you see that all sense of shame has disappeared, that even mechanisms of social hypocrisy that are needed to maintain the fabric of life have vanished. And in some way it is all connected to life under terrorism. Because if you live in a reality in which you see people torn apart, in which you see the living flesh torn, it is very difficult for you to go on believing in something. And you come to the conclusion that in order to maintain culture, and especially in order to maintain democracy, a certain type of illusion is needed, involving a social agreement that is based on a great deal of good will. And this has been undermined here. We came here so that even if there was danger one's instinct would be not to flee but to stay. Today that is no longer self-evident.

OZ I don't feel the same way David does. My existential fears are no longer Jewish and Israeli ones – they too have been globalised. Of the 29 conflicts that are bleeding today around the world, there is a Muslim side in at least 27 of them. And there is Christian fanaticism with manifestations of European anti-Semitism and Jewish religious-nationalist fundamentalism.

There is also a post-modern clock that posits everything in a relative light. One form of extremism engenders another. Either there is only one truth and whoever does not share it must be killed, or everything is true and everyone is equal, so murderers, too, have the right to murder.

Another clock that worries me is that of globalisation, a sort of infantilisation of the entire human race. So when you talk about a lack of culture, David, it doesn't have to do only with Hamas and with shattered bodies. It has to do with the feeling that we were born to buy or sell.

I will say something that is not popular: there is no culture without hierarchy. It just doesn't exist. There is no culture in voting and no culture based on a survey of buyers and no culture according to popularity ratings. Therefore my fear is not local. It's obvious that in a world of the fourth world war, a world in which a person with an envelope full of bacteria or chemical poison or radioactive contamination can threaten a whole city, I am scared to death.

DG Amos, it is impossible to ignore the fact that we are increasingly isolated here because of all kinds of threats and ostracisms . . . I hope I don't sound paranoid, but my feeling is that since the start of the intifada, and in its wake the wave of anti-Semitism and the attacks on Israel around the world, something in us has changed. I think the modern Israeli of my age, who already thought he was international, universal, who is plugged into the internet and has a dish on the roof and satellite TV and MTV, has suddenly begun to feel how the tragic element of the Jewish destiny is again closing in on him.

There is a feeling that the Jew who came to the land of Israel and built a state in order to connect with a certain solid base, with a concrete existence, has suddenly again become a symbol of something else. After all, the Jew was always a kind of metaphor for something: he was never perceived as the thing itself. And now that is coming back.

People always had a problem relating to us, the Jews, as human beings. There was demonisation and idealisation, but both are actually different forms of dehumanisation. Zionism, despite everything, healed us of that. It restored us to the practical, the human, the historical. But now we are again returning to that symbolic place. I find this dangerous. It also reinforces the sense of persecution that exists within us in any case. And it sucks us into the wound that exists in Judaism, into its sacrificial and traumatic content.

Amos Oz, those feelings are not alien to you, are they? You wrote about them long before the intifada.

OZ I always had the feeling that we were walking on thin ice. On probation for good behaviour, drawing on the bank of the memory of the Holocaust. Let me put it this way: large parts of the Arab world, and perhaps in Islam as well, have not got over the terrible affront they experienced as a result of Israel's establishment in 1948.

In the Christian world it goes far deeper. Because there is a deep, dark element in the Christian narrative. In Christianity, people are raised on a story that there is someone who can kill God. And whoever can kill God is terribly strong and smart, more than human, but also evil. Millions of Christian children around the world open their eyes and the first picture they see is of a person bleeding on the cross, a person dying in torment on the cross. And when the Christian child comes to understand that this is a picture of the dying God, he asks who the criminal is. Who did this? It trickles even into people who have become atheists. Because even people who have moved to the margins of the left and never set foot in a church were raised on that mother's milk. It's not that they are anti-Semitic in the banal sense of wanting to kill every Jew; they have a mix of awe and fear. And sometimes they also set a very high bar of moral demands vis-à-vis Jews. It's as though after they exonerated the Jews of collective responsibility for the crucifixion of Jesus, they have to prove that they deserve the exoneration.

Apart from Israel, there is not one country in the world that exists on condition. Israel is told: if you behave in such-and-such a way, you have the right to exist. If not, you don't have the right to exist and the whole thing was one big mistake. Behave well, you will live; behave badly, you will be dismantled.

But what especially frightens me is how far many Israelis in the intelligent, enlightened, peace-seeking left have internalised this approach. They too see Israel as a state-on-condition. A state whose existence depends on its behaviour.

Are you saying that within the left-wing, doveish intelligentsia in Israel there is some sort of echo of the Christian anti-Semitic approach to the Jewish state?

OZ During the period of the atrocities that France perpetrated in Algeria, the French intelligentsia was embittered. As was the American intelligentsia during the Vietnam War. But nowhere have I seen what I see here: this scale of hatred for the entire self-existence. Not for the government, but for the entire self-existence. Among some of the radical intelligentsia in Israel today I see hatred not only for the religious, for the settlers, the right, the nationalists. I see sweeping hatred for the architecture, for the music, the folk songs, the memories, for everything.

DG You're exaggerating.

OZ Maybe I am exaggerating with the word hatred. Maybe the right word is disgust. But sweeping disgust. There is something implicit here that truly outrages me. It outrages me, especially when it comes from within Israel more than it does when it comes from the European Christian intelligentsia.

DG I think you are going too far. These people say what they do out of a grieving heart. At the growing gap between dream and reality. And in any case, there are not so many of them and they are not all that important. So what interests me far more is how it comes about that after 54 years we are still on condition, how it is that we still don't really believe in our existence. It seems to me that this is the key question. What's behind it? Do we have, as Jews, a gene that makes us incapable of truly remaining in one place? You know, we have always had this thing, this unquiet, the wanderings. We have been unable to decide: are we a people of place or of time? In the diaspora, we decided we were a people of time. An eternal people. But even after we came to this place, we were still unable to crystallise for ourselves a feeling of identity as a people of place.

When did your world view take shape, how did it evolve, and what happened to it in the past two years?

DG I was 13 when the Six-Day War broke out in 1967. I remember the anxiety that preceded it. I remember the concreteness of the possibility that we would be thrown into the sea. Because that possibility was so real, in the winter before the war I started to take swimming lessons at the YMCA in Jerusalem.

Jewish immigrants arriving at Haifa harbour, October 1947. Credit: Getty Images

Then came the occupation. For my generation, there was some sort of interfusion of the sexual energies of adolescence and the energies of the occupation. There is no ignoring it: the sudden penetration and the breaking of the taboo and the entry into these holy places. There is something erotic in the contact between occupier and occupied. I absolutely remember the physical sensation, the sensation of power. And, at the same time, the fear. My parents, who were Mapainiks [Mapai, which was the forerunner of today's Labor Party, was in power from 1948 until 1977], drifted further and further to the right because of the fear. And during my military service I also espoused the views of what is now called the right wing. I served in intelligence and I knew what the Arabs thought of us. They didn't think such good things. So to this day the fears of the right are not alien to me.

For me the shock came in the Lebanon War [of 1982]. At first I completely bought the slogan that we were going to war in order to eradicate terrorism. But when I served as a reservist in a small village in the eastern sector [of Lebanon], I started to see things that I had not wanted to see before.

Not long after I returned home to Jerusalem, I was on a bus from the Talpiot neighbourhood and the bus stopped next to another bus, which was from Bethlehem or from Deheisheh [refugee camp]. Suddenly I saw them. We were there, one bus next to the other, and suddenly I saw the people who were in the other bus. I saw their faces, their despair. I had the feeling that they were like ghosts. I looked at them and I told myself that this is what an occupied person looks like.

When I wrote *Smile of the Lamb* in 1983 I was already trying to understand the malady of occupation. I asked myself how it was that the two sides had taught themselves to develop a kind of blank stare that doesn't see, because the occupied are ashamed of their situation and the occupiers prefer not to see what they are doing.

When I went to Deheisheh [to research] *The Yellow Wind*, for some of the children I was the first Israeli they had ever seen who wasn't in uniform. Finally, an old woman came by and took me to her hut, and she started to talk.

And what was your greatest shock in these past two and a half years?

DG The lynching in Ramallah. That was a kind of breaking point for all of us. It was an eruption of our deepest fears. I believe that we mustn't let go, mustn't give up, that we must continue to believe in the possibility of a rational solution.

Are there moments when you doubt such a possibility?

DG Sometimes I tell myself, look, there is no chance. I look at the map of little Israel, on which there isn't even enough room to write the country's name – you have to throw a few letters into the sea in order to be able to write it. And everything around it – the fundamentalism that is raging there, the lack of democracy in the Arab states. The fact that the Middle East did not really accept us.

But in the end, I feel a sort of personal affront in giving up. I am not blind to the shortcomings of our partner. I am not under a spell of delusions. And I don't believe in the goodwill of the Arabs. They have never shown us goodwill, nor have we shown much goodwill towards them. But in 1967 we entered some sort of loop in which we have been moving ever since. I think that with all our military might we have to be courageous enough to step out of this circle. We have to let go of that branch before we grab hold of the other branch, of the belief in peace. But we haven't yet dared to make that leap. We are still afraid.

In the final analysis, did the left fail or succeed? Was the left wrong or right?

DG The left clearly failed, but it is a failure that I am proud to be part of. Those who opted for the Oslo process knew the risk, that it would be very difficult to resolve a hundred-year conflict with one blow.

The left made two basic mistakes. One was too great a belief in rationality and the other was a basic flaw in evaluating the existing forces. I think that from this point of view the right has a healthier instinct in regard to the forces in the arena and the importance of deterrent force. That is essential in the rough-and-tumble, violent region in which we live. But in the final analysis, the mistakes of the left were in the details. Maybe also in evaluating the personality of Arafat, who is apparently a terrorist at heart. On the other hand, the right was wrong about the big picture. The right believed that it would be possible to maintain the occupation regime, and therefore, in the last analysis, I have no hesitations about where I am and what has to be done.

And another thing: we spoke earlier about the experience of victimhood but we ignored what that experience makes possible. In reaction to the hostility that was directed at us, we turned the West Bank into one big detention camp and carried out actions that border on crimes against humanity and often cross that border. As a society, we have placed our enlightened values in deep freeze. Our moral stature has sunk. And in the end, we confirmed quite a few anti-Semitic stereotypes about the xenophobic, manipulative, power-wielding, unreliable, imperialist Jew. All this has to stop.

Amos Oz, what was your greatest shock in these two and a half years? Was there anything that challenged your world view?

OZ Look, the Committee for Peace and Security espoused the two-state idea. We argued that if we were to follow the road we were proposing, there would be peace between the Palestinians and us. I adduced that argument for more than 30 years. Today I no longer adduce it. I still say that there have to be two states, but I am not sure that this will bring peace. In the best case it will bring peace, in the worst case it will bring about a situation in which, instead of fighting two wars and being in the right in one of them, we will fight one war in which we are completely in the right.

What it means is that this will be the first election campaign in which the left is promising peace: withdrawal, not peace.

I can testify for myself: I have withdrawn unilaterally. I assumed that if the Palestinians were offered what Ehud Barak offered them at Camp David they would come back with a counter-offer. I did not imagine that a proposal for a two-state solution with two capitals and the return of 92–97 per cent of the land would become the trigger for a wave of war against us. That was a very deep shock for me.

In retrospect, was Oslo a mistake?

OZ   I maintain that Oslo was not given even a day's grace. Immediately, even before the ink was dry, the one side planned jihad, while the other planned settlements. Therefore, I don't think Oslo failed, because Oslo was never tried.

I also don't accept the contention that the left drew no lessons from the events. When the leader of the Labor Party says unilateral withdrawal from the populated occupied territories, that is a radical shift from the positions that preceded the intifada. It is the right that has drawn no lessons. Not only since Oslo, but since the 1930s. Throughout this whole period the right has been saying only one thing: hit them very hard and they will calm down.

What do you think of Sharon? Do you detest him?

DG   I don't detest him. I think he has a very narrow world view and that he reduces everything to one shallow concept: force. He has no other solution. He is leading Israel to a very dangerous place. As a leader he is supposed to be taking us into the future, but instead he is constantly leading us into the past. What astonishes me is his success. He has succeeded in bringing about a situation in which he operates almost in a vacuum. He is a prime minister without an opposition and without a coalition, who does what he wants.

How do you explain that?

DG Maybe in a period when we all feel that the old order is collapsing there is a desire to cling to a person who projects some sort of continuity, stubbornness, consistency and rigidity. As a writer, I don't want to exclude myself from the feelings of supporters of the right. And Ariel Sharon truly projects strength. He contains a type of power. Put a toga on him and he will look like a Roman emperor. There is an almost biblical force about him. That image, with its very potent instincts and its brutality and its history, apparently has something that appeals to people.

OZ I will try to answer the Sharon question neither as a writer nor a psychologist but as a political analyst. He is popular because he is perceived to be victorious over the Palestinians without making America angry with us. And he is perceived as victorious because he has definitely won a victory: the Palestinians today are asking for what they rejected at Camp David. The public sees him as having subdued the enemy and delivered him a mortal blow and also as providing emotional satisfaction to our frustrations over the bodies of our shattered children.

I see a person who is projecting a sense of comfortable self-confidence but who doesn't know where he is going.

Is there a successor to Yitzhak Rabin and Shimon Peres?

DG The feeling is that a vacuum exists. Amram Mitzna is paying the price of the Labor Party's having served for two years as Sharon's fig leaf without constituting a counterweight to his instincts and drives. I feel sympathetic toward Meretz. Its leaders think two steps ahead. They are succeeding in not being part of the despair and sense of impotence. And they are able to rise above the very understandable feelings of fear and revenge.

OZ I will vote Meretz because what it says strikes me as correct. Yes, negotiations under fire. Yes, one more attempt to talk to the Palestinians. And if that attempt doesn't work, then a unilateral end to the occupation.

You believe that the left can recover and lead Israel into a reasonable future?

OZ My friend Jumus-Haim Oron says that what is happening now in Israeli public opinion is the same thing that happens in a major earthquake. When the tectonic plates shift, the depths move to one side and the upper layers to the other. In this election [28 January], the vote went to the right. Fundamentally, the Israeli public is moving leftward, not rightward.

I am very apprehensive about what Sharon is doing now. After destroying the Palestinian Authority he is now destroying the Palestinian middle class. What worries me is that when he concludes his work there really will be no one to talk to.

DG Today there is within the Palestinian leadership readiness to accept the Clinton blueprint. I say this from first-hand knowledge. But if no Israeli leader proposes it, I am afraid that Palestinian society will move towards extremism. If the privatisation of terrorism continues, it will become a nightmare – both a Palestinian nightmare and an Israeli nightmare. I am not under any illusions: even if there is peace with Arafat the terrorism will not cease completely. It will go on for many more years. But that is not a reason to stop the peace efforts – because terrorism is not an existential threat to Israel. What is an existential danger is the schism and the dissolution that the present situation is causing.

I said *summud* [an Arabic word meaning 'holding fast on to something'] to peace. The State of Israel arose so that we would not become victims. So that my grandfather would not be beaten again in that town in Galicia. So that we would come here, lead a normal life and defend ourselves. So I am disturbed by the fact that even though we are so powerful, even though we have maybe 200 nuclear bombs, we continue to be the victims of our fears and anxieties, of the screwed-up parts of our psyches. We have to face our history without being its victims. And to ensure that not all our energies are diverted solely to building this armour that protects us from the outside. Because right now the feeling is that we are so focused on the armour that there is no human being left inside. ❏

This interview, conducted by Ari Shavit, appeared in Ha'aretz *in January 2003*
© Ha'aretz

CONTAGIOUS EXCHANGES

AHDAF SOUEIF

AMERICA'S RELATIONSHIP WITH ISRAEL
IS CORRUPTING — FOR BOTH SIDES

Once again it's funny mirrors time. The world watches the meetings taking place by the Red Sea, and the Western media see one process taking place while the Arabs generally see another. Interpreting these meetings is largely a matter of how you view the relationship between the USA and Israel. A few weeks ago I heard a well-known British columnist say he was sick of being told that the Palestinian–Israeli conflict was the 'litmus test' for how people can expect the American imperium to influence the world. Yet 'Freedom for Palestine' was the demand on millions of the banners in the anti-war demonstrations that swept the world last February.

America's support for Israel dates to the beginning of the Zionist project in the late nineteenth century and grew stronger throughout the twentieth. From 1949 to the present, for every dollar the US spent on an African, it spent $250.65 on an Israeli, and for every dollar it spent on someone from the Western hemisphere outside the US, it spent $214 on an Israeli. As Israel grows stronger the support becomes more solid. According to Stephen Zunes, Chair of the Peace and Justice Studies Program at San Francisco University, 'Ninety-nine per cent of all US aid to Israel took place after the 1967 war.'

In the United Nations the US has used its veto against 34 resolutions related to the Arab–Israeli conflict. US support for Israel has involved turning a blind eye not only to Israeli flouting of international law, but to Israeli anti-American activities such as: spying (Jonathan Jay Pollard 1985 and David Tenenbaum 1997); selling arms to China (1990 onwards); espionage against American companies (cited in the *Wall Street Journal* 1992) and attacks on the dignity and the lives of American subjects as in the bombing of the USS *Liberty* in 1967; the beating by Israeli police of David Muirhead, who was working on an American-financed project to restore the main street in al-Khalil (Hebron) in 1997; the turning back of a US Congressional delegation from the Allenby Bridge in August 2002 and, in April, the Israeli Army's shooting of peace activist Brian Avery in Jenin and its killing of Rachel Corrie in Rafah.

Rafah, Gaza Strip, May 2003: Rachel Corrie, a member of the International Solidarity Movement, killed by an Israeli bulldozer. Credit: Sipa Press / Rex Features

Washington matches actions with words. On 18 May 2000, the Democratic candidate for the presidency, Al Gore, addressing the powerful pro-Israeli Washington lobby, AIPAC, was able to say: 'The United States has an absolute, uncompromising commitment to Israel's security and an absolute conviction that Israel alone must decide the steps necessary to ensure that security. That is Israel's prerogative. We accept that. We endorse that. Whatever Israel decides cannot, will not, will never, not ever alter our fundamental commitment to her security.'

You might have thought support couldn't come much stronger. But the group now known as the 'neo-cons', who became established in George W Bush's administration, were waiting for a chance to demonstrate higher levels of commitment. The policies they dreamed of before coming to power are well documented. They were handed the opportunity to leverage these policies into action by the murderous attacks on the Twin Towers and the Pentagon on the morning of 11 September 2001. That day, four major Israeli politicians, Shimon Peres, Ariel Sharon, Ehud Barak and Benyamin Netanyahu, took to the TV screens to assert that the terror just suffered by the Americans was the identical terror endured by Israel since its establishment, to drive home the point Israel had been pushing for years – that Israel's enemies were America's enemies.

But this was not always the case. Arabs (and some Israelis) believe that without American support Israel would have had to reach a just accommodation with the Palestinians. But since the 1960s at least the yardstick used by the US to measure the acceptability/goodness of an Arab country has been its government's stance towards Israel. The softer the stance the more 'moderate' or 'friendly' the country has been considered. It therefore came as a shock to the US public that the 19 hijackers who crashed aeroplanes into the Twin Towers and the Pentagon with such deadly results were from Egypt and Saudi Arabia: countries regarded as 'moderate'. The true, albeit unpopular, answer to this puzzle is that the more friendly (ie subservient) a regime is to an America that so identifies itself with (an intransigent) Israel, the harder that regime has had to oppress its own people and to close off all their legitimate means of political opposition. This is possibly one of the most terrible effects the American–Israeli alliance has had on the Arab world: that most of the Arab men and women who could have played important roles in developing their countries' civil and political institutions have been de-activated. Some have ended up feeling that the only path left open to them is the path of extremism clothed in the robes of what is now called 'militant Islam'.

These processes are absent from any discussion of America's relationship with the Arabs. So, in the *New Yorker*, for example, Seymour Hersh can give a detailed analysis of the internal problems of Saudi Arabia without ever touching on *why* a 'nationalist' government in Saudi might be unenthusiastic about selling oil to America. This holds for practically all the mainstream media in the US. The support of America for Israel has been likened to the elephant in the drawing room; everybody sees it but nobody mentions it. Any discussion of America's relationship with the Arabs therefore has an elephant-sized hole at its heart. And pundits come forward to fill the hole with chatter about the 'innate hostility' of the

Arabs to the US or the 'nihilism' of the terrorists or the 'fanatical nature' of Islam. Debate is reduced to 'they hate us because we are rich/free/democratic/unveiled'.

Most of the US administration's and media's information on the Arabs is now derived from the Middle East Media Research Institute (MEMRI), co-founded by Meyrav Wurmser, director of the Center for Middle East Policy at the Hudson Institute. According to a report by *Guardian* journalist Brian Whitaker, MEMRI is connected with Israeli Army Intelligence; it feeds the media and politicians with highly selective quotations from extreme Arab publications.

The proposition put forward by the USA and Israel today is that they share common values – basically a commitment to freedom and democracy. American politicians are constantly upping the rhetoric on the indivisibility of America and Israel: '. . . in war and peace, the United States has stood proudly at Israel's side. Our two nations and peoples are bound together by our common democratic values and traditions. So it has been for over 50 years. So it will always be,' said Secretary of State Colin Powell to AIPAC, 30 March 2003. Next day: 'As always, there are some, here and abroad, who would drive a wedge between America and Israel. But to do so would be to separate America from its best self . . . our commitment to Israel grows from our duty to preserve the great heritage of liberty and democracy of which we are the most fortunate heirs and the most powerful defenders,' said Senate Democratic Leader Tom Daschle to AIPAC, 31 March 2003.

In this view, America and Israel's love of liberty and democracy earn them the hatred of what prominent neo-cons have called the 'uncivilised' part of the world. The only way to end this 'hatred' is through a civilising mission; a process that the US has now started in Iraq. This can be seen as a logical move within long-term Israeli strategy. Israel has always sold itself to the West on the basis of the state's oppositional relationship to its chosen environment. Herzl assured the British Foreign Office at the end of the nineteenth century that Israel would provide a civilised bulwark against the barbarian hordes of Islam. Today, Israel's image is of a beacon of civilisation and, increasingly, America's only trustworthy friend in the region.

While some US policies, notably regarding the environment and trade, and the increasingly murky revelations about the links between corporate America and its government, make much of the world deeply uneasy, America's unwavering support for Israel has implicated it in a whole range of behaviours that have brought its modus operandi very close to its protégé's. In the past two years the United States has joined Israel in:

- manipulating or sidelining international institutions;
- ignoring accepted principles of international law (eg its operation at Guantánamo Bay, sanctioning assassinations worldwide);
- ignoring accepted principles of human rights (eg carrying out illegal detentions including the detention of children, condoning the use of torture);
- adopting military policies to achieve its political ends, embracing a policy of 'preventive' war;
- moving to curtail the civil rights of its own citizens (eg the US Patriot Act);
- encouraging the media to adopt government views and attempting to gag media which are not their own.

Meanwhile the voice of the Christian right has moved in from the margins and the discourse of this right and of members of the administration has become less guarded in its jingoism and its racism.

The US administration has now joined Israel in presenting itself as engaged in an existential war. Both states promote images of themselves as nations injured to a point of no return – Israel by the Holocaust and America by 11 September. In justifying the current war, George W Bush said it would be 'suicidal' of the US not to attack Iraq. The injury done them and the danger they are in justify putting aside institutions, concepts, ways of being that have taken centuries to evolve and from which they themselves – paradoxically – continue (in their own eyes) to derive their legitimacy. The paradox is accommodated in the image of the 'tough' but 'reluctant' fighter who takes up arms with a heavy heart because he has no other choice. Both countries evoke a national psychology which needs (for the sake of survival) to overcome a kind of wimpishness. For Zionism the wimpishness is that of the Diaspora Jews – who finally 'allowed themselves' to be destroyed. For Americans it's the fallout from guilt over Vietnam.

Americans and Israelis also seem to share a view of themselves as a 'chosen' people. In Israel's case this is through the Covenant. In America's case a recent poll confirmed that 92 per cent of those polled believed that God 'personally and individually loved them'. To be American is to be Good. We now hear talk of a 'shared mission' as in House Republican leader Tom DeLay's speech at Boca Raton (on the occasion of the death of the US space shuttle astronauts, among them the Israeli Ilan Ramon), in which he talked of a destiny shared by America and Israel and asked for divine assistance in protecting both.

In this fight for their existence, the Battle between Good and Evil, there are no middle grounds nor critical stances. You are either 'with us' or 'against us'. Americans who are not 'with' the United States' official policy are traitors; non-Americans are enemies. Jews who are not 'with' Israeli policy are self-haters; non-Jews are anti-Semitic. 'Enemies' and 'anti-Semites' are of course beyond negotiation or toleration; they have to be annihilated.

Americans on the whole appear genuinely uncomfortable being at odds with Israel. Israeli transgressions, injustices, etc, cannot be discussed as freely as those of any other country. Indeed, it seems almost in bad taste to express any reservations about the 'only democracy' in the Arab region. You can decry the absence of practical equality between black and white people in the USA, or talk about the history and plight of the country's Native Americans, but it is a terrible faux pas to mention that Israel, by law, is not the same state for its Muslim and Christian citizens as it is for its Jewish ones. It is possible that underlying this unease is the need to believe in the essential 'goodness' of Israel, a corollary of its 'moral' (as distinct from its de facto) right to exist. The intellectual inconsistency between deploring Israel's actions in the West Bank and Gaza today and applauding the even more extreme actions it took in the region in 1948 and the years leading up to that must be deeply problematic.

In this context one should note National Security Adviser Condoleezza Rice's words in her May interview with Israel's daily *Yediot Aharonot*: 'I have a deep affinity with Israel. I have always admired the history of the State of Israel and the hardness and determination of the people that founded it.' Any discussion of this issue feeds into the perception that the very existence of Israel is under threat. This is as patently absurd as the claim that Iraq under Saddam Hussein presented an existential threat to the United States. And yet it is the perception encouraged by the governments of both countries to mobilise their own people and to panic them. World media has carried pictures of Americans rushing to buy plastic sheeting and duct tape (to the financial advantage of one of the contributors to the Republican Party) and Israelis in sealed rooms strapping gas masks on to babies' faces – with all the allusions to the horrors of the Nazi gas chambers that this must evoke.

This poisoned view of the world could not have been promoted without the collusion of the media. Yet now the protest movements within the USA and Israel may be forcing parts of the media to re-examine their stance. *Ha'aretz*, in Israel, has for some time been providing a platform for dissident Israeli journalists such as Gideon Levy, Uri Avnery and Amira Hass. A fledgling Berkeley outfit called 'If Americans Knew' has just published a piece in the *Bay Guardian* showing that the *San Francisco Chronicle* is 20 times more likely to report on the deaths of Israeli children killed in the Israeli–Palestinian conflict than it is to cover Palestinian children's deaths.

The US- and Israeli-professed love of liberty and commitment to human values, betrayed by the governments of both countries, is now demonstrating itself powerfully in the actions of their people and fuelling an important grass-roots dissidence. In two notable recent acts, Professor Ilan Pappe of Haifa University has called for a boycott of Israeli institutions because of the increased restrictions placed on civil and academic freedoms, and William R Brody, Dean of the College of Arts and Sciences at Johns Hopkins University, has used his Commencement Address to warn of the dangers to American society from the US Patriot Act. But the most touching and heartening example is the movement of the Israeli soldiers in refusing to uphold the occupation of the West Bank and Gaza. They now number over 1,100.

Is it fanciful to suggest that the awakening of the world to the Palestinian–Israeli conflict has been – at least in part – an effect of the 'Likudisation' of the politics of the USA? And is it naive to hope that Israeli and American citizens with a true commitment to democracy and freedom may put a stop to this process before it destroys us all? And is it cynical to see more hope in this than in what is taking place now on the shores of the Red Sea? ❏

6 June 2003

***Ahdaf Soueif**'s latest book is* The Map of Love *(Bloomsbury, 2000)*
© *Ahdaf Soueif*

OCCUPATION IN SPACE AND TIME
RAFI SEGAL & EYAL WEIZMAN

TWO ISRAELI ARCHITECTS CREATED AN
EXHIBITION OF MAPS AND PHOTOS SHOWING
THE LINK BETWEEN THE PHYSICAL DESIGN
OF JEWISH SETTLEMENTS AND THE POLITICAL
MOTIVES BEHIND THEIR CONSTRUCTION. ITS
SPONSORS SHUT IT DOWN

The 'civilian occupation' of the West Bank began in the deep and arid Jordan Valley during the first years of Israeli rule under Labor governments (1967–77). Fifteen agricultural villages (kibbutzim and moshavim) were built according to the Labor Party plan that sought to establish a security border with Jordan while relying on the principle of 'maximum security and maximum territory for Israel, with a minimum number of Arabs'. Following the political turnabout of 1977 in which the hawkish Likud Party replaced Labor in government, the political climate in Israel changed. Thereafter, scores of new settlements were established in the mountain region, in and around the Palestinian cities, with a view to annexing the area and in order to allow for no territorial concessions.

For the price of a small apartment in Tel Aviv, settlers could purchase their own red-roofed house and benefit from massive government subsidies. Beyond the economic aspect of these settlements, the climb from the plains to the hills was argued with the rhetoric of the 'regeneration of the soul', as an act of 'personal and national renewal', imbued with the mystic quality of the heights. The mountain peaks of the West Bank easily lent themselves to state seizure. In the absence of an ordered land registry during the period of Jordanian rule, uncultivated land could be declared by Israel to be state land. Palestinian cultivated lands are found mainly on the slopes and in the valleys, where the agriculturally suitable alluvial soils erode down from the limestone slopes of the West Bank peaks. The barren hilltops, a patchwork quilt of isolated plots and discontinuous islands around peaks, were seized by the state. The West Bank was thus divided across its vertical axis. In almost every area the hilltops were annexed to Israel de facto, while the valleys between them were left under Palestinian ownership.

In the formal processes that base mountain settlements on topographical conditions, the laws of erosion were absorbed into the practice of urban design. The form laid out by nature in the specific summit morphology became the blueprint of development. The mountain settlement is typified by a principle of concentric organisation in which the topographical contours are retraced as lines of infrastructure. The roads are laid out in rings around the summit with the water, sewage, electricity and telephone lines buried under them. The division of lots is equal and repetitive, providing small private red-roofed houses positioned along the roads, against the backdrop of the landscape. The public functions are generally located within the innermost ring, on the highest ground. The 'ideal' arrangement for a small settlement is a circle. However, in reality, the geometry of the plan is distorted by the insistent demands of a highly irregular topography, as well as by the extent and form of available state land. Rather than exhibits of ordered forms, settlements are manifestations of anti-forms, the end results of tactical, land-use and topographical constraints.

The settlements create a large-scale network of 'civilian fortifications', generating tactical territorial surveillance in the state's regional strategic defence plan. The outward-looking arrangement of homes around summits imposes on the dwellers axial visibility (and lateral invisibility) oriented in two directions: inward and outward. The inward-oriented gaze protects the soft cores of the settlements, and the outward-oriented one surveys the landscape around it.

Vision dictated the discipline of design and its methodologies on all scales. Regionally, a strategic function was integrated into the distribution of settlements across the entire territory, thereby creating a 'network of observation' that overlooks the main traffic arteries of the West Bank; topographically, it was integrated into the siting of the settlements on summits; urbanistically, it was integrated into their very layout as rings around the summit, and in the positioning of homes perpendicular to the slope; architecturally, it was integrated into the arrangements and orientation of rooms, and finally into the precise positioning of windows.

Overleaf: Nahliel, Ramallah region, 2002: aerial view of 'civilian fortifications'.
Credit: courtesy Milutin Labudovic for Shalom Achsaht (Peace Now)

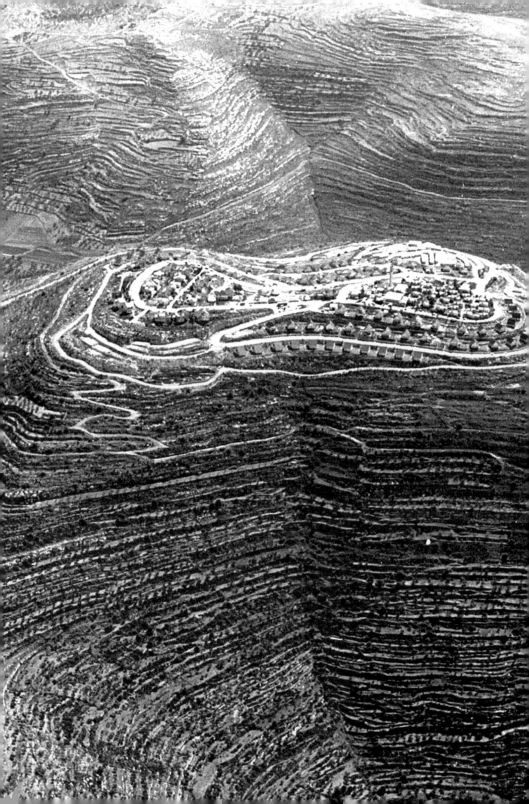

Indeed, the form of the mountain settlements is constructed according to the laws of a geometric system that unites the effectiveness of sight with that of spatial order, thereby producing sightlines that function to achieve different forms of power: strategic in its overlooking of main traffic arteries, control in its overlooking of Palestinian towns and villages, and self-defence in its overlooking the immediate surroundings and approach roads. Responding to mathematical layouts and maximising visibility across the landscape mean that power, as in Foucault's description of Bentham's Panopticon, can be exercised through observation. By placing settlers across the landscape, the Israeli government is not merely utilising the agencies of state power and control, namely the police and army, for the administration of power; it also 'drafts' the civilian population to inspect, control and subdue the Palestinian population. The desire for a single family home is being mobilised to serve the quest for military domination, while an act of domesticity, shrouded in the cosmetic façade of red tiles and green lawns, provides territorial control.

No longer seen as a resource to be agriculturally or industrially culti-vated, the landscape, imbued with imaginary religious signifiers, established the link that helped relive and re-enact religious and national myths that displace (on the very same land) ancient with modern time. In the ideal image of the pastoral landscape, integral to the perspective of colonial tradi-tions, the admiration of the rustic panorama is always viewed through the window frames of modernity. The impulse to retreat from the city to the country reasserts the virtues of a simpler life close to nature. It draws on the opposition between luxury and simplicity, the spontaneous and the planned, nativeness and foreignness, which are nothing but the opposite poles of the axis of vision that stretches between the settlements and their surrounding landscape. Furthermore, the re-creation of the picturesque scenes of a biblical landscape becomes a testimony to an ancient claim on the land.

Within the panorama, however, lies a cruel paradox: the very thing that renders the landscape 'biblical' or 'pastoral' – its traditional inhabitation and cultivation in terraces, its olive orchards, stone buildings and the presence of livestock – is produced by the Palestinians, whom the Jewish settlers came to replace. The very people who cultivate the 'green olive orchards' and render the landscape biblical, are themselves excluded from the panorama. The Palestinians are there to produce the scenery and then disappear. The panoptic arrangement of sightlines therefore serves two contradictory agendas: supervision and a self-imposed scotoma. The Jewish settlements superimpose another datum of latitudinal geography upon an existing landscape. Settlers could thus see only other settlements, avoiding Palestinian towns and villages, and could therefore feel that they have truly arrived 'as the people without land to the land without people'.

The fact that settlements are constructed beyond the 1967 international border violates Article 49 of the Fourth Geneva Convention, which states: 'The Occupying Power shall not deport or transfer parts of its own civilian population into the territory it occupies.' By taking up projects in the West Bank, Israeli architects cross yet another red line. Their planning conforms to a mode of design that serves to oppress and disrupt local populations. Thus, beyond the mere presence of Israeli settlements on occupied land, it is the way they were designed – their size, form and distribution across the terrain – that directly and negatively affects the lives and livelihood of Palestinians. According to the regional plans of politicians, settlements and the roads leading to them are designed and built with the self-proclaimed aim to bisect, disturb and squeeze out Palestinian communities. This centralised, strategic and political use of planning was voluntarily transferred on the ground by private architectural firms for financial profit. Planning and building in the West Bank is effectively executing a political agenda through spatial manipulations.

The evidence, as is always the case, is in the drawing. It is by investigating the working methods and tools of architects – the lines drawn on plans, 'master plans', maps and aerial photographs – that the equation setting material organisation against the abuse of power begins to unravel. Formal manipulations and programmatic organisations are the very stuff of architecture and planning, and it is in the drawings that their effects are stated. In them the forms produced by the processes and forces inherent within the logic of the occupation can be traced. In logic and in the repetition of micro conditions, architecture and planning are used as territorial weapons. Settlement forms and location are manipulated for the bisection of a Palestinian traffic artery, for the surrounding of a village, for the supervision of a major city or a strategic crossroad. In the very act of design, the architect is engaged in the reversal of his professional practice. Despite the banality and simplicity of the statement, and in the absence of an architectural equivalent of the medical profession's Hippocratic oath, planning and architecture must be carried out for the benefit of society. If the architect draws a particular angle, line or arc, or makes any other design decision that is explicitly and practically aimed at disturbance, suppression, aggression or racism, and if these clearly and brutally stand in breach of basic human rights, a crime has been committed. ❏

Rafi Segal and Eyal Weizman *are architects based in Tel Aviv, whose redesign of the Ashdod Museum of Art opened in June 2003*

Excerpted from Rafi Segal and Eyal Weizman, A Civilian Occupation: The Politics of Israeli Architecture *(Verso, forthcoming September 2003)*

A Civilian Occupation *is a detailed examination through the use of maps and photographs of the spatial form of Israeli settlements in the West Bank, showing the link between their physical design and the political motives behind their construction. It was originally sponsored by the Israeli Association of United Architects as the country's contribution to the 2002 Berlin World Congress of Architecture, but the association withdrew its support, cancelled the show and banned its catalogue, claiming that* A Civilian Occupation *was a political agenda in the guise of architectural study. The exhibition was re-created and restaged in New York in February 2003*

48 HOURS

ADEL ZAANOUN

Two days in the working life of a Palestinian TV journalist. The month before, APTN cameraman Nazih Darwazeh had been shot and killed by Israeli forces in the occupied West Bank city of Nablus. The International Federation of Journalists commented afterwards: 'It is impossible to ignore the evidence here of [Israeli] soldiers deliberately targeting journalists.'

Wednesday 21 May 2003

Covering incidents in the city of Beit Hanoun, at the northern end of the Gaza Strip. In the early hours of the morning, we go to the junction of the road to Beit Lahia and wait for a scheduled meeting with Prime Minister Abu Mazen (Mahmoud Abbas), as agreed with his office. He's supposed to visit the area following the end of a five-day military operation in the city by an Israeli task force and their supposed withdrawal the day before. But as we reach the junction locals warn us that the Israeli tanks have come back to the very same positions they had quit just the day before.

Of course we go straight down there, with a crew from the Palestinian satellite TV network, hitching a lift with our colleagues from the BBC in their armoured jeep. We go in carefully until we can see the Israeli tanks and wait a while. The Palestinian traffic moves past us; we realise that the rough path that we are parked on is actually the site of what used to be a bridge connecting the township to the nearest main road. We find out that it was blown up by the Israeli Army during their five-day operation in the area. There is so much dust thrown up by the Israeli tanks and bulldozers it's hard to see. It looks like smoke from a huge battle. We start to film the bulldozers and the tanks from about a hundred metres away and my journalist colleague does a quick piece to camera. We plan to go back to the junction near Beit Lahia where we still hope to meet Abu Mazen's convoy. There is gunfire, immediately identifiable as coming from the Israeli task force. The bulldozers continue to plough up the roadway, filling it with new holes. We reach Sufian Abu Ziada, who heads the local Palestinian Civic Relations Committee, and who explains that Abu Mazen has now cancelled the visit because the Israeli Army has refused to withdraw again to allow him to inspect the damage they caused on their earlier operations. He had aimed to visit the homes, security force bases and local industry, including several farmers, fields bulldozed, hit by the Israeli operation. We go back to the Israeli tanks at Beit Hanoun to pick up the story there. The Israeli troops have opened fire at scores of children who have also rushed down to see what is going on. One is wounded in the stomach. Locals tell us that some Palestinians had fired on the Israelis before escaping. The presence of journalists in any area is a danger to the people around them, as they can be to us. We can each draw fire for different reasons at different times. So we move away from the children and back to our offices to file our stories. It's just another hard day.

Thursday 22 May

We're told that more clashes have broken out between the Palestinian kids and the Israeli Army unit at the junction. We stop by our contacts with the Palestinian police and talk to some local witnesses, then check with the nearby hospitals in Jebalia and Beit Lahia, where a number of the injured youths have been taken. Back then to the contested junction, where a number of other journalists are already set up to cover the trouble to follow. All the roads to Beit Hanoun are now sealed up by the Israeli Army. Again we try to keep our distance from the scores of kids and youths as they start to throw stones at the Israeli troops, who return fire, trying to pick out the stone-throwers in the crowd of boys.

We have our flak jackets and helmets on and try to move to an area where we can both work safely and be seen to be working as journalists. The Israelis in their armoured vehicles don't care much about the presence of reporters, though they would prefer it if we were not here recording what they are doing. Some of the Israeli fire seems to be directed at us as well and after a while we move away. We're able to grab quick interviews with some of the children still clustering in the area. It is, of course, impossible for any journalist – Palestinian or foreign – to speak to any of the Israelis on the spot.

We hang around for half an hour following the skirmishes. Some of the stone-throwers are wounded, one seriously, we hear later from the hospital. We can see Palestinian paramedics trying to reach two wounded where they lie, just a hundred metres in front of the Israeli tanks. They're unable to reach them through the Israeli fire.

Then we go down to see the injured, at the Hospital of the Return and in Jebal Ali and Kamal Odwan Hospital in Beit Lahia, two small hospitals developed out of clinics over the last two years. We interview some of the wounded youngsters, but we can only speak to the slightly hurt. Two children with serious stomach and back injuries can't be visited; they're later transferred to the larger Shifa Hospital across Gaza. We follow them there; now we can work and we can even take off our flak jackets. Later, we head back to the office to edit and file our footage.

And there's time to think: it's clear that as soon as we reached the scene of the latest incident, the stone-throwing boys ran towards us, encircled us and asked us to film them. This increases the danger to them and us. Israeli bullets don't distinguish between boy and journalist. But of course it's hardly justifiable for men to use bullets against boys throwing stones. ❑

Adel Zaanoun is a cameraman with Palestine Broadcasting and
Agence France Press

CULTURE

New York City, 2002. Credit: Paul Fusco / Magnum Photos

A STORY ABOUT MY PARENTS

RABA'I MADHOUN

My father died on the morning of Thursday, the second of May, 1960. Death plucked him one day before our weekly visit to him at al-Bureij Hospital. Three days before, my mother had told her sister-in-law Haniyyah, my Uncle 'Ulaim's wife, 'Abu Raba'i is coming on Thursday, Haniyyah.' Haniyyah was stunned. 'Congratulations, Um Raba'i. Such news is worthy of happiness.' 'Who brought the good news?' she asked. My mother responded: 'Some people came from the hospital, where they saw Abu Raba'i, and he asked them to tell me that he's coming on Thursday. They swore that he said, "I've recovered now, thank God. I'll be leaving on Thursday and I'll never be returning to hospital."'

My mother was over the moon. On Wednesday, she flitted around the house like a butterfly. She entered our small kitchen, washed the plates, dishes, clay plates, the ladle and the knives. 'Khalil likes everything to be clean,' she murmured. She went outside carrying the kerosene burner in her right hand and a knife. She picked a lemon off the tree, cut it in half, put one half on the edge of the cement sink near the door and used the other half to rub the kerosene burner's copper body. She rubbed it the way she had bathed me when I was younger. Its colour turned a golden yellow, just like my skin after I had been bathed. She stroked the fragrant basil plant in the eastern corner of the flowerbed with her palm and the scent of basil permeated the whole house. She went to the bedroom and changed the sheets and covers on my father's bed. She slipped off the pillowcases, replacing them with ones that were embroidered with rose patterns around the edges. The words 'in safety' were crocheted in the middle of one of them, and the words 'healthy sleep' were embroidered in the middle of the other. My mother made the bed as though she were preparing it for her wedding night. Our home was like white Arabian jasmine, and my mother became a bride. Joy breezed through the house as we went to bed that night. My mother fell asleep with the image of my father's homecoming the next morning in her mind's eye.

In the morning they brought my father, laid out on a stretcher carried by two male nurses. They turned over his corpse to my mother. My mother had wanted him that day restored to his youth, returning to her for ever, but she received him as a corpse. My father did return on

Thursday, the day he had appointed. But he returned as though he had been expelled from the hospital, as though his long-standing residency there – which had continued on and off for almost nine years – had suddenly expired and they had evicted him, refusing to renew it. My father died because he had decided to return home for good, as though his life were not possible outside the hospital. He had spent years living as though he had been officially sentenced to pulmonary tuberculosis. If only he had extended his sentence in hospital and not died, so that he could have continued to visit us for a week once every three months as he had grown accustomed to doing. He would visit my mother in her bed as we slept whenever he yearned for her and they would resume their interrupted nights. And we would feel our father's presence once again.

I had often asked myself: how do they make love? The issue preoccupied me and so I asked. Tuberculosis is a serious and contagious disease. How had my mother become used to breathing into my father's chest? How had she sucked the nectar of love from his lips? How had she inhaled his breath for ten years without catching tuberculosis? Had my father covered his face every time? Had he become like a shy virgin before my mother's uncovered face? Had she generously given him two small lips pursed like an engagement ring, while he covered his face to prevent her from inhaling his tuberculosis? My mother loved my father, serious illness and all. She breathed in his tuberculosis without fear. As for my poor father, he must have used his back to hug her. Hadn't I often seen him loving with his back? Can a back overflow with emotions like a bosom? My father's back overflowed with tenderness. This was to separate words from their meaning. How can tenderness be separated from the bosom to give the back a function it is not accustomed to? How can a heart beat backwards, sending its pulses in an opposite direction, so that the beloved hears them like an echo?

When my sister Rihab turned two years old and started toddling inside the house, my father's yearning for her grew. He would call her, using baby talk: Dada, dada, dada. When she reached him, he would catch her and hold her between his knees. Her head would fall on to his stomach and she would raise her laughing face towards him. He would long to hug her, but he would hesitate, fearing an explosion of the tuberculosis stored up inside his chest.

My father would lie on his right side on the bed, and ask Rihab to sit astride his middle. She would rush to climb over him, sitting on him and giggling. My father would shake his body, tilting her slightly forward and she would slip off and land behind his back. He would nimbly embrace her with his left arm and tickle her. She would laugh, enjoying the game and the tenderness of his back. Rihab had to seek the tenderness of the bosom from my mother. And we had to do likewise. And my mother also had to look with us for my father's bosom, for his back, for the whole of him. My father would not return that day. We would even miss his dangerous, tuberculosis breath.

Last Friday I had visited my father. I found him waiting for me at the gate when I arrived, bringing forward the visit several minutes before it was due. Perhaps he was in a hurry to see my mother as usual but she was not there. I was on my own. I had not been in the habit of coming on my own. My mother, saying she was tired that week, had not come. She would visit my father again every week without fail after that, she had said. My father did not ask me about her when we met. From a distance, over the hospital's iron gates, he postponed a mutual embarrassment. My father was shy and I had fully inherited his shyness. We spoke for a few minutes, filling the time with talk about general things until the hospital gate was opened at one o'clock when official visiting hours began. I shook hands with my father and handed him the basket I had brought with me. Inside it were the usual contents: a tightly closed saucepan of soup, two pigeons stuffed with rice and pine kernels, several oranges and a few apples. At the very top was my father's clean underwear, which my mother had folded and arranged, and my father's favourite Egyptian weekly magazine *Akhir Sa'ah*. In my pocket was ten pence which was my father's weekly pocket money. As usual my aunt had paid it, half in a note, and half in coin. My father said to the gateman: 'This is some clean underwear, newspapers, some paper and a bit of fruit.' He held up one side of the basket to reassure the gateman. Bringing foodstuffs into the hospital was not allowed. The gateman was reassured, my father carried his basket in and we entered the ward together, walking among the beds until we reached his bed which was number 265. I sat on the edge of the bed until my father had finished arranging his things. When he had finished he put the magazine under his pillow.

A coughing man sat in the bed next to my father's, surrounded by his visitors. They propped him up and he relaxed and stopped coughing. My father picked up a folded blanket that was on his bed and we went outside.

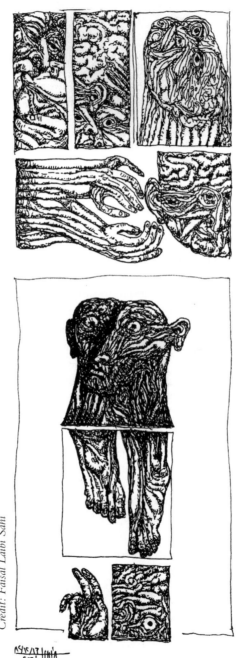

Credit: Faisal Laibi Sahi

He spread it over the hard unpaved ground beneath a shady acacia tree close to the western wall of the hospital backyard, near the opening through which children used to sneak in and out of the hospital.

'Stretch out, son, crawl through. Yes. That's it, well done. Get up and shake the earth off your clothes.' I had crawled through the hole that the patients had made near the bottom of the wall. They had removed a brick close to the western corner of the wall and dug out the ground beneath it. It became a secret gateway for children that the patients closed as soon as visiting hours were over. They would open it for children who arrived early, wanting to enter before the start of official visiting hours, just as my father sometimes wanted his basket early. At times like that, I would hand it to him over the wall, then push my small body through the opening on to the backyard. I laughed and said to my father: 'You'll have to remove another brick from the wall, Father, so that I can get through.' My father laughed and said: 'You've become a young man, son. You've grown.'

The backyard filled up with patients and visitors. The weather was hot for that time of year. Visitors preferred to sit in the yard instead of spending their visiting time among the beds. An occasional breeze and the rustling of the acacia and cinchona leaves refreshed us and the scent of the flowers some of the visitors had brought with them spread the scent of spring.

My father and I sat alone with the postponed question: why had my mother not come? I thought of apologising but my father asked about my mother before I could formulate my apology in a way that would mitigate her absence. I failed to change the explanation and told him what my mother had told me to tell him.

We talked throughout the hour allocated to the visit. I gave him all the good news I could think of. I told him that little Rihab was very pleased with the doll that Mrs Madeleine, the director of the hospital, had given her as a gift. He whispered to me that she was an American Jew, that he was the only one who knew this, that she had admitted this to him and that they had become very good friends. I felt an inward shiver. My father assured me that she was good. He said: 'Not all Jews are alike, son.'

I told him that I was going to the cinema the next day in the afternoon and that Awni Shawwa and I had agreed to go together. We might see *Taras Bulba* at Cinema al-Samer or *The Viking* at Cinema al-Jalaa. We both liked Yul Brynner, with his red bald head that resembled a monkey's bottom and Kirk Douglas and Tony Curtis. I awaited my father's comment. I feared he might say I couldn't go. He asked me how much money I had. I told him and he said that I didn't have enough. He surprised me by giving me half his pocket money. I was acutely embarrassed and felt like melting away. Had it been a mistake to tell him? Would he be affected by the reduction in his weekly allowance? I felt guilty. I did not want to go to the cinema if this would burden or upset him. He sensed my feelings and pressed the five-pence note into my hand. My hand was perspiring. I felt it was crying, and that its tears were soaking into the note. I feared it would disintegrate. I opened my hand and the note breathed after almost suffocating. I felt the note regaining its life in my hand and I stuffed it into my shirt pocket. My father's face lit up like the morning sun. At that moment, I understood my father better than ever before. He had given me money out of his own pocket although it was my aunt's money. He had sacrificed half his allowance so that he could enjoy a moment he had stopped experiencing since falling ill, of no longer being able to put his hand in his pocket to bring out some money. ❑

Raba'i Madhoun works as editor of the Opinion page of Al-Sharq al-Awsat. He lives in London

This is an excerpt from his memoirs, translated by Samira Kawar and reprinted from Banipal *magazine, 15/16, Autumn 2002/Spring 2003. Arabic original* Ta'am al-Furaaq (Taste of Separation) *(al-Muassassa al-Arabiyya lil-Dirassat wal-Nashr, Beirut, 2001)*

SAVE YOUR OUTRAGE FOR THE END

SARA ROY

Some months ago I was invited to reflect on my journey as a child of Holocaust survivors. This journey continues and shall continue until the day I die. Though I cannot possibly say everything, it seems especially poignant that I should be addressing this topic at a time when the conflict between Israelis and Palestinians is descending so tragically into a moral abyss and when, for me at least, the very essence of Judaism, of what it means to be a Jew, seems to be descending with it.

The Holocaust has been the defining feature of my life. It could not have been otherwise. I lost over a hundred members of my family and extended family in the Nazi ghettos and death camps in Poland – grandparents, aunts, uncles, cousins, a sibling not yet born – people about whom I have heard so much throughout my life, people I never knew. They lived in Poland in Jewish communities called shtetls.

In thinking about what I wanted to say about this journey, I tried to remember my very first conscious encounter with the Holocaust. Although I cannot be certain, I think it was the first time I noticed the number the Nazis had imprinted on my father's arm. To his oppressors, my father Abraham had no name, no history, and no identity other than that blue-inked number, which I never wrote down. As a young child of four or five, I remember asking my father why he had that number on his arm. He answered that he had once painted it on but then found it would not wash off, so was left with it.

My father was one of six children, and he was the only one in his family to survive the Holocaust. I know very little about his family because he could not speak about them without breaking down. I know little about my paternal grandmother, after whom I am named, and even less about my father's sisters and brother. I know only their names. It caused me such pain to see him suffer with his memories that I stopped asking him to share them.

My father's name was recognised in Holocaust circles because he was one of two known survivors of the death camp at Chelmno, in Poland, where 350,000 Jews were murdered, among them the majority of my family on my father's and mother's sides. They were taken there and gassed to death in January 1942. Through my father's cousin I learned that there is now a plaque at the entrance to what is left of the Chelmno death camp with my father's name on it – something I hope one day to see. My father also survived the concentration camps at Auschwitz and Buchenwald and because of it was called to testify at the Eichmann trial in Jerusalem in 1961.

My mother, Taube, was one of nine children – seven girls and two boys. Her father Herschel was a rabbi and *shohet*, a ritual slaughterer, and deeply loved and respected by all who knew him. Herschel was a learned man who had studied with some of the great rabbis of Poland. The stories both my mother and aunt have told me also indicate that he was a feminist of sorts, getting down on his hands and knees to help his wife or daughters scrub the floor, treating the women in his life with the same respect and reverence he gave the men. My grandmother Miriam, whose name I also have, was a kind and gentle soul but the disciplinarian of the family since Herschel could never raise his voice to his children. My mother came from a deeply religious and loving family. My aunts and uncles were as devoted to their parents and they were to them. As a family they lived very modestly, but every Sabbath my grandfather would bring home a poor or homeless person who was seated at the head of the table to share the Sabbath meal.

My mother and her sister Frania were the only two in their family to survive the war. Everyone else perished, except for one other sister, Shoshana, who had emigrated to Palestine in 1936. My mother and Frania had managed to stay together throughout the war – seven years in the Pabanice and Lodz ghettos, followed by the Auschwitz and Halbstadt concentration camps. The only time in seven years they were separated was at Auschwitz. They were in a selection line where Jews were lined up and their fate sealed by the Nazi doctor Joseph Mengele, who alone would determine who would live and who would die. When my aunt approached him, Mengele sent her to the right, to labour (a temporary reprieve). When my mother approached him, he sent her to the left, to death, which meant she would be gassed. Miraculously, my mother managed to sneak back into the selection line, and when she approached Mengele again, he sent her to labour.

A defining moment in my life and journey as a child of Holocaust survivors occurred even before I was born. It involved decisions taken by my mother and her sister, two very remarkable women, which would change their lives and mine. After the war ended, my aunt Frania desperately wanted to go to Palestine to join their sister, who had been there for ten years. The creation of a Jewish state was imminent, and Frania felt it was the only safe place for Jews after the Holocaust. My mother disagreed and adamantly refused to go. She told me many times during my life that her decision not to live in Israel was based on a belief, learned and reinforced by her experiences during the war, that tolerance, compassion and justice cannot be practised or extended when one lives only among one's own. 'I could not live as a Jew among Jews alone,' she said. 'For me, it wasn't possible and it wasn't what I wanted. I wanted to live as a Jew in a pluralist society, where my group remained important to me but where others were important to me, too.' Frania emigrated to Israel and my parents went to America. It was extremely painful for my mother to leave her sister, but she felt she had no alternative. (They have remained very close and have seen each other often, both in this country and in Israel.)

I have always found my mother's choice and the context from which it emanated remarkable. I grew up in a home where Judaism was defined and practised not as a religion but as a system of ethics and culture. God was present but not central. My first language was Yiddish, which I still speak with my family. My home was filled with joy and optimism although punctuated at times by grief and loss. Israel and the notion of a Jewish homeland were very important to my parents. After all, the remnants of our family were there. But, unlike many of their friends, my parents were not uncritical of Israel, insofar as they felt they could be. Obedience to a state was not an ultimate Jewish value, not for them, not after the Holocaust. Judaism provided the context for our life and for values and beliefs that were not dependent upon national boundaries, but transcended them. For my mother and father, Judaism meant bearing witness, railing against injustice and forgoing silence. It meant compassion, tolerance and rescue. It meant, as Ammiel Alcalay has written, ensuring to the extent possible that the memories of the past do not become the memories of the future. These were the ultimate Jewish values. My parents were not saints; they had their faults and they made mistakes. But they cared profoundly about issues of justice and fairness, and they cared profoundly about people – all people, not just their own. The lessons of the Holocaust were always presented to me as both particular (ie Jewish) and universal. Perhaps most importantly, they were presented as indivisible. To divide them would diminish the meaning of both.

Looking back over my life, I realise that through their actions and words my mother and father never tried to shield me from self-knowledge;

instead, they insisted that I confront what I did not know or understand. Noam Chomsky speaks of the 'parameters of thinkable thought'. My mother and father constantly pushed those parameters as far as they could, which was not far enough for me, but they taught me how to push them and the importance of doing so.

It was perhaps inevitable that I would follow a path that would lead me to the Arab–Israeli issue. I visited Israel many times while growing up. As a child, I found it a beautiful, romantic and peaceful place. As a teenager and young adult I began to feel certain contradictions that I could not fully explain, but which centred on what seemed to be the almost complete absence in Israeli life and discourse of Jewish life in Eastern Europe before the Holocaust, and even of the Holocaust itself. I would ask my aunt why these subjects were not discussed, and why Israelis didn't learn to speak Yiddish. My questions were often met with grim silence.

Most painful to me was the denigration of the Holocaust and pre-state Jewish life by many of my Israeli friends. For them, those were times of shame, when Jews were weak and passive, inferior and unworthy, deserving not of our respect but of our disdain. 'We will never allow ourselves to be slaughtered again or go so willingly to our slaughter,' they would say. There was little need to understand those millions who perished or the lives they lived. There was even less need to honour them. Yet, at the same time, the Holocaust was used by the state as a defence against others, as a justification for political and military acts.

I could not comprehend or make sense of what I was hearing. I remember fearing for my aunt. In my confusion, I also remember profound anger. It was at that moment, perhaps, that I began thinking about the Palestinians and their conflict with the Jews. If so many among us could negate our own and so pervert the truth, why not with the Palestinians? Was there a link of some sort between the murdered Jews of Europe and the Palestinians? I did not know, but so my search began.

The journey has been a painful one but among the most meaningful of my life. At my side, always, was my mother, constant in her support, although ambivalent and conflicted at times. My father had died a young man; I do not know what he would have thought, but I have always felt his presence. My Israeli family opposed what I was doing and has always remained steadfast in their opposition. In fact, I have not spoken with them about my work in over 15 years.

Despite many visits to Israel during my youth, I first went to the West Bank and Gaza in the summer of 1985, two and a half years before the first Palestinian uprising, to conduct fieldwork for my doctoral dissertation, which examined American economic assistance to the West Bank and Gaza Strip. My research focused on whether it was possible to promote economic development under conditions of military occupation. That summer changed my life because it was then that I came to understand and experience what occupation was and what it meant. I learned how occupation works, its impact on the economy, on daily life, and its grinding impact on people. I learned what it meant to have little control over one's life and, more importantly, over the lives of one's children.

As with the Holocaust, I tried to remember my very first encounter with the occupation. One of my earliest encounters involved a group of Israeli soldiers, an old Palestinian man and his donkey. Standing on a street with some Palestinian friends, I noticed an elderly Palestinian walking down the street, leading his donkey. A small child no more than three or four years old, clearly his grandson, was with him. Some Israeli soldiers standing nearby went up to the old man and stopped him. One soldier ambled over to the donkey and pried open its mouth. 'Old man,' he asked, 'why are your donkey's teeth so yellow? Why aren't they white? Don't you brush your donkey's teeth?' The old Palestinian was mortified, the little boy visibly upset. The soldier repeated his question, yelling this time, while the other soldiers laughed. The child began to cry and the old man just stood there silently, humiliated. This scene repeated itself while a crowd gathered. The soldier then ordered the old man to stand behind the donkey and demanded that he kiss the animal's behind. At first, the old man refused but as the soldier screamed at him and his grandson became hysterical, he bent down and did it. The soldiers laughed and walked away. They had achieved their goal: to humiliate him and those around him. We all stood there in silence, ashamed to look at each other, hearing nothing but the uncontrollable sobs of the little boy. The old man did not move for what seemed a very long time. He just stood there, demeaned and destroyed.

I stood there too, in stunned disbelief. I immediately thought of the stories my parents had told me of how Jews had been treated by the Nazis in the 1930s, before the ghettos and death camps, of how Jews would be forced to clean sidewalks with toothbrushes and have their beards cut off in public. What happened to the old man was absolutely equivalent in principle, intent and impact: to humiliate and dehumanise. In this instance, there was no difference between the German soldier and the Israeli one. Throughout that summer of 1985, I saw similar incidents: young Palestinian men being forced by Israeli soldiers to bark like dogs on their hands and knees, or dance in the streets.

In this critical respect, my first encounter with the occupation was the same as my first encounter with the Holocaust, with the number on my father's arm. It spoke the same message: the denial of one's humanity. It is important to understand the very real differences in volume, scale and horror between the Holocaust and the occupation and to be careful about comparing the two, but it is also important to recognise parallels where they do exist.

As a child of Holocaust survivors I always wanted to be able in some way to experience and feel some aspect of what my parents endured, which, of course, was impossible. I listened to their stories, always wanting more, and shared their tears. I often would ask myself: what does sheer terror feel like? What does it look like? What does it mean to lose one's whole family so horrifically and so immediately, or to have an entire way of life extinguished so irrevocably? I would try to imagine myself in their place, but it was impossible. It was beyond my reach, too unfathomable.

It was not until I lived with Palestinians under occupation that I found at least part of the answers to some of these questions. I was not searching for the answers; they were thrust upon me. I learned, for example, what sheer terror looked like from my friend Rabia, 18 years old, who, frozen by fear and uncontrollable shaking, stood glued to the middle of a room we shared in a refugee camp, unable to move, while Israeli soldiers were trying to break down the front door to our shelter. I experienced terror while watching Israeli soldiers beat a pregnant woman in her belly because she flashed a V-sign at them, and I was too paralysed by fear to help her. I could more concretely understand the meaning of loss and displacement when I watched grown men sob and women scream as Israeli Army bulldozers destroyed their home and everything in it because they built their house without the permit that the Israeli authorities had refused to give them.

It is perhaps in the concept of home and shelter that I find the most profound link between the Jews and the Palestinians and, perhaps, the most painful illustration of the meaning of occupation. I cannot begin to describe how horrible and obscene it is to watch the deliberate destruction of a

Bethlehem, 2002: a curfew is briefly lifted. Credit: JC Tordai / Panos Pictures

family's home while that family watches, powerless to stop it. For Jews as for Palestinians, a house represents far more than a roof over one's head; it represents life itself. Speaking about the demolition of Palestinian homes, Meron Benvenisti, an Israeli historian and scholar, writes: 'It would be hard to overstate the symbolic value of a house to an individual for whom the culture of wandering and of becoming rooted to the land is so deeply engrained in tradition, for an individual whose national myth is based on the tragedy of being uprooted from a stolen homeland. The arrival of a firstborn son and the building of a home are the central events in such an individual's life because they symbolise continuity in time and physical space. And with the demolition of the individual's home comes the destruction of the world.'

Israel's occupation of the Palestinians is the crux of the problem between the two peoples, and it will remain so until it ends. For the last 35 years, occupation has meant dislocation and dispersion; the separation of families; the denial of human, civil, legal, political and economic rights imposed by a system of military rule; the torture of thousands; the confiscation of tens of thousands of acres of land and the uprooting of tens of thousands of trees; the destruction of more than seven thousand Palestinian homes; the building of illegal Israeli settlements on Palestinian lands and the doubling of the settler population over the last ten years; first, the undermining of the Palestinian economy and now its destruction; closure; curfew; geographic fragmentation; demographic isolation and collective punishment.

Israel's occupation of the Palestinians is not the moral equivalent of the Nazi genocide of the Jews. But it does not have to be. No, this is not genocide, but it is repression, and it is brutal. And it has become frighteningly natural. Occupation is about the domination and dispossession of one people by another. It is about the destruction of their property and the destruction of their soul. Occupation aims, at its core, to deny Palestinians their humanity by denying them the right to determine their existence, to live normal lives in their own homes. Occupation is humiliation. It is despair and desperation. And just as there is no moral equivalence or symmetry between the Holocaust and the occupation, so there is no moral equivalence or symmetry between the occupier and the occupied, no matter how much we as Jews regard ourselves as victims.

And it is from this context of deprivation and suffocation, now largely forgotten, that the horrific and despicable suicide bombings have emerged and taken the lives of more innocents. Why should innocent Israelis, among them my aunt and her grandchildren, pay the price of occupation? Like the settlements, razed homes and barricades that preceded them, the suicide bombers have not always been there.

Memory in Judaism – like all memory – is dynamic, not static, embracing a multiplicity of voices and shunning the hegemony of one. But in the post-Holocaust world, Jewish memory has faltered, even failed, in one critical respect: it has excluded the reality of Palestinian suffering and Jewish culpability therein. As a people, we have been unable to link the creation of Israel with the displacement of the Palestinians. We have been unwilling to see, let alone remember, that finding our place meant the loss of theirs. Perhaps one reason for the ferocity of the conflict today is that Palestinians are insisting on their voice despite our continued and desperate efforts to subdue it.

Within the Jewish community it has always been considered a form of heresy to compare Israeli actions or policies with those of the Nazis, and certainly one must be very careful in doing so. But what does it mean when Israeli soldiers paint identification numbers on Palestinian arms; when young Palestinian men and boys of a certain age are told through Israeli loudspeakers to gather in the town square; when Israeli soldiers openly admit to shooting Palestinian children for sport; when some of the Palestinian dead must be buried in mass graves while the bodies of others are left in city streets and camp alleyways because the army will not allow proper burial; when certain Israeli officials and Jewish intellectuals publicly call for the destruction of Palestinian villages in retaliation for suicide bombings, or for the transfer of the Palestinian population out of the West Bank and Gaza; when 46 per cent of the Israeli public favours such transfers and when transfer or expulsion becomes a legitimate part of popular discourse; when government officials speak of the 'cleansing of the refugee camps', and when a leading Israeli intellectual calls for hermetic separation between Israelis and Palestinians in the form of a Berlin Wall, caring not whether the Palestinians on the other side of the wall may starve to death as a result?

What are we supposed to think when we hear this? What is my mother supposed to think?

In the context of Jewish existence today, what does it mean to preserve the Jewish character of the State of Israel? Does it mean preserving a Jewish demographic majority through any means and continued Jewish domination of the Palestinian people and their land? What is the narrative that we as a people are creating, and what kind of voice are we seeking? What sort of meaning do we as Jews derive from the debasement and humiliation of Palestinians? What is at the centre of our moral and ethical discourse? What is the source of our moral and spiritual legacy? What is the source of our redemption? Has the process of creating and rebuilding ended for us?

I want to end this essay with a quote from Irena Klepfisz, a writer and child survivor of the Warsaw Ghetto, whose father spirited her and her mother out of the ghetto and then himself died in the ghetto uprising.

'I have concluded that one way to pay tribute to those we loved who struggled, resisted and died is to hold on to their vision and their fierce outrage at the destruction of the ordinary life of their people. It is this outrage we need to keep alive in our daily life and apply it to all situations, whether they involve Jews or non-Jews. It is this outrage we must use to fuel our actions and vision whenever we see any signs of the disruptions of common life: the hysteria of a mother grieving for the teenager who has been shot; a family stunned in front of a vandalised or demolished home; a family separated, displaced; arbitrary and unjust laws that demand the closing or opening of shops and schools; humiliation of a people whose culture is alien and deemed inferior; a people left homeless without citizenship; a people living under military rule. Because of our experience, we recognise these evils as obstacles to peace. At those moments of recognition, we remember the past, feel the outrage that inspired the Jews of the Warsaw Ghetto and allow it to guide us in present struggles.'

For me, these words define the true meaning of Judaism and the lessons my parents sought to impart. ❏

Sara Roy *is a senior research scholar at the Center for Middle Eastern Studies, Harvard University, and author of* The Gaza Strip: The Political Economy of De-Development *(Institute for Palestine Studies, 1995)*

This article first appeared in the Journal of Palestine Studies *(University of California, autumn 2002)*

TWO POEMS

GRACE PALEY

SWORDS AND PLOUGHSHARES

What a terrible racket they made
beating all those swords into ploughshares
people were deafened world-wide   letters
of protest   as well as serious essays
pointing out in the sensible way
of ordinary people   we no longer
use ploughshares   swords have been
for generations the playthings
　　of boys and men

now the government that year happened
to be a poet   it explained
in a kindly way   citizens   we had
in mind a living performing metaphor
using familiar religious themes and
literary memories   of course once we
get those useless ploughshares there
may be a couple of economic or
industrial uses   we will even be able
to beat them back into swords should
swords still be required by boys and men

FATHERS

Fathers are
more fathering
these days   they have
accomplished this by
being more mothering

what luck for them that
women's lib happened   then
the dream of new fathering
began to shine in the eyes
of free women and was
irresistible

on the New York subways
and the mass transits
of other cities   one may
see fatherings of many colours
with their round babies on
their laps   this may also
happen in the countryside

these scenes were brand new
exciting for an old woman who
had watched the old fathers
gathering once again in
familiar army camps and comfortable war rooms to consider
the necessary eradication of
the new fathering fathers
(who are their sons) as well
as the women and children who
will surely be in the way ❑

Grace Paley is a poet, short story writer and an activist in the peace movement

SITUATION HOPELESS, BUT NOT SERIOUS
RITA GILLITT

On 1 February 2003, the Chinese authorities in Guangdong Province reported that 300 people had become ill and five had died in an outbreak of a mysterious respiratory illness. On 28 February a Chinese doctor, infected in Guangdong, stayed at the Metropole Hotel in Hong Kong. Twelve other guests at the hotel contracted the illness. When the infected guests left the hotel and flew home they carried the virus to five countries in three different continents. Two remained in Hong Kong. In Canada the disease spread through two extended families. In Vietnam and Hong Kong health workers became infected. An infected health worker from Singapore flew to New York then on to Frankfurt. Meanwhile, the disease continued to spread throughout China. On 24 March, the World Health Organisation (WHO) announced that Sars is a new form of the coronavirus, a pathogen known to affect humans, but not a global killer. Strict containment of all known cases is vital. A team of WHO doctors had been in Beijing but was waiting for permission to visit other provinces where there were thought to be clusters of cases. After a week of waiting, the doctors were allowed to go to Guangdong. Under intense pressure and criticism from WHO, the Chinese Health Ministry announced the outbreak had begun five months earlier. They had far more cases than the 40 previously announced – nearly 400. On 5 April, China apologised for its slow response to the Sars outbreak. There were allegations that officials had covered up the extent of the spread of the disease.

Rita Gillitt arrived to live and work in north-western China in March 2003. She asked her colleagues if they had heard of the new disease called Sars. They knew nothing. The Chinese media were not reporting anything unusual.

2 April
I read on a website that US citizens are being advised to cancel non-essential travel to China; Beijing has sold out of face masks. I have lunch with a new friend, a Chinese woman doctor in the local disease control centre. She says she knows nothing about Sars.

4 April
My organisation bans me from travelling to Hong Kong or Guangdong. The Chinese authorities are not suggesting that precautions should be

taken, even though WHO is advising travellers to stay away. My Chinese colleagues tell me the disease is described as a kind of flu on their news.

9 April

Still no alert from the Chinese authorities but my organisation is instructing me not to travel or have visitors to stay. If we catch the disease we have to be treated in the Chinese health-care system; it isn't possible for us to be treated abroad. I tell my Chinese boss all this; he looks bemused.

14 April

My organisation reluctantly says if we feel vulnerable we can stay in Beijing where there are better hospitals. I decide the risks of going to Beijing are greater than staying in my town, where there are no reported cases. I stay put.

18 April

A student invites me to stay with his family during the May holidays. What to do? Defy the travel ban? Or tell the student I'm not allowed to go, for reasons he won't understand or know about?

20 April

The BBC World Service announces the Chinese Minister of Health and the Mayor of Beijing have had their Communist Party membership taken away – fired, in other words – for covering up the Sars outbreak in China. I check this out with my doctor friend who seems to know very little. She is politely disbelieving when I tell her international airlines are on the brink of not flying to Hong Kong or Singapore because the disease is spread by air travellers.

21 April

The BBC World Service reports that the week-long May holiday has been cancelled in China to reduce the spread of Sars. I phone another foreign teacher in my province who says swimming pools in Beijing have been closed, but there are still no reported cases in our area.

22 April

My school managers and teachers have a meeting about Sars prevention. All students and staff will have their temperature taken twice a day, we must keep well away from each other, open windows to improve ventilation, eat well, avoid crowded places such as the bus station, restaurants, etc.

23 April

My methodology class for local teachers is cancelled and visitors are not allowed on to our campus. Students are not allowed out at all for two weeks, no one will be able to return home for the May holiday. Lessons will continue as usual to keep the students occupied. The students accept this news without protest.

24 April

Members of staff take their temperature in public in the staff room with a shared thermometer. I negotiate to take my own, with my own thermometer, and record it in my diary should anyone wish to see.

25 April

My flat is compulsorily sprayed with Lysol by the school nurse. I object on the grounds that it's already very clean, I live alone and don't have visitors, but I'm told it's 'regulations'. The vile smell takes my appetite away, I don't eat well. The open latrine a few yards from my kitchen windows still stinks and generates fat bluebottles so I can't open my kitchen windows, and there's a spitter who performs outside my front door every morning. These far greater risks to my health are used in negotiations with the school president for a less smelly disinfectant to be used on my flat. I receive an email from my organisation offering voluntary evacuation. I decide to stay on – I don't want to leave my job so soon, having invested energy in getting to know the students, learning Chinese, making friends, etc – but with some misgivings, as I have to leave the campus daily to read my mail and the internet café is potentially a risk. A teacher from the Middle School where I give classes on Sunday mornings comes to tell me I won't be allowed in the school because of Sars. Her students are not allowed to leave the school either.

26 April

A friend who studies at the university college in town tells me he has been confined to campus. He is married to a European who has her own house and he has to climb over the wall at night to be with her.

Village north of Beijing, May 2003: the sign reads 'Sars Quarantine Area'.
Credit: AP / Greg Baker

27 April

My doctor friend has to work seven days a week at the disease control
centre. She knows all about the disease now, and calls it Sars. She has
been told not to travel out of town, so our weekend plans to drive to the
provincial capital to go shopping have been cancelled. She invites me to
go dancing next weekend until I remind her we're not supposed to go to
crowded places. She tells me there are two wards prepared in two of the
town's Chinese medicine hospitals for Sars cases. Two teams of doctors and
nurses have been assigned; she's relieved she's not one of them. We laugh
together as we imagine preventive health nurses spraying nomads' tents
with Lysol; apparently, village doctors will deal with any problems in the
grasslands. She says nomads aren't at risk because they're in the fresh air so

much. We go for a bike ride in the evening and on the way visit a colleague of hers who is on a 12-hour shift at the bus station checking every passenger's temperature. I learn Beijing's internet cafés have been closed down, but not in my town (yet). My organisation's representative phones for a chat. He mentions that the Chinese government is coming close to imposing martial law to control the outbreak.

28 April
I ask my Foreign Affairs officer to obtain a re-entry visa for me should I decide to evacuate. Normally this takes a month but he does it in 24 hours. I get a lift with him to the provincial capital as a former foreign teacher has donated his old PC to my school. I have been told I can have this for my own use, to avoid using the internet café. The officer is denied entry to his ministry by a masked guard because he isn't wearing a mask. On the way back the car is sprayed inside with bleach at two road blocks. I learn that half the teachers in China with my organisation have accepted the offer of voluntary evacuation.

1 May
May Day, usually a public holiday, is a normal school day. No one objects.

2 May
I phone my organisation's representative, as we have agreed to a weekly chat. He says there is an easing of anxiety over the way the Chinese authorities are handling the Sars outbreak, even though more cases are announced. Everything is being done to keep it under control. I reiterate my decision to stay in China. In my town I notice the salesgirls in the supermarket are no longer wearing face masks and latex gloves. Later that evening I check my email. My organisation has decided to make temporary evacuation compulsory. The teachers who left during the preceding week experienced great difficulties crossing China; many internal flights have been cancelled because no one is travelling. The implications for us if we should need any medical attention have forced the decision to evacuate compulsorily, as we're not allowed to use local hospitals even for minor health problems. I would like to remain in Asia for the period of the evacuation, but flights to neighbouring countries have also been suspended and land borders closed as a disease control measure. I have no option but to go via Beijing to the UK. Once I've been back long enough to prove I

don't have Sars I'll be freer to travel in Asia. At present anyone coming directly from China to another Asian country is subject to a 20-day quarantine.

3 May

A day of packing and planning. My doctor friend says anyone coming from Beijing to our province, even if symptom-free, has to endure 20 days' quarantine. I sense there won't be an early return. We go to the bus station, on the way to a farewell lunch at a colleague's house, for a packet of precious Chinese herbs to be sent express to a niece who has a weak chest.

4 May

A walk to the hill above the town for the last time. On the way back I see one of my students escaping over the school wall. It's good to see some signs of rebellion.

5 May

My boss and I have a meeting to tie up loose ends. He shows me his protective packet of Chinese herbs worn around his neck in a small red cloth sachet. He asks me how tall I am; later I am presented with a superb set of traditional Tibetan clothes at a farewell banquet given by the president. I make a speech saying that it is not an occasion for celebration. It isn't my wish to leave China so soon.

6 May

The school car takes me to the nearest airport with my boss to act as interpreter. I have no ticket; luckily there are two connecting flights to get me to Beijing tomorrow. Road blocks en route for the usual bleach spray, with temperatures taken here, at the hotel and at the airport.

7 May

A long stopover in Xi'an but decide to spend the day at the airport as there are several reported cases of Sars and many people in quarantine here – I fear I may not be allowed back in to the airport. I wear my mask all day, it's hot and uncomfortable. The BBC website reports 10,000 people quarantined in Nanjing; the headline in the *China Daily* is 'nine farmer cases confirmed in Beijing'. I'm relieved I don't have a cough or a cold on this journey, they could be grounds for putting me in quarantine.

8 May

We leave on a BA 777 with only 47 passengers. The flight is three hours longer than usual as we go via Seoul to pick up a fresh crew. British Airways staff don't get off the plane in Beijing any more. The purser tells us we are each costing the company £20,000. They have cut flights to three per week but can't reduce them any further or valuable landing and take-off slots will be lost at Beijing airport. I take my mask off. My temperature is not taken on arrival at Heathrow.

In May the Chinese government introduced stiffer penalties for evading or escaping quarantine, including death.

23 May

I receive an email from a student at my school. She thinks the situation is getting more serious and from next week she won't be allowed off campus at all. This may be her last communication for a while.

26 May

I receive an upbeat email from my organisation in Beijing; indications are positive for our return to China. A decision will be taken at the end of June. More teachers are being recruited for an August departure.

Afterword

On 2 June China announced no new cases on the mainland for 24 hours, the first day there had been no new cases since the start of the outbreak. This announcement came amid fears of a renewed threat in Toronto. A spokesman for WHO in Beijing said: 'The figures look pretty good. Hard to believe sometimes, but we are taking them in good faith.' The next day WHO expressed concern about the reported sharp drop in new Sars cases in recent days, saying: 'It may be that there has been a dramatic drop-off in the number of Sars cases in China, but clearly because of the way it was handled when it first emerged in China there is a credibility problem.' ❑

Rita Gillitt *is a pseudonym*

After more than 30 years tracking and challenging abuses of freedom of expression through its pages, *Index on Censorship* magazine is getting closer to the story with a programme that takes its team to the front lines of the fight to defend free speech.

Already the world's principal focal point for reports on free expression issues, the magazine can now be found working directly with free speech champions in their own countries.

'The magazine was originally created as an outlet for banned writing and monitoring violations of free speech,' says *Index on Censorship*'s editor-in-chief Ursula Owen. 'So it's a natural step to find new ways of using our publishing skills, our contacts and our historical knowledge of the problem by standing side by side with the people who write for us at such risk.'

That sense of duty now takes the magazine to Iraq, where its team members are monitoring free speech abuses, lobbying for changes in media laws, supporting the independent press through training programmes and opening up the internet to previously silenced opinion.

And *Index on Censorship* associate editor Rohan Jayasekera returns to Iraq to combine a programme of training for young journalists with the publication of a special edition of *Index on Censorship* in Arabic, covering the free speech issues raised by the war. A Kurdish version is also planned.

'*Index on Censorship* needs to do more than just report the process,' adds Ursula Owen. 'It can also play a direct part, too. And if it can, it should.'

- *A New Voice in the Middle East: A Provisional Needs Assessment for the Iraqi Media*, a joint assessment report by the Baltic Media Centre, *Index on Censorship*, the Institute for War & Peace Reporting and International Media Support, is available on the *Index* website at http://www.indexoncensorship.org/pdf/iraqmedia.pdf, and its partners' sites.

IF YOU WOULD LIKE MORE INFORMATION ABOUT
INDEX ON CENSORSHIP
OR WOULD LIKE TO SUPPORT OUR WORK
**PLEASE CONTACT HUGO GRIEVE, DEVELOPMENT MANAGER,
ON 020 7278 2313
OR EMAIL HUGO@INDEXONCENSORSHIP.ORG**

WWW.INDEXONCENSORSHIP.ORG
CONTACT@INDEXONCENSORSHIP.ORG
TEL: 020 7278 2313 • FAX: 020 7278 1878

SUBSCRIPTIONS (4 ISSUES PER ANNUM)
INDIVIDUALS: BRITAIN £32, US $48, REST OF WORLD £42
INSTITUTIONS: BRITAIN £48, US $80, REST OF WORLD £52
PLEASE PHONE 020 8249 4443
OR EMAIL TONY@INDEXONCENSORSHIP.ORG

Index on Censorship (ISSN 0306-4220) is published four times a year by a non-profit-making company: Writers & Scholars International Ltd, Lancaster House, 33 Islington High Street, London N1 9LH. *Index on Censorship* is associated with Writers & Scholars Educational Trust, registered charity number 325003 **Periodicals postage:** (US subscribers only) paid at Newark, New Jersey. Postmaster: send US address changes to *Index on Censorship* c/o Mercury Airfreight International Ltd Inc., 365 Blair Road, Avenel, NJ 07001, USA